# HELPING TO MAKE YOUR PUNTING PAY IN AN EVER-CHANGING BETTING LANDSCAPE

Nothing gets the pulse racing quite like a bet. Whether it be the shaking of the reins, the strike of the ball or the swing of a club that gets your heart beating faster, betting on sport puts you right in the thick of the action and this book has indispensable advice and tips to help you beat the bookies.

With expert guidance on everything from how to improve your Saturday football accumulator strike-rate to finding the winner of the Masters or Super Bowl, you'll discover what you need to help you find that winning feeling on a regular basis.

Whether you're a novice keen to explore the world of betting or a seasoned judge, you will find angles and pointers that can help you find more winners and stop you falling into the traps that often catch out punters.

In an ever-changing digital era, we have never had so many opportunities to have a punt. If there is a bet to be had, the bookies are there to accommodate. Such choice can be a blessing and a curse, but by sharing the secrets of some of the most experienced experts in the business this book has you covered, whatever you choose to bet on.

Our clean and simple breakdown of each sport means you will increase your knowledge of sports betting in an easy-to-understand way. We're here to help you become a smarter bettor.

You'll be doing more cheering and less jeering, more withdrawing and less depositing. ■

**Tom Park, editor**

Published in 2019 by Racing Post Books
27 Kingfisher Court, Hambridge Road, Newbury, RG14 5SJ
Copyright © Racing Post 2019

ISBN 978-1-83950-010-7
10 9 8 7 6 5 4 3 2 1

**Designed by David Dew**

Cover design by Jay Vincent ■ Images by Edward Whitaker, Patrick McCann (racingpost.com/photos) & Getty
Printed in Slovenia by DZS Grafik

# THE EXPERTS

**80**

**88**

144

216

172

# RACING BASICS
## by Racing Post betting editor Keith Melrose

Want a bet? If you are reading this book, I'll take any odds offered that at some point in your life you have been asked: why do you love sport so much? The answer to the question is easy, although it might be incomprehensible to anyone who thinks to ask. It is because sport contains all the parts of life that we want to see in colour.

What that means in practice differs from fanatic to fanatic, but it's all there. The collectivism of a grassy bank or a tiered stand, where everyone knows the words. Plot twists that would have you rolling your eyes in the cinema, instead seizing your breath because not a word of it is scripted. Most of us who come to betting are brought through the turnstiles by these elevated moments, finding a suitable chaser to enhance the shot.

For many, it is all they need. The stated aim is to render that putt sneaking in on its terminal roll, or that photo-finish that doesn't go their way, in a more vivid shade of green. Betting is a nice bonus when it comes off, a small levy when it doesn't. Oh well, enjoyed it either way. Same time next week, yeah?

For others, that is not enough. Perfectionism soon takes hold and sport becomes less summer blockbuster than classic literature. It is there to be interpreted and, ultimately, solved. Using whatever information we can get our hands on, we join in at the edge of sport's whirlpool and are sucked ever closer to the centre.

What keeps sport obsessives safely clear of the dad-in-the-shed trope is that you can't bet on, say, birdwatching or model railways. Give Bill enough time and he will get to see a capercaillie in the Cairngorms, but in our realm the depth of our knowledge and experience is measured coldly, in the profit-and-loss column.

The opportunities for a recreational punter have never been greater. Betting exchanges, spreads and innumerable traditional sports markets mean you can bet on whatever you want, however you want.

Sport betting grew up with horseracing, in the days before football, rugby or tennis even existed in an organised sense. In the last half-century or so, it has grown exponentially, in tandem with these

*'Opportunities have never been greater. Betting exchanges, spreads and innumerable traditional sports markets mean you can bet on whatever you want, however you want'*

hosts. In the same way that ploughed fields and cotton jerseys have given way to bowling-green pitches and sweat-wicking fibres, betting is no longer hidden behind the gates to the course or the beads across betting shop doors.

However, growth has had other effects and the general theme is that they have made betting easier, but winning more difficult. The big bookmakers are now multinationals, turning over billions of pounds and duly carrying the clout to employ traders dedicated to even the most obscure markets. Bet on a first-round ITF Futures match from Blois and chances are the trader at the other side of the screen knows both players' percentage of games won from 0-15.

At the time of writing racing remains a relatively data-poor sport, but the effects of modern developments have not missed betting's oldest friend. Exchanges have revolutionised how the sport is bet on, with traders on and off the track able to apply their overround (what the casinos would call a 'house edge') on top of the exchange prices, which effectively act as a massive open-source tissue on every race.

While the vast majority of us will only ever bet for leisure, to bet leisurely these days is to guarantee that your betting bank will not increase in the long run. And profit is surely the aim towards which all serious recreational punters strive.

A career spent at close quarters with some of the best bettors and tipsters in the country has taught one lesson above all: that no one arrives fully formed as a judge and a punter. Everyone will come to betting with dubious preconceptions, and let there be no doubt that after nearly 15 years some of mine still persist. The key is to keep learning from those who will lend advice, to keep tightening the circle as you drift on the whirlpool.

There are almost as many ways to approach betting as there are bettors and, while they cannot all be right, the umbrella themes are all covered in these pages. Our team of experts, all long-standing professionals in the field of finding winning bets, approach the old – such as form, staking plans and exotic bets – as well as the newer aspects of exchanges and the ever-growing opportunity to bet on international events.

Place your bets, and the very best of luck. We're under starter's orders . . .

*We're under starter's orders – get ready for our invaluable advice*

# PRICEWISE ON RACING
## by Tom Segal

## INTRODUCTION

Before the advent of the betting exchanges, punting on horseracing was, dare I say it, pretty easy. It was a simply you versus the bookmaker, mano a mano, one brain versus another and the punter had the added advantage of taking a guaranteed price. However, the exchanges and the internet have changed the betting landscape forever, meaning prices are updated constantly and it is only in the last few minutes before the off that the true market becomes clear.

Consequently it's much harder to win because there are no secrets anymore and what would have been a 16-1 shot ten years ago is now half that price at best. Punters have two choices. The first is to find something else to do, the second is to adapt and if you're reading this then I guess you haven't taken up fishing quite yet.

Of course this isn't aimed at the exchange wizards, who trade more bets in day than I would in a year, but there are still loads of us out there who love the sport and nothing beats the feeling of unearthing the winner.

*Betting is no longer simply about pitting your wits against the bookmaker – there are now a whole raft of other factors to consider*

We have to modernise our thinking. Of course, prices are still important, but becoming less price sensitive is vital too, with exchanges sorting the wheat from the chaff very quickly. Once you have realised that a 5-1 shot who was double that price 30 minutes ago is still a good price you can move on and use all the tools that made us winning punters in the first place.

Profitable betting has always been as much a mental game as a judgement one. It's much harder now than it used to be but, with proper thinking and a definite plan, there is no reason why we all still can't win.

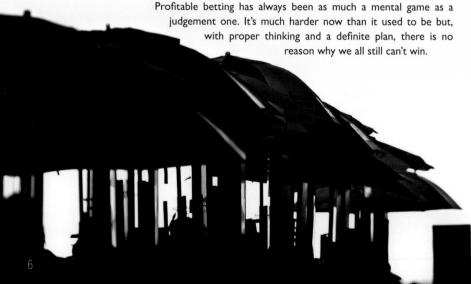

# TEN WAYS TO BET SMART ON HORSERACING

## 1. Work out your individual method

It would be nice to think there is some short of magic key to unlock horseracing and that when you find it you will start backing loads of winners. The reality of the situation is that if you really want to win, you have to find a method that works. You can't play at betting on horses or think you have it cracked because as soon as that enters your mindset, you are usually in a whole world of trouble.

There are no shortcuts and there really are no excuses anymore because nearly all of us have access to the internet and we can watch every race and read all there is to know about any horse at any stage.

While it is important to do your homework, you have to realise the tipping point of your own brain. There is a time when the more work you do on any given race or horse, the more confused you get and you can't see the wood for the trees.

The key to winner finding as far as I'm concerned is to find the method that works for you, for your temperament and for your way of thinking. We are all different and what works for one person might not work for anyone else.

Personally I think my talent lies in watching horses. I think that you can identify a good horse by the way they move, the way they carry themselves during a race and obviously their form, so I would suggest watching as many races as you can. However, time pressures mean that is not easy for everyone and, more pertinently, that approach might not be where your talents lie.

Many of my punting pals love speed figures and sectional times but I will freely admit that I'm too lazy to do them. However, they are quite rightly becoming the trend and there are loads of people out there that do them for you. Use them, use the ratings, dare I say it even use tipsters if you want, but the key to successful punting is to find the way that suits you best and fundamentally the one that you enjoy the most.

## 2. Work out what type of punter you are

Once you have worked out the way of finding a horse to back in any given race, the next key is to work out what kind of punter you are. Once again it all depends on your mindset and how a bet affects you.

If you are the kind of person that hides behind the sofa when you've had twenty quid on something or can't forget about a bet once you have struck it, you really shouldn't be betting in the first place but the truth is we all have our own staking plan and usually it's best to stick to it.

*'There are no shortcuts and there really are no excuses anymore because nearly all of us have access to the internet and we can watch every race and read all there is to know about any horse at any stage'*

*'There are going to be times when you really fancy a horse but in my experience you get taken out of your comfort zone when you bet more than you are prepared to lose'*

Of course there are going to be times when you really fancy a horse but in my experience you get taken out of your comfort zone when you bet more than you are prepared to lose and it becomes more important that any normal bet. That is when the fun stops.

Also there is no real point in having any sort of price restriction. Of course if you are betting in tenners then you have to have an incredible strike-rate when backing short-priced horses but often the best-value bets can be at the head of the markets. Japan hacked up at Royal Ascot 2019 with the owners incredulous at his starting price of 6-4 and, while I'm in danger of sounding a bit like that great philosopher David Brent, a good bet is a good bet whatever the price.

If you restrict yourself to big prices there is every chance of long losing runs and that can lead to poor thinking and many poor bets too. Consequently a smart and safe way to bet is to stick to a bet size you are comfortable with and make sure every horse at every price is available to you.

## 3. Timing is the key

Punting can often feel like you are playing poker with the bookmakers but they can see your hand. You can still win if you get four aces or a royal flush but more often than not you are going to lose.

Winning punters will often only bet when the odds are stacked in their favour and that brings in the question of timing. The bookmakers can't tell you when to have your bet but they will usually price up all the major races at the weights stage, while every Monday the following Saturday's TV races are priced up. Use that to your advantage.

Of course bookmakers are defensive on a Monday or a Tuesday as they try to get their card marked early by the sharp punters and so there is never going to be a chance to get too much money on. However, there are lots of bookmakers out there and you can back the same horse to small stakes with all of them, so it is well worth considering beating the market and using their willingness to price up races early against them.

Old-style ante-post betting has gone right out of fashion and once again stake limitation is always going to apply but the willingness of punters not to act on what they see always surprises me. If you think you have spotted a good horse at any stage, why not act on it? For example, Visinari broke the clock when winning on his

racecourse debut at Newmarket in June 2019 and on that evidence he has to be top class. It's obviously unlikely he will win the 2,000 Guineas in 2020 but odds of 50-1 undoubtedly underestimated him on what he showed that day. Surely that is the essence of a good bet.

The Cheltenham Festival is always a brilliant betting opportunity for punters when the non-runner no bet guarantee is applied. The worry about losing your stake has gone and yet as with all ante-post bets you get a good chance to beat the price. That is simply what all the best punters are trying to achieve.

## 4. Don't be scared of big prices and make sure you get the best price

Still to this day you will hear punters saying they can't back a certain horse because it's too big a price. Stop for a second and think how daft that sounds. You would contemplate backing a horse if it was 10-1 but you wouldn't if it was double that price?

Of course there is an element of inside information that exists in horseracing that isn't there in other sports but if you have done your homework and the horse fits your betting criteria, why in any shape or form should a big price put you off? I get it if you think the horse is too short because there will be plenty of other opportunities but never if it's a bigger price than you expected.

Yes, there might be a reason why the horse is too big a price but if you can't see it, don't let it mess up your betting methodology, especially as there is always a huge degree of mental anguish involved in missing a big-priced winner.

Make sure you get the best price and to do that you must have lots of betting accounts with all the big firms. If you're really serious about winning, taking the best price is a must, especially as you have nothing to lose with nearly all the firms paying best odds guaranteed even if your horse is a drifter.

Of course if you keep winning there is a good chance your account will get closed, so in my experience the key is to spread the love around, not abuse them and use all the accounts available.

As in any betting medium the key to winning is to beat the market and if you are scared of big prices or even worse don't take the best price, you are seriously hampering your chances of ever being successful.

*Paul Townend celebrates after success with Al Boum Photo in the Gold Cup at Cheltenham where the non-runner no bet guarantee is a huge help for ante-post punters*

*Facing page: Visinari swoops to success on his racecourse debut*

## 5. Be a Jack of all trades

The obvious difference between horseracing and virtually any other betting medium is the number of opportunities a punter has. There are tens of thousands of races every year with often 30 races to choose form every day in the summer. Remember that it's not obligatory to bet on all of them!

It's a good idea to specialise on the races you enjoy most as they are likely to be the ones you do best at. No-one likes throwing money away and if you are constantly hurting and losing, 99 per cent of us will stop doing the thing that is causing us pain.

My bread-and-butter races have changed over time. Sprint handicaps used to be my thing – I was extremely confident I would win in the long run but in recent years that hasn't been the case and it certainly wouldn't upset me if I never saw another 20-runner sprint handicap.

The reasons are complex but basically there are so many sprint-bred horses in training that all the horses are roughly of the same standard, which means visual, form or speed edges are hard to find these days. It seems to me that sprint handicap form doesn't translate from one race to the next, so I have had to adapt.

Of course that doesn't mean I won't get sucked in by the lure of a big-priced sprint handicapper from time to time but nowadays two-year-old races and Graded/Group races over jumps and on the Flat are where I find the best betting edges are.

Of course that won't be the same for everyone but the key is to find the races that suit your temperament and methodology and concentrate on them.

## 6. The importance of jockeys

It always amazes me how many punters don't care about the single most important person in any race and that is the jockey.

Every day on the TV, I'm told by good judges and good punters that they don't factor in the jockey and yet, after form, that has always been a key consideration for me.

The jockey can't make a horse run faster than they are able to, but they can sure make them run a lot slower and that happens day in, day out in every race I watch.

It starts in the paddock and on the way to the start because, as the price movements on betting exchanges show with great clarity, lots of races have been lost before the race has even started. Having a top-class jockey or at least one that is familiar with the horse he or she is riding has to be a big advantage.

Next there is the start, which is the most undervalued part of any race. How often do you see the best jockeys give away any

## TOP TIP

Don't under-estimate the importance of the jockey riding the horse you want to back – the rider can make a massive difference

advantage at the gates? The answer is hardly ever.

Then comes the race itself where tactical awareness of space is crucial because the easiest way to get any horse beaten is for them to go faster in the early part than they want to. If you've ever run an 800m race you will now that the faster you go at the start, the slower you finish. It's not rocket science.

If you've read Ruby Walsh's book you will know he counted the strides between hurdles and after riding at the tracks for a long time he got to know the optimum pace. Frankie Dettori on the round course at Ascot is like having 7lb up your sleeve and the same is the case when Jamie Spencer rides one of the straight courses. Then there's Richard Kingscote from the front, especially at Haydock, or Davy Russell in any big race anywhere.

The key to all the best jockeys is their hands because I can't remember a horse ever failing to settle for Dettori or Ryan Moore or Russell or Walsh, and conserving energy is the key to any sports race.

Lionel Messi and Cristiano Ronaldo are better than anyone else at football, Tiger Woods and Brooks Koepka are better golfers, so why shouldn't there be jockeys who are much better than the rest? There are but too few punters seem to treat them as such.

## 7. It's all in the genes

As horseracing punters we tend to all use the same tools to find winners. The form, the speed figures, the draw and the ground are invaluable tools, but the bookmakers are also using them and they have the advantage of knowing precisely where the sharp money has gone too.

*Masters of their craft (from top to bottom): Ruby Walsh, Frankie Dettori, Jamie Spencer, Richard Kingscote and Davy Russell*

Consequently they have the edge and so we have to find other factors that might turn the betting market in our favour. For me it's all in the genes. Galileo has been the key sire in the best races for years and yet in 2019 he was still able to have Classic winners at 13-2, 14-1 and 33-1 in Britain and Ireland, while Circus Maximus won the St James's Palace Stakes at Royal Ascot at a double-figure price too.

Of course Galileo's brilliance means he had lots of runners in the English and Irish Derbys but Hermosa was his only runner when she won the 1,000 Guineas and Circus Maximus was his sole representative in the St James's Palace. Amazingly Galileo's horses are probably still undervalued in the market

Kingman has already sired 15 horses with a Racing Post Rating of over 100 in his first crop and he seems destined to be a superstar sire too. I reckon if you stick to backing Kingman horses within reason, you are going to be quids in over the next decade or so.

upgrade their horses regularly. Due Diligence made a great start with his two-year-olds in 2019 and Bated Breath has a brilliant Ascot record. He had three winners at the 2019 royal meeting, two at massive prices, yet that will be largely ignored at future Ascot meetings.

Basically pedigrees and breeding are very rarely used as a winner-finding mechanism but the evidence strongly suggests they should be. Digging a little deeper into pedigree pages should go a long way to improving your punting.

## 8. Back more than one horse in a race

There are many days when I wish I was a golf punter. The number one player in the world usually starts at 10-1, there are loads of top-class players at huge prices and three or four big-priced winners a year can pay for all the rest.

Compare that to any on-the-day horseracing market where you will hardly ever find a horse at 50-1 or bigger. When you do, many of them are handicaps, designed for all the horses to

finish in a line, and there is a huge chaos factor involved in every race too.

Of course in golf the best player doesn't always win, which is why no serious golf punter would limit themselves to one bet in any tournament, so why would you do the same in a horse race?

In nearly every race I look at, I end up fancying two or three and there is nothing worse than doing all the work and then choosing the wrong one. The answer is simple: back all the ones you fancy and never be scared to back more than one in any race.

There was a time when it was seen as a cop-out to back more than one selection but a golf punter would never dream of it, so why would you when the prices are more limiting and there are plenty more factors involved in trying to find a winner?

That might mean changing your staking plan or splitting your normal stake in two or three ways, but no-one ever said backing winners was easy and if you fancy a couple in a race the advice is to back them both.

## 9. Take note of times and breeze-up sales prices

Nearly every sport incorporates times. Showjumping, skiing, athletics, yachting, even golf is bringing in a shot clock now. You name it and there is usually a clock in the corner telling the viewers how fast they participants have run at a certain stage or providing them with extra information of some form or another.

*A plethora of riders line up in the silks of Gigginstown House Stud before the 2019 Irish Grand National – and punters should also not feel restricted to backing just one runner in a race*

Imagine watching the Olympics and not knowing how fast Usain Bolt had run. It would take away half the enjoyment and we couldn't put into context what an amazing athlete he was.

Even more important are the sectionals that tell us whether Mo Farah has gone through any section of his race quickly or slowly, or whether a skier is on course to win the downhill gold medal.

Yet in racing we seem very reluctant to embrace the times. Of course they are not the be-all and end-all of winner-finding but if we know a horse can run 11-second furlongs consecutively or if a two-year-old has run faster than a 100-rated horse over the same course and distance, we can be pretty sure they are well above average.

Bookmakers will be catching up quickly, as they always do, but we are talking about the best horses here and we can usually back them ante-post, when the bookmakers are off their guard.

On a similar theme, breeze-up sales have become extremely fashionable and as punters we should be able to use the information they give to our advantage. If you've ever been to a breeze-up you won't have failed to notice how technically advanced they are in relation to actual races, with the horses on sale being timed and their stride lengths measured.

As you would imagine the ones with the best data sell for the most and the sales results are there for everyone to see. Once again it doesn't mean you are going to back more winners but if a Kingman filly has sold for nearly a million pounds, as Summer Romance did only a month before winning a Listed race, you can be pretty sure she can run very fast.

Racehorse punters all around the world use technology to their advantage and so should we.

## 10. Make sure it's fun

In any walk of life you do your best work when you enjoy it, so one of the crucial factors for all successful punters is to make sure betting is fun. Of course that nearly always comes when you're winning but too often as punters we forget what the point of racing was to begin with and that was simply as an entertainment source. Punters should never get down on themselves when the going gets tough. Backing winners was never meant to be easy and when I go through a bad patch the quickest way out of it, bar backing a 10-1 winner, is to remember what I enjoyed about the sport in the first place.

Since the betting exchanges came along the punting landscape has changed massively and we all know of professional punters who back horses for a living, but you don't have to take it that seriously and it can still be great fun.

## MAINTAIN POSITIVITY

*Too often we as punters forget what the point of racing was to begin with and that was simply as an entertainment source. Punters should never get down on themselves when the going gets tough, backing winners was never meant to be easy and when I go through a bad patch the quickest way out of it, bar backing a 10-1 winner, is to remember what we enjoyed about the sport in the first place.*

# EXPERT VIEW

The key to winning is to find a way that best suits you and your own specific temperament and to stick with it. All the factors talked about when trying to find the winner of any race are valid but they might not work for you, so find the ones that resonate with you and stick with them.

There are many winning punters who use factors that I would consider to be totally irrelevant and there are loads that have no clue what I'm on about, so it is clear a successful method for betting on horseracing is specific to the individual.

Fundamentally, though, in any market place the key to being successful is to be ahead of the curve. While the betting exchanges haven't made that easier to decipher for the traditional punter, we still have many factors in our favour and it is important to get the best price and bet at the right time.

Finally, we must always remember that horseracing is not that important and we should never let it get in the way of the really important things in life. Keeping it fun makes the winning so much better and the losing easier to bear. ■

Find your own strategy

Search out the best possible odds

Watch your bets and keep perspective

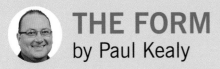

# THE FORM
## by Paul Kealy

## INTRODUCTION

Compared to when I started at the Racing Post around 30 years ago punters have never had it so good in terms of information available to help them study the form.

When I look back I wonder how we ever managed to back winners – not that I had many in my early years!

It's hard to imagine a world with no internet and no TV, but that's what it was like in the mid-1980s, when Racing Post Spotlight writers would arrive at the office every day with a back-breaking bag full of form books over their shoulders.

To find out what a horse did last time, or the time before, they would spend half the day leafing through the pages, but without ever getting real insight into what a horse had done, other than reading the in-running comments.

I'm not sure I'd have had the energy or enthusiasm to go through that knowing I'd still have little more than half a clue by the end of it, so I'm quite thankful I got to spend years bluffing my way through life on the sports desk writing about golf, tennis, boxing and the like until things became better!

There were professional punters around for sure, but far fewer than there are now, and they would all clock up serious miles on the road as, other than around 80 days a year of terrestrial coverage on big days, the only way to view racing back then was to be at the track.

Wind forward 30 years and, by comparison, punters are in danger of information overload. All form, replays and ratings are available at your fingertips and form study has never been easier. That doesn't mean it's easy, as you still have to put the effort in, but the amount of time it can take you to study a race properly now is a heck of a lot shorter than it used to be.

Of course, there is no such thing as information overload and Britain still lags some way behind other countries in the amount that is available to bettors, particularly is terms of sectional timing, which is virtually non-existent here but commonplace in some other countries.

Generally, there is no secret to form study, it's just a case of putting the work in and then working out what you're good at. Here are my top pieces of advice . . .

*'All form, replays and ratings are available at your fingertips and form study has never been easier'*

# TIME TO STUDY

Assuming that, unlike myself, you are not lucky enough to be paid to study form for a living, you are already at a disadvantage because time is the most important factor.

It's simply a case of the more you put in the more you get out, but if you're faced with anything from six to ten TV races on a Saturday and intend to have a bet in all of them despite starting your study only that morning, you are sure to struggle in the long run.

Of course, if all you're doing is betting for recreation then it doesn't really matter, but if you want to take it seriously you have got to limit the number of races you are prepared to look at.

*The action comes thick and fast on a Saturday and a knowledge of the form is vital*

This decision-making process will be very personal and will depend on how you like to bet. There are some who like nothing better than a solid favourite they can bet on with confidence and there's nothing wrong with that, but it's not for me.

Any race, on TV or otherwise, with a short-priced favourite is immediately off my list – unless I can justify taking on the jolly. I don't get any sort of kick out of betting at short odds and, while it would be stupid to argue that you'll never find a value odds-on shot, I'm happy to leave that to others.

Big handicaps are what get my juices flowing although the problem with those is that they can take a lot of time. I spend a minimum of an hour on an eight-runner race, but can spend as much as three hours on a big-field contest because you simply have to look at as many horses as possible.

There's nothing more galling seeing a 25-1 winner of a race and then realising you didn't even look at it. You almost certainly wouldn't have come down on it anyway, but you'll be amazed at the number of times you'll look at a winner post-race and think to yourself "I could have had that."

It happens to me on a regular basis and I take as few shortcuts as possible.

## OVERROUND EXPLAINED

*In theory a betting book should be 100 per cent, so a toss of a coin would be even-money heads, even-money tails. However, the bookmakers' profit margins mean the figure is usually above 100 per cent. In cases where it is less this is referred to as overround.*

## PRICE THE RACE AND FIND THE FAVOURITE

Depending on when you start your study and what type of race you're looking at, this job can already be done for you by the bookmakers, as by 6pm the night before nearly every race for the following day is priced up.

However, it is never a bad idea, if you have the time, to try to price up a race yourself. This used to be the 'golden rule' spouted most often by professionals years ago and I dare say there are still plenty who live by it.

It used to be said you should price a race to a 100 per cent margin (theoretically giving no edge to either bookmaker of punter) and then if you find a horse on offer at a bigger price than you make that's when you should bet.

In practice, with bookmakers betting to more than 120 per cent in most of the races I bet in, the truth is you'd almost never have a bet using that method.

I used to try to price races up and, if nothing else, it's a good way to discover whether you're going about it the right way. Anyone can make a mess of a race full of unraced maidens, but you really shouldn't be too far out with in one full of exposed handicappers.

Nowadays my main focus is to identify the favourite, work out what price it is likely to be and then try to find something to beat it.

If I can't then, depending on the likely price, more often than not I will move on to another race.

Part of the reason I do this is because, as a tipster, I think it's important to give readers more than the blindingly obvious. It's a personal thing and it works for me.

I always tell people that if I tip something at a short price it's because I've simply run out of inspiration. I'd rather not bother, but you have put up something every day.

*Speeding to the line in Doncaster's Brocklesby Stakes – traditionally the first two-year-old race of the Flat season*

## LOOKING AT THE CONTENDERS

By the time most people will get round to studying the form most races will have been priced up and I'd bet good money that the majority of punters start their study with the favourite and then work downwards in price until they find one they like.

I'm convinced this is the wrong way to do it as all the shorter-priced contenders will be the most obvious ones and the chances are you will find something you like before going too far down the list and you might miss something.

What I tend to do is use a ratings service. There are plenty of them but, for obvious reasons, I have always used Racing Post Ratings. I know all our handicappers well and have plenty of respect for them so see no reason to change now.

The beauty of using Racing Post Ratings for me is that they appear on the racecard on the racingpost.com website and you can reorder the card in RPR order by clicking on the RPR link.

RPRs on the card take into account each horse's best run in the past 12 months and what you will find, especially with handicaps, is that a lot of bigger-priced horses are far nearer the top than their prices suggest they should be.

There will be a reason they are on offer at big prices – usually because they have been out of form – but this will at least serve as a reminder that, especially in handicaps, nearly every horse has at least one line of form in the past 12 months that gives it a decent chance.

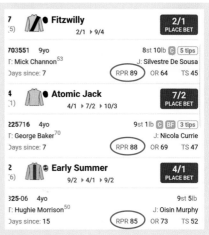

*How RPRs appear on the racecard when using the Racing Post mobile app*

This encourages me to look at a lot of bigger-priced horses earlier than would normally be the case and the decision you then have to make is whether there are reasons to think it will be able to run to its previous best.

A word of warning, though, all ratings services are tipsters too and they tend to tweak their figures to take into account variables likes ground conditions, trip and course.

It is something that has always annoyed me, but everyone does it. I simply want to know what they have done and then make my own decisions about what they're likely to do, but to use these on the cards you'll have to be early.

The ratings that first appear on racingpost.com when the declarations are made are the ones I want to see, but they are likely to be different if you're looking on the morning of the race and they have been tweaked.

## MAKE A HABIT OF WATCHING REPLAYS

One of the biggest single advantages we have nowadays is being able to watch virtually any past race whenever we want, whether on racingpost.com, attheraces.com, or racingtv.com and it is something everyone should make a habit of doing.

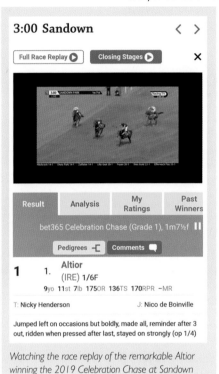

### 3:00 Sandown

Full Race Replay ▶   Closing Stages ▶   ✕

| Result | Analysis | My Ratings | Past Winners |
|---|---|---|---|

bet365 Celebration Chase (Grade 1), 1m7½f ▌▌

Pedigrees ⊏  Comments 💬

| | | | |
|---|---|---|---|
| **1** | 1. | **Altior** | |
| | | (IRE) 1/6F | |

9yo 11st 7lb 175OR 136TS 170RPR −MR

T: Nicky Henderson          J: Nico de Boinville

Jumped left on occasions but boldly, made all, reminder after 3 out, ridden when pressed after last, stayed on strongly (op 1/4)

*Watching the race replay of the remarkable Altior winning the 2019 Celebration Chase at Sandown*

I spend hours watching replays and will sometimes watch the same race more than half a dozen times just to confirm what I think I've seen.

Just looking at results will not tell you exactly how a horse has run and you will find plenty who can be considered much better than the bare result and more than a few who might be a bit flattered.

I like to look for horses dropping or going up in trip and seeing how they have travelled through their races at other trips. It doesn't always work but horses who travel really well in a race and then drop back quickly could simply be in need of a drop in trip. They could also have breathing issues which means once put under pressure – at any trip – they are likely to falter, but continually watching horses will give you an idea of how they run and when they're in form – even if form figures and in-running comments can't give you the full picture.

In-running comments for instance, have to be reasonably short just for space purposes and a phrase such as 'not clear run' can cover a wide range.

## CHECK THE TRAINER FORM

I know plenty of people who pay little attention to trainer form, especially with the big yards. They will argue that random number generators will tell you that a trainer who runs hundreds of horses is statistically certain to have a run of 40 consecutive losers at least once a season and they're right on that score.

However, there has to be more to it than that as horses aren't random numbers, but living, breathing animals as prone to minor infections as the human population, perhaps even more so.

Indeed, on the Flat you're basically dealing with a load of children, and anyone who has had kids will tell you how often they come back home from school with runny noses.

Large populations of people are breeding grounds for viruses and it would be a surprise if it wasn't the same for horses.

Working out when a trainer is likely to have a minor bug in the yard is much more difficult and numbers of wins is simply far too crude a method.

A trainer who has zero wins from 40 runners but has had half of his runners finish second or third is just dealing with bad luck rather than bad form.

Fortunately there is a quick way for looking into trainer form and that's to click on the trainer's profile on racingpost.com.

On there we give a list of the trainer's runners in the past 14 days and, in the final leg will be a +/- figure, which is the difference in pounds between what it has just run to and its previous best in the past 12 months.

Anything within 7lb (on the Flat, 10lb for jumps) is perfectly reasonable, but if a trainer has loads of horses who have run a long way below form you would be right to be wary of them.

## GOING, GOING OR YOU'LL BE GONE

Possibly the most important factor when studying form is the ground. There are plenty of horses who seem able to act on any surface but there are many more with definite preferences.

Again, using only wins as a guide is too crude a method, but you can arrange a horse's runs by going on the horse profiles at racingpost.com and clicking on the going tab, or simply by clicking on the stats tab.

What you need to look for is a horse's best RPR by surface and if there's a big difference, assuming there's enough evidence to go on

*Fast or slow, heavy or holding – getting to grips with the ground and which horses act on which surfaces is crucial*

*To calculate betting percentage from fractional odds, divide the number on the right by the sum of both numbers . . .*

| Fractional | Decimal | Probability |
|---|---|---|
| 1-5 | 1.20 | 83.3% |
| 2-9 | 1.22 | 81.8% |
| 1-4 | 1.25 | 80% |
| 2-7 | 1.29 | 77.8% |
| 3-10 | 1.30 | 76.9% |
| 1-3 | 1.33 | 75% |
| 4-11 | 1.36 | 73.3% |
| 2-5 | 1.40 | 71.4% |
| 4-9 | 1.44 | 69.23% |
| 1-2 | 1.50 | 66.67% |
| 8-15 | 1.53 | 65.22% |
| 4-7 | 1.57 | 63.64% |
| 8-13 | 1.62 | 61.9% |
| 4-6 | 1.67 | 61.54% |
| 8-11 | 1.73 | 57.89% |
| 4-5 | 1.80 | 55.56% |
| 5-6 | 1.83 | 54.55% |
| 10-11 | 1.90 | 52.38% |
| Evens | 2.00 | 50% |
| 11-10 | 2.10 | 47.62% |
| 6-5 | 2.20 | 45.45% |
| 5-4 | 2.25 | 44.44% |
| 11-8 | 2.38 | 42.11% |
| 6-4 | 2.50 | 40% |
| 13-8 | 2.63 | 38.1% |
| 7-4 | 2.75 | 36.36% |
| 15-8 | 2.88 | 34.78% |
| 2-1 | 3.00 | 33.33% |
| 9-4 | 3.25 | 30.77% |
| 5-2 | 3.50 | 28.57% |
| 11-4 | 3.75 | 26.67% |
| 3-1 | 4.00 | 25% |
| 100-30 | 4.33 | 23.08% |
| 7-2 | 4.50 | 22.22% |
| 4-1 | 5.00 | 20% |
| 9-2 | 5.50 | 18.18% |
| 5-1 | 6.00 | 16.67% |
| 11-2 | 6.50 | 15.38% |
| 6-1 | 7.00 | 14.29% |
| 13-2 | 7.50 | 13.33% |
| 7-1 | 8.00 | 12.5% |
| 15-2 | 8.50 | 11.76% |
| 8-1 | 9.00 | 11.11% |
| 17-2 | 9.50 | 10.53% |
| 9-1 | 10.00 | 10% |
| 10-1 | 11.00 | 9.09% |
| 11-1 | 12.00 | 8.33% |
| 12-1 | 13.00 | 7.69% |
| 14-1 | 15.00 | 6.67% |
| 16-1 | 17.00 | 5.88% |
| 20-1 | 21.00 | 4.76% |
| 25-1 | 26.00 | 3.85% |
| 28-1 | 29.00 | 3.45% |
| 33-1 | 34.00 | 2.94% |
| 40-1 | 41.00 | 2.44% |
| 50-1 | 51.00 | 1.96% |
| 66-1 | 67.00 | 1.49% |
| 100-1 | 101.00 | 0.91% |

Watch as much racing as you can and spend plenty of time on replays – getting to know the form will reap dividends

(one run would not be nearly enough, three or four would be the minimum) you'll get a good idea of what a horse's preference is.

Of course, there will be many times when there won't be enough evidence and you'll have to make an educated guess.

Pedigrees certainly help, and you can look a stallions progeny stats (again on racingpost.com) and see what sort of strike-rate they have with their progeny on different surfaces.

Be very suspicious, however, of listening to pundits who talk about sires being influences for certain ground types. Sometimes they will be right, but too often they will lazily quote something that is no more than anecdotal and simply untrue.

It is one of the great myths, for instance, that the sire Pivotal is an influence for soft ground. He's just an outstanding sire whose wins/ runs strike-rate on all surfaces is a solid 12-14 per cent.

Pivotal, by the way, raced on a surface softer than good to firm only once in his life and was well beaten.

Looking at a horse's action can also help. Those with a high knee action tend to hit the ground pretty hard and, generally speaking, are likely to better with a bit of ease in the ground. Those with less of an action will tend to be more at home on quicker surfaces than slow ones. Again, there are always exceptions to the rule.

*Bristol De Mai has a superb record at Haydock, where he is perfectly suited to the characteristics of the track*

## HORSES FOR COURSES

Probably one of the most underrated variables is course form. If a horse has won or run very close to it's best at a particular course that is a big plus in my book.

We tend to think of certain courses as more likely to attract specialists, with Ascot and it's sand-based turf straight track an obvious example, but the truth is all tracks in Britain are unique.

If you think grass racing is the same all over the country you're not taking into account the actual turf horses are racing on. It's the reason Haydock's heavy ground is totally unique and impossible to handle for some horses who are otherwise perfectly suited to desperate conditions.

Bristol De Mai is a prime example of this. At the time of writing he is unbeaten in four starts at the course and destroyed two very strong

Betfair Chase fields in 2017 and 2018 by an aggregate of 61 lengths.

A horse with a record of running well at a particular track will tend to continue to do so provided all conditions – going, trainer form etc – are in its favour.

A few examples on the Flat include Ripp Orf, who since 2018 to mid July 2019 had form figures of 13125 in fields of 27-27-20-15-26, and Communique, who run four times across Newmarket's two tracks in 2018-19, recording four wins at odds of 11-8, 8-1, 11-1 and 12-1. I've never kicked myself so much for neither tipping nor backing the latter for the Princess of Wales's Tattersalls Stakes in July 2019.

He couldn't really win on form, giving weight to some classy rivals, but that didn't take into account just how effective he is at the track.

Pivoine, who won the 2019 John Smith's Cup at York, is another example. He ran at York for the first time at the Ebor meeting in 2018 and absolutely hacked up. You will rarely see a horse travel as well he did through that race on very fast ground at York, but he went to the John Smith's Cup as a 14-1 outsider (had been 25-1 at the five-day stage) following a tailed-off effort at Ascot.

York proved the key, though, as he once again cruised through the race and was produced to win going away.

*Ripp Orf has a terrific record in big-field handicaps at Ascot*

## MOVE WITH THE TIMES

As mentioned earlier in this chapter, there a certain aspects of form study in Britain that lag behind other countries and the big one is sectional times, although there are signs that is about to change over the next few years, which can only be a good thing.

I know plenty of people who think sectional times are a waste of time, but I'm certainly not one of those, although I've never looked too much into them.

I have used an online stopwatch to time races in the past when I have a particular interest, but otherwise I leave it to the professionals.

However there are simply too many people I have great respect for championing their cause to be so dismissive of them and I get the impression I'm going to have to move with the times at some point.

Being set in your ways when it comes to betting is almost certainly not a good move. In any case, when it comes to information the more of it the better as far as I'm concerned.

Certainly, being able to know for sure how a race has been run has to be a positive. We all know that in some races the leaders go off too fast, which is why the closers fight out the finish, and at other times the leaders get away with setting early fractions that make it hard for the finishers to get involved.

*Paul Kealy delivers his tips — and ice creams — at Sandown during a promotional campaign*

I've always considered myself a fair judge of pace when watching but am not stupid enough to believe I'm infallible – or indeed ever that accurate – and sectionals are the only true way to build up a picture of how a race has been run.

Using them you can identify when horses have run particularly fast to overcome a pace bias, have gone too fast for their own good, have not been able to run to their best because the race wasn't run to suit.

I'm not going to give you examples of how because I'm not an expert, but incorporating sectionals times into analysis is something I am intending to do when they become more readily available and I'd certainly suggest you do the same.

*'Every piece of evidence you can get your hands on - and how you use it - is a potential weapon in the battle with the bookmakers'*

## EXPERT VIEW

People often ask me why, if I'm 'that good' I don't give up work and punt professionally.

There are many answers to that, the first being that I thoroughly enjoy my job and have to pinch myself every day knowing I'm getting paid to do something I'd happily do in my spare time anyway.

The second is that being a professional punter is not an easy life. They don't just sit on their yachts counting money. I've known a few who rarely take a holiday for fear of missing too much racing.

I still consider myself more of a recreational punter anyway, largely because I've never been the most disciplined in any aspect of life.

Making money, or simply breaking even, takes plenty of work and if you're not prepared to do it it's probably not for you.

I think that just about sums up how I go about my work and I hope it has been of some help.

I'm sure many other people have different ways, but as far as I'm concerned there are no shortcuts.

What you make out of this game will be in direct proportion to what you put into it. Nothing in life comes easy.

What I will say is that every piece of evidence you can get your hands on – and how you use it – is a potential weapon in the battle with the bookmakers.

That's why I know I'm going to have to get to grips with sectionals at some point. I will always be more of a 'feel' punter than anything else, but if you don't move with the times you will get left behind. ■

Form study is hard work

You'll get out what you put in

Use every piece of information you can

# HUNTING THE ODDS
## by Keith Melrose

*The Sporting Life, once used by bookmakers to help price up races*

## INTRODUCTION

Betting has been far from immune to the information revolution of the last 20 years. The single biggest event would almost certainly be the emergence of betting exchanges, which mark the card of both punter and bookie, though it is by no means the only factor.

Go back 30 years or more and there are tales of certain, normally independent, bookmakers who would lay small stakes at the SP forecast in a newspaper. All it might have taken was a misprint at the Sporting Life to do our intrepid local layer out of a few hundred quid!

Even in the early years of the century, it was common to walk into a William Hill betting shop just before lunchtime and have prices available on only a selection of the day's races. Now there are firms pricing up many races by teatime the day before and, for the most part at the time of writing, standing those prices at best odds guaranteed, which basically insures punters against their selection returning a larger SP.

The main driver besides exchanges is competition among firms. Bookmaking has become big business, partly but not wholly as a result of the 2005 Gambling Act which helped to deregulate the industry and brought bookies' adverts to our TV screens for the first time.

The mushrooming of betting brought on by the act is what led to the aforementioned best odds guaranteed, the widespread waiving of smaller Rule 4 deductions, the double result (i.e. paying first past the post and any amended result) and so-called 'justice refunds' for horses that refused to race or suffered some other early calamity.

Choppier waters for firms in the late-2010s has meant the good times are no longer rolling like they once were. Smaller players have gone bust, bigger ones have merged and all that are left are trying to get some of the toothpaste back into the tube.

More's the pity, but the days of spotting 'ricks' (clearly inaccurate odds) on a regular basis are over. Indeed, it is taken as read that firms who price up early are doing so to small stakes in order to have their markets right for when the raceday money pours in.

As long as there is human input into betting markets and marketing budgets able to seed loss-leading offers, there will always be ways to get ahead. The main rule to follow is observe and adapt, but certain principles will normally apply . . .

## TOP TIP

Always make sure you keep your typical stake (often termed as '1pt' by tipsters) in each account, so you are able to act quickly once identifying a bet

# 1. Have accounts with several firms

This may seem obvious to some, but it bears emphasising as we're only a generation on from punter-bookmaker monogamy. Whatever shop was closest to your dad's house, or the pub he drank in, was probably 'his' bookie.

Nowadays, the distance between William Hill and Ladbrokes is a few columns on oddschecker.com, which at the time of publication is the most popular site for odds comparison – though others, including the Racing Post, offer a similar service on their own site, handily located right beside the in-depth form.

The reasons for having accounts across competitors are obvious. Firstly, it increases the chances of finding the best odds available on a given race or event. It also gives access to a greater array of markets, such as distance betting, without-the-favourite markets and even spreads for those so inclined.

Then there are the competing offers. These operate in the everyday, but firms tend to save the real giveaways for big festivals. (An aside on offers: always give precedence to those that offer rewards in cash, rather than free bets).

The advice goes beyond merely opening accounts with a few firms. Getting to know how your various bookmakers operate – when they tend to price up races, in which races they tend to offer more generous place terms, and so

on – is a significant head start when it comes to placing your bets. An awareness that, say, Sky Bet tend to offer enhanced place terms on the big handicap on Saturdays can make betting that bit more efficient and help whittle down who to place that bet with beyond just looking for the bolded-up best odds.

The potential downside of having multiple accounts is spreading your betting bank. Having to deposit funds for every bet will not only get tedious pretty quickly, but can on odd occasions lead to the frustration of a missed price.

There are many ways to deal with this, but perhaps the most pragmatic approach is to always make sure that you keep your typical stake (often termed as 'Ipt' by tipsters) in each account, so you are able to act quickly once identifying a bet.

On those lines, it is also good practice to take extraneous funds from your accounts on a regular basis. If you have £40 in all of your accounts bar Coral, with whom you have £500, personal experience suggests it is likely that you will bet that bit more often with Coral, even when it is not the most advantageous thing to do.

## 2. Bet as early as is practical

The starting prices returned after a race and ones that are seen in the official result are the culmination of the efforts by all of those who bet into the market. The lion's share of this money goes down in the 20 minutes or so before a race, as it is when most firms are confident enough in the market to lay to large stakes, and the big hitters weigh in on the exchanges.

At this stage, these markets are said to be mature. That is to say that most of those who matter have had their input and the market has adapted accordingly. Making money at this point is playing the game on the highest difficulty setting. All sorts of top judges, not to mention those who have knowledge not in the public domain, have already dipped their hand into the pot, taking out what they perceive to be the value.

The lesson from all of this is that you should place your bets at the earliest convenient time to do so. Some firms price up most races, except those where there is little form to go on, as early as 5pm the day before racing, others join in on the day of the race. Major bookmakers will tend to have all British and Irish racing priced up before mid-morning.

When is your best time to bet is a matter of personal circumstance. Those with the time to look at the next day's racing in the afternoon can be ready to take the first show, but be warned that stakes are squeezed and success at this stage is likely to bring an account to the trading department's attention before too long.

The above is not an option for those who only have time to look at races in the evening, or who stake enough that they will not be entertained at evening prices (some in the latter category take what they can get at evening odds and top up later). Day-of-race action tends to pick up from around 9am and most who can 'get on' will manage to at this point.

For most of us, it will get no further than that. The people who have to hunt round various shops taking the maximum allowed stake, or who can only play on Betfair in the minutes before the off in order to get matched, have an unenviable task in one sense but they are also the sort of people you would do well to become friends with.

*'If you have £40 in all of your accounts bar Coral, with whom you have £500, personal experience suggests it is likely that you will bet that bit more often with Coral, even when it is not the most advantageous thing to do'*

## 3. Get a feel for market dynamics

If it were possible to predict with accuracy how a market will pan out, right up to the off, you would need only a Betfair account and a small starting bank to make plenty of money in the long run. No one can aspire to that level, but the vast majority of astute punters have a feel for the behaviour of markets to some level.

A full chapter on the behaviour of betting markets could be written. There are a few central tenets that any punter can learn.

What might be called 'inside money' tends to come late. For example, a handicap debutant is put in at 6-4 overnight in a 12-runner field, before drifting to 9-4 in the morning. This probably does not mean a great deal, because if connections know the horse has a stone in hand they are likely to put down a reasonable wedge near the off, rather than pick up scraps in an immature market. If the initial odds quoted feel on the skinny side, a bettor with a good grasp of market dynamics would know that in the majority of cases they will have an opportunity to get on at bigger odds at some stage.

Note that this runs against the idea of placing bets as soon as is practical. Unfortunately, the first rule of betting on horseracing is that no rule is unbreakable.

By the same token, there are times when it is advisable to potentially miss the fancy odds on a horse, knowing that they are a better bet at a short price than a big one. These will generally, but by no means always, be horses coming off a break, after wind surgery, or racing under new conditions that may in theory suit them.

Understanding the structural weak points in how a horse has been priced up is another fundamental of market dynamics. Certain aspects, like jockey bookings, are initially given weight by cautious odds compilers but are usually not as strong a factor as, for instance, form. If prices start to change in an unexpected way, ask why the initial odds were as they were. If you are quick in your deductions, you can reap the rewards.

Reading markets is an intricate game of feel that is notably hard to master, but those who take the time to learn will tend to get on early in the curve.

*There will be times when missing fancy prices is advisable – one example being when a horse is sporting headgear for the first time*

## 4. Don't be scared of the exchanges

With traditional bookmakers offering so many concessions, it can be difficult to tear oneself away to bet on the exchanges, where there is no best odds guaranteed, no double result, less clarity in returns (commission must be factored in) and adjustments that are not always as punter-friendly as Rule 4s.

The betting exchange is the market in its purest form and, even if you rarely place bets on Betfair, it provides data that can prove extremely useful. In-running odds are a solid measure of how a horse shaped in a race, while perhaps more importantly the money in a market that is the most telling (i.e. played just before the off at the time of highest liquidity) is often picked up only by the exchanges, as it all happens too late for traditional markets to properly react.

It is suggested that you should place a majority of bets that are struck immediately pre-race on an exchange. This is for the simple reason that, even once commission is deducted, you are still more likely than not to hold the best odds. This applies all the more strongly the further down the market you go. If you fancy an outsider, it is no exaggeration to say that by race time you will regularly get twice the price or more on Betfair.

There will not be an exchange punter alive who has not carefully picked their moment to strike, only to see their horse drift by a whole point within 30 seconds. That volatility is part and parcel of the medium. In the long run, you are much more likely to win overall than if you were to rely on the comfort blanket of best odds guaranteed.

*Play on the exchanges and you are more likely to win in the long term than relying on best odds guaranteed with a traditional bookmaker*

## 5. Be alive to the place angles

Each-way betting is more than a matter of personal taste. Most serious punters, including tipsters and the like, will always have good reason for putting up an each-way selection. It might be that the selection is solid, but potentially vulnerable for win purposes. Or it could just reflect the competitive nature of a race.

To take the next step along this path would be to gain a full understanding of place terms, to even treat the place part of a bet as a separate entity if necessary.

Place betting in this traditional sense is a bit of an anachronism, as it was essentially born from the initial win market and remains tied to that. The idea of a certain fraction of the odds for a certain number of places, depending on field size, is little more than a line of best fit, which in most cases is reasonably fair to punter and bookmaker.

There are occasions when this does not apply. Try comparing the traditional each-way odds you would get on a race with the same

race's place market on the exchanges and you will not have to look far for pretty obvious disparity.

Without going too deep into the theory, there are certain races in which the win book remains marginally in the bookies' favour, but the place portion is 'overbroke,' that in effect means with an easy-to-calculate staking plan a punter could guarantee profit. These races tend to have an odds-on favourite, a clear second favourite and eight or nine runners – maiden and novice races are duly more prone than most to the phenomenon.

These are called 'bad each-way' races by bookmakers, and targeting them would soon be nipped in the bud by an understandable desire not to give away free money. But the principle that gives rise to them is still exploitable.

At all levels of racing, there are horses whose place odds will not fit the model. Think about the horse in a 0-60 that more or less always runs its race. This horse might be 6-1 to win and deserves to be, it is fully exposed, but with the rogues generally in opposition at that level, place odds of 6-5 could well be generous.

*A consistent performer at a low level could be better value for a place rather than the win*

## EXPERT VIEW

While odds are quite literally the hard numbers of betting, making the best of them is more art than science.

Getting the best odds about your selections depends on several factors, including your own approach to betting and the types of horses you tend to back. As such, any advice that can be given has been earned from years of personal experience and your sweet spot will only be found through similar means.

Accordingly, it is always a good idea to watch markets and how they develop wherever possible. That goes for evening before markets right the way along to comparing on-track betting with what is happening on the exchanges. As with anything in racing, the lessons drawn are all the better if you are familiar with the horses involved.

That said, many of the factors in reading the markets boil down to reading the human actors involved – to paraphrase a quote so

beloved by horsemen, the horse cannot affect what price it is.

If bookies are offering prices now, what is in it for them? If someone wants to get a wedge on, when would they do it? What signs might there be that today is The Day, when it is all fancied to come together for this horse?

Judging the market is something that even the best bettors get wrong more often than other factors. You will back a few that go off five times the price and are never involved. The satisfaction of being an early adopter more than makes up for these moments, though, and even though it stings to see your 8-1 bet get chinned eight hours later as 15-8 favourite, the fact you read the market so deftly soon comes along as a bit of an anaesthetic.

A word of warning, though: do not mistake this cold comfort for any sort of compensation. It is surprisingly easy to find yourself looking for horses who will go off shorter than current odds, rather than those that actually represent good value. The two often overlap, but are ultimately distinct. Never lose sight that winners are the currency of betting and that beating the market is comparable with nothing more important than grabbing a bargain in the sales. ∎

Watch markets closely

Learn to read the market

Don't rest on your laurels

# FAVOURITES
## by Richard Birch

*How Pricewise has taken the bookies to the cleaners down the years with his big-price selections*

## INTRODUCTION

Every person who bets on horseracing is obsessed in some way with favourites. Punters, bookmakers, television presenters and tipsters all spend a high proportion of their time either dissecting their chances or discussing them. Betting shops may not be full of the characters who inhabited them in a bygone, smoky era, but it's long odds-on that most who still frequent these premises will be betting and cheering home favourites.

So what is a favourite? Basically, it's the horse which is perceived – initially by the oddsmakers and finally by punters – to have the best chance of winning on all available known evidence.

The favourite in a race contested by six horses will be the one who is the shortest-priced runner of the sextet. For instance, if the prices of the runners are 11-10, 2-1, 9-2, 8-1, 16-1 and 20-1, the 11-10 shot is described as the favourite. There are all sorts of reasons why a horse is made favourite, but the principal one is invariably that it possesses the best form.

Odds compilers will come up with a list of prices on the runners and punters must decide whether they wish to bet on any of them.

Some punters naturally steer away from favourites because they perceive there is a lack of 'value' in them, while others migrate to them like animals in Africa to a water hole during periods of drought.

During the early days of the Racing Post the Pricewise column was founded by Mark Coton. It was an innovative form of betting in which the idea was to suggest backing not the most likely winner of the race but instead the horse who provided the greatest value.

In punting terms, value basically refers to a horse who has been underestimated for some reason in the market and boasts a better chance of winning than its odds suggest. It is a word scorned by some individuals, but there is no doubt that in the long run a punter will lose if he or she continually backs a series of horses who represent bad value.

The logical perception from all this is that a high proportion of favourites represent bad value, but that's not necessarily the case.

One of the most successful horseracing punters of all, Patrick Veitch, revealed in his excellent book, Enemy Number One, that he sometimes placed hefty amounts on a favourite if he felt they represented value.

Other well-known backers, such as Denman's co-owner Harry Findlay, have specialised in betting on short-priced favourites.

Ultimately, it's all about what suits the individual punter, but there are definitely some occasions when it is smart to bet on favourites. Here are five of the best.

## FIVE WAYS TO BET SMART ON FAVOURITES

### 1. By specialising in the high-class races

It is generally accepted that high-class horses who tackle the best races are more likely to run to form. Perhaps Frankel isn't the best example as he was simply a freak – the best horse I'll ever have the privilege to witness – and simply in a different league to his contemporaries over three seasons of competition. However, he did manage to go unbeaten through a 14-race career and started favourite for every single one of those races.

Many students of form will argue that favourites for Group races on the Flat and Graded contests over jumps are more likely to justify their market billing than, for example, a low-rated 4-6 shot in a Sedgefield selling hurdle.

Lower-class horses are less likely to reproduce their best form on any one occasion purely because they lack the natural ability and consistency of the more choicely bred, better-calibre types.

That's not to say that punters should always dismiss the chances of the 4-6 favourite for the Sedgefield seller and automatically focus on the 4-6 favourite for the 2,000 Guineas at Newmarket.

But it's a general rule of thumb that many punters – who have survived the test of time – will swear by.

*The remarkable Frankel won all 14 races and started favourite every time he ran*

37

*A favourite who revels in mud like this could provide a perfect betting opportunity*

## 2. Strong recent form and suitable ground

All sorts of things govern whether a horse is a good favourite. Strong recent form is a prime factor.

While overall form provides an important indicator, a horse is more likely to reproduce a run it did three weeks ago than a performance it delivered three years ago.

That's the reason why many favourites have the figure '1' next to their name – they are last-time-out winners and come into the race at the top of their game.

Most punters tend to focus on horses who have 1s in their recent form. It's only natural – they're looking for winners, and winners often make favourites.

Ground conditions are important when assessing the chance of any horse. While some will act on all types of ground, many have a marked preference for firm ground, good ground, soft ground or heavy ground.

A real mudlark who is priced as 6-4 favourite on good to firm ground is potentially a favourite to oppose and not a smart bet.

By contrast, a favourite who revels in the mud and has the opportunity to encounter heavy ground could provide an excellent bet.

## 3. Horses ahead of handicapper under a penalty

When betting in handicaps the first thing to remember is that if the official handicapper could have his way the field would cross the line with less than a length between first and last. His task is to allocate weight which, in theory, will mean each horse in the race holds an equal chance.

Of course, that's impossible in practice, and the reason why lots of punters specialise in handicaps.

One of the best ways in which trainers seek to beat the handicapper is by running a recent winner under a penalty before its official mark has been reassessed.

For example, a horse rated 100 bolts up by 25 lengths in a Sandown handicap hurdle on November 2 and doesn't appear to have expended too much energy in doing so. The trainer has already entered the winner for a similar race five days later where it is due to carry a 7lb penalty.

It's reasonable to assume that when the handicapper has reassessed the horse for its Sandown win, the new rating will be perhaps 12lb higher on 112. Punters can therefore back a horse who is almost certain to be 5lb 'well in'. Most horses who are 'well in' start favourite, and a good proportion of them will win simply because they are in rude health and hold an edge over the handicapper.

This is one of the classic methods of betting smart on favourites.

## 4. When the horse is a 'value' price

We're back to the word that has the potential to provoke argument after argument among punters. Some will be adamant that no favourite can ever be 'value' to back, but that's utter nonsense.

Perhaps the best examples can be found in the early-price markets. Nowadays bookmakers price up every single race the day before racing. Those odds usually begin to filter through on racingpost.com at around 4.30pm. Where punters hold a clear edge over the bookmakers is that they don't have to bet on every single race on every single day. However, bookmakers are now compelled – I really don't know why – to offer prices well in advance on all races.

It takes an exceptional amount of study to assess just four races each day, let alone up to 40, so bookmakers will often make mistakes. Those mistakes are frequently made about the bang-in-form, short-priced favourite for a handicap.

Bookmakers will sometimes go even-money about a horse that sheer punter logic dictates could start at 2-5 the following day. How can you possibly disagree that 'evens' isn't a smart value bet when you're convinced the horse will be sent off at much shorter odds?

## TOP TIP

Bookmakers do make mistakes when pricing up the next day's racing. Get ready to pounce and snap up any odds you consider to represent value

Alternatively some favourites will drift for no discernible reason and win. The perception may be that "there must be something wrong with the horse" if it drifts from 6-4 to 7-2, but that's not always the case.

And with many punters eligible for the best odds guaranteed concession, this is another example where there is definite value to be had about favourites.

## 5. Change of scenery and first-time headgear

It is often smart to bet on favourites when they have enjoyed a change of scenery by moving from one stable to another.

This particularly applies to horses who, in the punter's opinion, are moving from a moderate trainer to a richly talented one. Sometimes it is not just the access to better gallops or superior training methods that benefit a racehorse; it is merely the change of scenery and relishing a different routine on a daily basis after getting stale.

Horses who have dropped in the handicap for a moderate trainer and then move to a better outfit off an attractive handicap mark often make excellent bets.

A potential double whammy for punters who specialise in this type of research is when a horse moves stable and is fitted with some form of headgear for the first time.

Blinkers, visors and cheekpieces are often used to focus concentration in the horse and improve performance. A tongue-tie can also be fitted to aid breathing during the race, while a hood is used by some trainers in an attempt to get the horse to settle.

Punters have never had more access to information and a relatively recent introduction was the declaration on a racecard of horses who have undergone wind surgery prior to the race.

Unfortunately, only the fact it has been given a wind operation is declared. There are lots of different types of wind ops, and some are known to work much better than others.

However, it is pertinent to point out that this is another factor in determining whether a favourite is a smart bet or not.

*'Horses who have dropped in the handicap for a moderate trainer and then move to a better outfit off an attractive handicap mark often make excellent bets'*

*A variety of headgear can be used by trainers to improve a horse's concentration and bring about improved performance*

# EXPERT VIEW

I back plenty of favourites over the course of a 12-month punting year, but only do so in the belief that they represent some form of value.

That might be because I believe their odds have been underrated by the odds compilers or it might be due to the fact that I think I have spotted something which others may have missed.

Perhaps I rate the form of the horse's last-time-out run more than some owing to the fact that I studied the video of the race for half an hour and concluded that it won with more in hand than the winning distance implied.

Or perhaps the favourite I intend to back has been underestimated even though it possesses an excellent record over the relevant course and distance.

Course form, incidentally, is one area in which I think many people consistently overlook its overall importance. For instance, a Brighton regular who relishes the tricky rollercoaster gradients of the seaside track can often put that expertise and experience to good use over rivals who are running there for the first time.

These are just some of the factors and variables that need to be brought into the equation when assessing whether a favourite is a smart bet.

*Punters search out the value in the betting ring at the Galway festival*

In a nutshell, I have never heard of a punter who has won money in the long term by exclusively backing favourites.

Sheer common sense dictates that the key to winning money is by backing a decent number of winners.

However, if the punter solely backs favourites he will need to have an exceptional strike-rate to emerge on top of the bookmaker in the long run.

That's when 'value' rears its head. Basically, as with every bet a punter strikes, it should be done only on the basis that the price taken is better than could reasonably be anticipated.

Punters who consistently take 4-6 about 5-4 chances will undoubtedly do their brains; punters who get 5-2 about 6-4 shots will have a far better chance of winning in the long run.

Betting on horse racing is a fascinating pursuit. Every individual punter is different and an approach that suits one may be totally unsuitable for another.

We all have the same long-term aim, though, and that is to win money off a bookmaker to pay for things like holidays and new cars. The fruits of success can only be achieved by hard work, discipline and, above all, by enjoying it. ∎

Market leaders can be value

Other factors also come into play

Hard work and discipline are important

# HANDICAPS
## by Keith Melrose

## INTRODUCTION

Horseracing started as a game of bravado among wealthy men, simply to test the claim that 'my horse is faster than your horse', but for the last century the bulk of races run have been in the less obviously meritocratic form of handicaps.

As punters, we are better off for it. The ostensible balancing of all horses' chances by the allocation of weights based on ability leads to the sort of open markets that we would not enjoy if sellers, claimers and conditions races were allowed to spread like weeds on the betting landscape.

A handicap in racing is just the same as your local golf club's monthly medal, or when you play a few frames down the snooker club with a friend whom you begrudgingly admit to be a stronger player. Once a horse has run three times, a handicapper employed by the British Horseracing Authority normally gives a rating/handicap mark based on the form it has shown. It can then run in handicap races, where it will meet the other horses in a race off weights that, according to the handicap marks, neutralise any differences in ability.

These weights are calculated on a scale. On the Flat the very best horses are rated around 140 (corresponding to around 10st, or 140lb, which is generally the top weight in a Flat handicap) and the lowest

*At the heart of the action in the County Hurdle – one of the most fiercely contested handicaps at the Cheltenham Festival*

handicappers around 45. Over jumps the figures are higher, mostly because jumpers have historically carried weights up to 12st 7lb (175lb). As such, exceptional jumpers will be rated 180 or higher, the lowest performers with any quantifiable ability in the 70s.

Of course, a horse's ability can change over time and every new piece of evidence can be used to determine more accurately just how good it is. So, after each run, the BHA handicapper will reassess every horse and adjust their marks as he or she sees fit. Progressive or in-form horses move up, exposed ones edge downwards, awaiting their turn.

The other factor to consider is the concept of pounds per length. Take two horses, one of which is deemed to be 10lb better than the other. If these two horses were both 5f sprinters, we would expect to see two and a half or three lengths between them at the finish line. If they were 3m chasers, however, it would be ten lengths or even more.

This is a reflection of time and relative distance, the finer details of which we need not concern ourselves with too much here. Just remember that while you might finish within 20 metres of Usain Bolt in a dash, Mo Farah would beat you by miles in a marathon.

Handicaps and handicapping are among the main draws of racing for many in the sport, from the owners of horses who would otherwise struggle to win races to the punters who like getting stuck into competitive markets. Neither maidens, nor sellers, nor even Group 1s, are worthy of their own chapter in a book on betting, but handicaps most certainly are. They are in many ways their own ecosystem, and a few special guiding principles apply.

*'Handicaps and handicapping are among the main draws of racing for many in the sport'*

# FIVE WAYS TO BET SMART IN HANDICAPS

## 1. Unexposed is best, in general

Put yourself in the position of the BHA handicapper. You would much prefer to have a few dozen races, ideally with most of them in handicaps with criss-crossing formlines, on which to assess a horse than a small number of maidens against similarly unknown quantities.

The three-run principle is there for a reason: it gives what handicappers deem to be just enough evidence to form a view. Handicappers, skilled as they are, will still leave chinks in the armour when given 'just enough' evidence and this is where the canny punter can drive their sword.

There are two main signifiers that show handicap debutants, in particular, are to be given due respect in all cases. This group are more likely than most to be facing a new set of conditions, whether that be in terms of trip, distance or even the addition of headgear. All of these can be sources of improvement for an unexposed horse.

The second factor, which is more telling than explicitly helpful, is that handicap debutants at the lower levels in particular (those given an initial mark of 60 or less on the Flat, roughly 100 over jumps) are more likely than average to have marks ending in a 0 or a 5. This can be a sign of handicappers having to take a bit of a guess. A typical maiden winner runs to something between 75 and 85 on the Flat and those beaten a comfortable distance are harder to weigh up.

In addition to arriving in handicaps with less solid evidence of their true ability, lower-grade types are also up against lesser rivals, who for one reason or another are generally less reliable than higher-rated horses.

*The Tatling (left) ends his career on a winning note in a 0-60 handicap on the all-weather at Wolverhampton as a 14-year-old in 2011. He won 18 races in a long career that included victories at Listed, Group 3 and Group 2 level*

Furthermore, it obviously takes less to show the ability to win off 60 than it does to win off 80. Modest improvement will often do and, in game show parlance, it can pay to open the box and see what is inside.

There is just a tinge of caution, though, because the unexposed handicapper is a fairly obvious angle that is almost always factored into prices, sometimes to an exaggerated extent. As ever, there needs to be some evidence found for why a horse is going to improve, instead of blind supposition.

Is the horse bred to be useful, or to better suit the new trip/surface? Did it go off at a fairly short price on any of its qualifying runs, or trade short during them? Has it been given a break since its last run, or has something been added that could give it the impetus to improve? These are just some of the factors that can signal improvement is just around the corner.

## 2. Pay attention to standard, not just class

In Britain, the most prominent display of a race's quality is its Class (numbered from 1 at the top to 6 at the bottom). This is a system used primarily to denote how much a race is worth, although that ties in fairly naturally with the quality of the horses that are eligible.

It is handy to know the value of a race, as enterprising trainers tend to fire their best arrows at the more valuable events and these will duly be more competitive. It is at least as important to note the conditions of the race, especially as you go down the scale.

A 0-80 can still be a competitive race. Roughly speaking, this is the grade in which those who have shown substantial promise in maiden and novice races, perhaps even won one, may set off in handicaps. Slide down to 0-75, or 0-70, and those runners become rarer. By the time we reach handicaps with a ceiling in the 60s, we are in the realm of moderate handicappers and late bloomers.

The application of the theory comes predominantly with those going down in grade. Moving from a 0-65 to a 0-60 might not be immediately obvious (both would be Class 6 races), but there is a tangible difference in the quality of rivals. A horse who has been finding the upper bracket just a little too much is likely to be more competitive to a noticeable degree down a mini-class, especially if they have been dropped a pound or two by the handicapper on the way.

It can work the other way too. A horse who is climbing the ranks may win a 0-75 like it could have carried another stone without changing the result, but that is not to say if it goes up 9lb and runs in a 0-90 next time that promise will necessarily be reflected in the result. In the new grade, he could be facing future Listed or Group horses.

Switching class is an important factor, but the shades of grey that cover the individual ratings bands can be just as significant.

*'Switching class is an important factor, but the shades of grey that cover the individual ratings bands can be just as significant'*

### 3. Be wary of lower-grade handicappers

Grades can also be a guide in a wider sense, particularly when it comes to one's betting approach.

Put frankly, very few horses are bred to be moderate handicappers and those who end up in the lower grades often do so as a result of physical or mental shortcomings.

The lesson to be taken from this is that the lower down you dig, the more cautious you should be. A low-grade handicapper is likely to be less reliable than one that flits between handicaps and minor Pattern races.

How this affects your betting can be a matter of taste, but measures such as a slight reduction in stakes in lower-grade handicaps or applying a higher threshold to what constitutes a bet at those levels can be a wallet-friendly approach.

There are few saints in 0-100 handicap chases, a truism you can be assured even experienced punters forget from time to time.

*Breaking from the stalls in a handicap at Brighton*

## 4. Weight for age is your friend

For those interested in the minutiae of handicapping, the weight-for-age scale is like finding pi to a quadrillion decimal places.

It exists as an admission of natural development in horses: that a two-year-old is not going to have developed physically to the extent that a five-year-old will have, and that for the two age groups to compete on an even footing there must be some weight allowance given to the immature horses.

If it did not exist, precious few three-year-olds would run in races like the Eclipse or the Arc, as they would be at a physical disadvantage that only outstanding horses could overcome.

The weight-for-age scale remains roughly similar to when it was first conceived in the 1860s. In most cases, especially those on which we have a lot of data to go on, it does a good job. Where it has been questioned, and can be used to a punter's advantage, is in less well-tested areas. In almost all cases, the benefit is seen to lie with the younger horses receiving weight.

| Dist | Age | Jan | | Feb | | Mar | | Apr | | May | | Jun | |
|------|-----|------|-------|------|-------|------|-------|------|-------|------|-------|------|-------|
| | | 1-15 | 16-31 | 1-14 | 15-28 | 1-15 | 16-31 | 1-15 | 16-30 | 1-15 | 16-31 | 1-15 | 16-30 |
| 5f | 2 | 0 | 0 | 0 | 0 | 0 | 47 | 44 | 41 | 38 | 36 | 34 | 32 |
| | 3 | 15 | 15 | 14 | 14 | 13 | 12 | 11 | 10 | 9 | 8 | 7 | 6 |
| 6f | 2 | 0 | 0 | 0 | 0 | 0 | 0 | 0 | 0 | 44 | 41 | 38 | 36 |
| | 3 | 16 | 16 | 15 | 15 | 14 | 13 | 12 | 11 | 10 | 9 | 8 | 7 |
| 7f | 2 | 0 | 0 | 0 | 0 | 0 | 0 | 0 | 0 | 0 | 0 | 0 | 0 |
| | 3 | 18 | 18 | 17 | 17 | 16 | 15 | 14 | 13 | 12 | 11 | 10 | 9 |
| 8f | 2 | 0 | 0 | 0 | 0 | 0 | 0 | 0 | 0 | 0 | 0 | 0 | 0 |
| | 3 | 20 | 20 | 19 | 19 | 18 | 17 | 15 | 14 | 13 | 12 | 11 | 10 |
| 9f | 3 | 22 | 22 | 21 | 21 | 20 | 19 | 17 | 15 | 14 | 13 | 12 | 11 |
| | 4 | 1 | 1 | 0 | 0 | 0 | 0 | 0 | 0 | 0 | 0 | 0 | 0 |
| 10f | 3 | 23 | 23 | 22 | 22 | 21 | 20 | 19 | 17 | 15 | 14 | 13 | 12 |
| | 4 | 1 | 1 | 0 | 0 | 0 | 0 | 0 | 0 | 0 | 0 | 0 | 0 |
| 11f | 3 | 24 | 24 | 23 | 23 | 22 | 21 | 20 | 19 | 17 | 15 | 14 | 13 |
| | 4 | 2 | 2 | 1 | 1 | 0 | 0 | 0 | 0 | 0 | 0 | 0 | 0 |
| 12f | 3 | 25 | 25 | 24 | 24 | 23 | 22 | 21 | 20 | 19 | 17 | 15 | 14 |
| | 4 | 3 | 3 | 2 | 2 | 1 | 1 | 0 | 0 | 0 | 0 | 0 | 0 |
| 13f | 3 | 26 | 26 | 25 | 25 | 24 | 23 | 22 | 21 | 20 | 19 | 17 | 15 |
| | 4 | 3 | 3 | 2 | 2 | 1 | 1 | 0 | 0 | 0 | 0 | 0 | 0 |
| 14f | 3 | 27 | 27 | 26 | 26 | 25 | 24 | 23 | 22 | 21 | 20 | 18 | 16 |
| | 4 | 4 | 4 | 3 | 3 | 2 | 2 | 1 | 1 | 0 | 0 | 0 | 0 |
| 15f | 3 | 28 | 28 | 27 | 27 | 26 | 25 | 24 | 23 | 22 | 21 | 19 | 17 |
| | 4 | 4 | 4 | 3 | 3 | 2 | 2 | 1 | 1 | 0 | 0 | 0 | 0 |
| 16f | 3 | 29 | 29 | 28 | 28 | 27 | 26 | 25 | 24 | 23 | 22 | 21 | 19 |
| | 4 | 5 | 5 | 4 | 4 | 3 | 3 | 2 | 2 | 1 | 1 | 0 | 0 |
| 18f | 3 | 31 | 31 | 30 | 30 | 29 | 28 | 27 | 26 | 25 | 24 | 23 | 21 |
| | 4 | 5 | 5 | 4 | 4 | 3 | 3 | 2 | 2 | 1 | 1 | 0 | 0 |
| 20f | 3 | 33 | 33 | 32 | 32 | 31 | 30 | 29 | 28 | 27 | 26 | 25 | 23 |
| | 4 | 6 | 6 | 5 | 5 | 4 | 4 | 3 | 3 | 2 | 2 | 1 | 1 |

*The official scale of weight, age and distance (Flat 2018) for Northern hemisphere-bred horses*

There are high-profile examples of young horses using weight-for-age in top races, such as two-year-olds in top sprints and four-year-olds going over fences, but handicaps provide by far the most fertile ground.

The benefit of being unexposed that was discussed above is not factored into weight-for-age. With canny placement, a stoutly bred three-year-old can start running over 1m6f against older horses in July and be both the least exposed runner in the field and in receipt of 14lb weight-for-age.

With weight-for-age largely favouring young horses when it offers any bias, giving the least exposed runners an additional allowance that is generous, even to the tune of a pound or two, makes for an excellent angle that is not always sufficiently factored in.

Weight-for-age is also becoming increasingly important in jump racing. The scale is built for more traditional jumps-bred horses, while most juvenile hurdlers and four-year-old chasers are bred either in France or for the Flat and are duly that little bit more precocious. They no longer need quite same allowances as the scale implies.

| Dist | Age | Jul | | Aug | | Sep | | Oct | | Nov | | Dec | |
|---|---|---|---|---|---|---|---|---|---|---|---|---|---|
| | | 1-15 | 16-31 | 1-15 | 16-31 | 1-15 | 16-30 | 1-15 | 16-31 | 1-15 | 16-30 | 1-15 | 16-31 |
| 5f | 2 | 30 | 28 | 26 | 24 | 22 | 20 | 19 | 18 | 17 | 17 | 16 | 16 |
| | 3 | 5 | 4 | 3 | 2 | 1 | 1 | 0 | 0 | 0 | 0 | 0 | 0 |
| 6f | 2 | 33 | 31 | 28 | 26 | 24 | 22 | 21 | 20 | 19 | 18 | 17 | 17 |
| | 3 | 6 | 5 | 4 | 3 | 2 | 2 | 1 | 1 | 0 | 0 | 0 | 0 |
| 7f | 2 | 38 | 35 | 32 | 30 | 27 | 25 | 23 | 22 | 21 | 20 | 19 | 19 |
| | 3 | 8 | 7 | 6 | 5 | 4 | 3 | 2 | 2 | 1 | 1 | 0 | 0 |
| 8f | 2 | 0 | 0 | 37 | 34 | 31 | 28 | 26 | 24 | 23 | 22 | 21 | 20 |
| | 3 | 9 | 8 | 7 | 6 | 5 | 4 | 3 | 3 | 2 | 2 | 1 | 1 |
| 9f | 3 | 10 | 9 | 8 | 7 | 6 | 5 | 4 | 4 | 3 | 3 | 2 | 2 |
| | 4 | 0 | 0 | 0 | 0 | 0 | 0 | 0 | 0 | 0 | 0 | 0 | 0 |
| 10f | 3 | 10 | 9 | 8 | 7 | 6 | 5 | 4 | 4 | 3 | 3 | 2 | 2 |
| | 4 | 0 | 0 | 0 | 0 | 0 | 0 | 0 | 0 | 0 | 0 | 0 | 0 |
| 11f | 3 | 11 | 10 | 9 | 8 | 7 | 6 | 5 | 5 | 4 | 4 | 3 | 3 |
| | 4 | 0 | 0 | 0 | 0 | 0 | 0 | 0 | 0 | 0 | 0 | 0 | 0 |
| 12f | 3 | 12 | 11 | 10 | 9 | 8 | 7 | 6 | 6 | 5 | 5 | 4 | 4 |
| | 4 | 0 | 0 | 0 | 0 | 0 | 0 | 0 | 0 | 0 | 0 | 0 | 0 |
| 13f | 3 | 13 | 11 | 10 | 9 | 8 | 7 | 6 | 6 | 5 | 5 | 4 | 4 |
| | 4 | 0 | 0 | 0 | 0 | 0 | 0 | 0 | 0 | 0 | 0 | 0 | 0 |
| 14f | 3 | 14 | 12 | 11 | 10 | 9 | 8 | 7 | 7 | 6 | 6 | 5 | 5 |
| | 4 | 0 | 0 | 0 | 0 | 0 | 0 | 0 | 0 | 0 | 0 | 0 | 0 |
| 15f | 3 | 15 | 13 | 12 | 11 | 10 | 9 | 8 | 7 | 6 | 6 | 5 | 5 |
| | 4 | 0 | 0 | 0 | 0 | 0 | 0 | 0 | 0 | 0 | 0 | 0 | 0 |
| 16f | 3 | 17 | 15 | 13 | 12 | 11 | 10 | 9 | 8 | 7 | 7 | 6 | 6 |
| | 4 | 0 | 0 | 0 | 0 | 0 | 0 | 0 | 0 | 0 | 0 | 0 | 0 |
| 18f | 3 | 19 | 17 | 15 | 13 | 12 | 11 | 10 | 9 | 8 | 7 | 6 | 6 |
| | 4 | 0 | 0 | 0 | 0 | 0 | 0 | 0 | 0 | 0 | 0 | 0 | 0 |
| 20f | 3 | 21 | 19 | 17 | 15 | 13 | 12 | 11 | 10 | 9 | 8 | 7 | 7 |
| | 4 | 0 | 0 | 0 | 0 | 0 | 0 | 0 | 0 | 0 | 0 | 0 | 0 |

*'With canny placement, a stoutly bred three-year-old can start running over 1m6f against older horses in July and be both the least exposed runner in the field and in receipt of 14lb weight-for-age'*

The scale has been tightened over fences, but always give a juvenile hurdler taking on elders, especially at lower levels, a good look over in handicaps. As of 2019, the BHA's penal handicapping of juvenile hurdlers masks that particular discrepancy, but it is expected that some time in the future the current allowances, which can still be up to 10lb in the spring, will be shown up as over-generous.

With the way horses are bred and trained changing all the time, mostly in the direction of making them more precocious, the weight-for-age scale is likely to remain a thorn in the side of handicappers, and an ally of bettors.

## 5. Trust the handicaps

While this chapter might give the impression there will be attractive, improving young handicappers as far as the eye can see, the truth is a bit less Love Island and a bit more The Best Exotic Marigold Hotel.

Most horses have given the BHA handicapper more than enough to go on and are generally referred to as 'exposed'. A good number of handicaps are made up entirely of horses in this bracket.

What is the best way to approach such races? Often the early market will favour a horse with promising recent form figures: it is not hard to think that a horse with recent runs that read 4232 is knocking on the door.

Even when dealing with exposed horses, however, not all form figures are equal. Our ostensible overdue winner might have been running in older-horse maidens, which are notoriously weak, or receiving weight and a sound beating in claimers.

When it comes to handicaps, the best form guide is other handicaps. They are generally the most competitive and solid races, away from the top level. As such, separating the strongest handicaps from the everyday is one of the most coveted skills in betting.

It will not take long to regard subsequent form and the backgrounds and stables of the players as signifiers of good handicap form. Some more subtle clues, particularly useful when looking at more exposed handicappers, include the age of the horses involved, the track at which the race was run (in general, a 0-75 at Doncaster will be stronger than one at Catterick) and whether the principals pulled clear of the rest.

In a handicap, when we can quickly narrow down the possibilities as to why a result has sprung up, general rules like those above can become pretty handy guidelines as to which horses should be interesting in similar grades next time.

This rule does not apply so strongly in other types of races. It is common to see horses flattered in sellers, claimers and maidens, although the last of those can take a while to manifest.

## TOP TIP

Handicaps are usually very competitive and using the form of similar races will serve you well

The exception would be some Listed/Group races. These tend to impact only top-end handicaps and are not always reliable, but if you can watch a horse operating in Pattern company and cannot say it has been flattered, then it could well be an interesting handicapper down the line.

There is a fairly modern phenomenon along those lines, most common in Irish jump racing, whereby novices are campaigned in Graded races so as to get a high enough mark for certain big handicaps (chiefly at Cheltenham) while leaving uncertainty as to the exact worth of their form. A horse worthy of a 140 rating would be more likely to get in lightly if beaten eight or ten lengths in a Grade 2 than if winning an everyday maiden hurdle by half the track.

## EXPERT VIEW

Betting on handicaps is a great way to isolate variables. Trying to find the Derby winner begins with assessing each of the dozen or more runners from scratch and judging which are the most able. In handicaps, the shortlist begins with those who are potentially ahead of their mark, whether it's in a 0-90 handicap hurdle or the Royal Hunt Cup.

The hitch, if we may call it that, is that there as many ways to go about this as there are bettors on horseracing.

The advice, put as starkly as possible, is to avoid the illogical and, thereafter, the obvious. Any angle should be backed up by reason and a numerical treatment of form does that to an extent, but does not rule out the odd bit of logical fancy.

No punter should paint with just one colour either. Finding those who might be ahead of their mark might involve looking backwards, or projecting forwards, but the punter who heeds just one of the two is unlikely to gain much of an edge.

It is also too easy to get tied up solely in the numbers, or collateral form. The reason handicaps with 'n' runners do not all end up in an 'n-way' dead-heat for first place is not because the BHA handicappers are bad at their job, but because so many factors affect how a horse performs on the day, to either a minor or major extent.

All of this harks back to rule number one of betting on horses: there are no rules, only guidelines. Handicaps are the most challenging and rewarding betting medium bar none, but if they were easy to figure out they would have disappeared by now.

That is not to say that they are infinitely complicated. Find a well-treated horse who will run up to its form under the conditions and you have a viable handicap bet. From there, it is about using some of the guidelines above to separate good handicap form from bad and to grapple with what value those qualifiers might offer. ∎

Avoid illogical and obvious

Keep well-treated horses on your side

Separate good and bad handicap form

# MULTIPLES
## by Graeme Rodway

## INTRODUCTION

A multiple bet is one that combines two or more selections into one single wager with any returns from the first selection automatically staked on the second selection and so on until all selections have won, thus giving a return, or until one selection loses, in which case the whole bet is lost.

Known as a parlay bet in the United States, this combination of several selections multiplies the odds and makes winning less likely, but the reward on offer is significantly larger than for a single bet. That makes multiple bets particularly appealing for small-stakes punters who are seeking a bigger payout than for choosing a single selection to win. The more selections you include, the higher the odds are likely to be and the bigger the potential payout.

Multiple bets are probably most popular in football where, until 2002, accumulators with three or more selections were the only type of wager accepted by law.

Nowadays single bets on soccer are commonplace, but multiple bets remain one of the most popular ways to play and that has been transferred across to horseracing with a huge array of bets available to punters.

There are all kinds of weird and wonderful multiples on offer, but in this chapter I'll be focusing on seven specific bets that are among the most popular with horseracing punters.

## Double

The most simple of the lot. One bet consisting of two selections in different events. Both selections must win (or place if the bet is each-way) to guarantee a return. If the first selection wins, everything that would have been returned is then staked on the second selection.

This is a good way of multiplying the value of two selections and each-way doubles are popular as the place part of the bet runs on to the second selection even if the first doesn't win. A place double will often yield enough for the full stake to be returned should both selections make the places, so it's a solid way of attempting to cover your stake on the win part of the bet.

*'Multiple bets remain one of the most popular ways to play and that has been transferred across to horseracing with a huge array of bets available to punters'*

## Treble

Similar to a double but containing three selections rather than two, a treble is a single bet on three outcomes in different events. All three selections must win (or place if the bet is each-way) to guarantee a win with the returns from the first selection staked on the second, then the returns from the second staked on the third. This is a useful way to multiply the odds on several horses.

## Accumulator

An accumulator is a bet that combines four or more selections in one bet. As with doubles and trebles, this is a group of selections on different events and all of them must win (or place if the bet is each-way) to guarantee a return. Due to the high number of selections the odds are bigger and the risk is greater but, with so much accumulating, the reward for a win is often substantial.

*At the Cheltenham Festival in 2012, Nicky Henderson's head lad Conor Murphy landed the bet of a lifetime when winning £1 million on a five-horse acca after wins for (clockwise from left) Sprinter Sacre, Simonsig, Riverside Theatre, Bobs Worth and (below) Finian's Rainbow*

## Lucky 15

Now we're starting to get more complicated. This is one of the most popular multiple bets among racing punters and the clue is in the name as a Lucky 15 consists of 15 bets on four selections in different events. That equals four singles, six doubles, four trebles and a fourfold accumulator.

The beauty of the Lucky 15 is that only one selection of four must win to guarantee a return and the majority of bookmakers will offer incentives to play the bet. Most will pay out at double the odds if you select only one winner, while several pay a bonus of up to ten per cent for four winners.

The problem is that even if one selection wins at double the odds, it's highly unlikely the original full stake will be covered and you can still end up losing on the bet despite having had a winner.

## Yankee

Basically a Lucky 15 without the four single bets, a Yankee consists of a total of 11 bets on four selections in different events. That equals six doubles, four trebles and a fourfold accumulator

Given we've forsaken the singles, a minimum of two selections must win to guarantee a return but that should at least cover the initial outlay and in most cases two winners will secure a profit.

## Heinz

*Facing page: Dee Ex Bee races in second place at Ascot. In his first two seasons he ran 13 times, finishing in the first four on all but one occasion making him an ideal each-way proposition*

Named after the 57 varieties of the Heinz company slogan, a Heinz bet consists of 57 bets on six selections in different events. That equals 15 doubles, 20 trebles, 15 fourfold accumulators, six fivefold accumulators and one sixfold accumulator. It covers every permutation on six selections.

With no singles involved, a minimum of two selections must win to guarantee a return but, with an initial outlay of 57 bets, it's highly unlikely two winners will cover the original full stake.

## Goliath

Another bet where the name tells everything. A Goliath is one of the biggest bets on offer, made up of 247 bets on eight selections in different events. The bets consist of 28 doubles, 56 trebles, 70 fourfold accumulators, 56 fivefold accumulators, 28 sixfold accumulators, eight sevenfold accumulators and one eightfold accumulator, covering every permutation on all eight selections.

A minimum of two selections must win to guarantee a return but, similar to the Heinz, it's highly unlikely two winners will cover the

original full stake. The Goliath has the potential for a huge payout but the large number of selections means that a significant initial outlay is usually needed.

That's a brief rundown of some of the most popular multiple bets, so let's move on to how we can attempt to take advantage of the bets on offer. When placing a multiple we are trying to multiply the value on our selections and here's a few tips on the best ways to secure a profit.

## FIVE WAYS TO BET SMART ON MULTIPLES

### 1. Play each-way

It's hard enough to pick one winner a day, let alone several in the same bet, so play your multiple each-way. The most important thing when playing multiple bets is to ensure as many of your bets survive as possible. For example, if you're placing a Heinz 57 bet you need to be landing as many of those 57 bets as possible. Even if they are only small wins, they will quickly add up.

The beauty of an each-way multiple is that even if the win part of the bet loses, the place part rolls on with the returns from the first selection staked on the second, then the returns from the second staked on the third and so on. How hard can it be to find five runners to be placed?

It's still difficult, but there is far more chance of having five selections placed than there is of selecting five winners and, given the stakes will be multiplying with each runner that makes the places, the returns for all your selections being placed can often be lucrative. It's a solid way of attempting to gain a return without backing a winner and well worth the extra initial outlay.

*'The beauty of an each-way multiple is that even if the win part of the bet loses, the place part rolls on with the returns from the first selection staked on the second'*

## 2. Don't get greedy

The biggest trap that punters fall into is to get greedy. We see the potential of a huge win and just can't resist chasing those rainbows. We need to resist that temptation and this is especially true when placing multiples, as by adding just one or two extra selections we can take the possible winnings of our bet up from hundreds to thousands, and even tens of thousands.

There is a reason the potential winnings are rising and that's because, even by adding one or two extra selections, we are making the bet significantly less likely to succeed. The more selections we place, the more variables we bring into play and the more likely we are to end up losing.

Restrict the number of selections and don't take unnecessary chances. Concentrate on winning the bet first and worry about the potential winnings afterwards. If you fancy four horses then place a multiple bet on four horses, don't get tempted to add short-priced favourites to bolster the payout. It's a quick way to undo your hard work. There's no such thing as a certainty.

## 3. Don't be afraid to win big

Probably the most popular type of multiple bet is one that includes favourites. Many small-stakes punters see multiple bets as a great way to increase the odds on a host of short-priced favourites.

That isn't necessarily wrong and if you like backing favourites then by all means go ahead, but don't be afraid to do the opposite and perm up several big-priced selections. Remember that multiple betting is probably the most lucrative type of betting and the paydays can be huge for a small outlay. Don't be afraid to take chances on outsiders, especially in each-way multiples.

## 4. Don't always go 'full cover'

A full cover bet is one that includes all possible multiple bets, including doubles, trebles and accumulators, for a given number of selections. I've already outlined seven popular multiple bets and the Yankee, Heinz and Goliath are examples of full cover multiples. But you don't always have to go full cover and it can sometimes pay to just play one part of those bets to higher stakes.

As a general rule of thumb I'm happy to go full cover on anything up to five selections but, when we move into the realms of six, seven and eight, I tend to move away from covering all bets. Instead I'll choose just to play either the doubles, trebles or fourfold accumulators in the bet.

**TOP TIP**

Don't be lured into adding extra selections to your bet to bump up potential winning – restrict the numbers and keep it realistic

For example, if I'm betting on eight selections, rather than doing the 247 bets of the full cover Goliath, I may instead choose just to play the 56 trebles and nothing else. That means I can increase the stakes on the trebles and still keep the initial outlay at less than the Goliath.

You will forfeit the chance of a colossal payout if they all win, but it's worth doing so in order to bolster the returns if only three or four of your selections are successful. Be flexible and don't be constrained by the full cover bet. Don't be afraid to stray away from the traditional multiples and play the ones that suit your selections best. That's the key to making multiples pay.

## 5. Keep stakes small

Probably the most important of the five pieces of advice. Don't go overboard with your stakes on multiples. Always remember that the beauty of multiple betting is the payouts can be huge for only a small outlay, so there is no need to go in overly strong with your stakes. Keep them small.

Multiple bets are high risk and often only one of your selections needs to be unsuccessful for the whole of the multiple to lose. It's extremely difficult to string together four or five consecutive winners and you don't want to be frittering away huge chunks of your bank on this type of bet.

> *'Don't be afraid to stray away from the traditional multiples and play the ones that suit your selections best. That's the key to making multiples pay'*

*'Don't let the gut-wrenching defeats get to you, keep your staking and selections sensible, and there is every chance your day will come'*

*Get your multiple bet correct and there might just be a pot of gold at the end of the rainbow*

Fun and big rewards possible

Keep your stakes small

Expect plenty of hard-luck stories

Bet each-way to reduce risk

## EXPERT VIEW

There is no better bet than a multiple for small-stakes punters looking for an interest bet that could last several races and also has the potential for a lucrative payout. Multiple bets are among the most fun and potentially rewarding wagers, but you'll need plenty of luck to land that windfall.

Don't get carried away with too many selections and keep your stakes small. I've been taught to play small-stake multiples and larger-stake singles and that has proved sound advice.

Never lose sight of the fact that it's very hard to string together several consecutive correct results and you can reduce the risk involved by playing your selections each-way. The payout can still be lucrative if you can string together several places and that's much easier to do.

Multiple bets lend themselves to hard-luck stories. There are going to be any number of occasions where you may be one or two winners away from a substantial payout only to miss out in agonising fashion, but when the stars align there is the potential for a life-changing sum.

Don't let the gut-wrenching defeats get to you, keep your staking and selections sensible, and there is every chance your day will come. ■

# EXCHANGES
## by Paul Kealy

*'A betting exchange is a market place which pits punters against each other'*

*Love Divine (pink colours) powers to victory in the Oaks on the day Betfair opened for business*

## THE BACKGROUND

June 9 2000 – Love Divine lands a sixth Oaks for Sir Henry Cecil (then just Henry Cecil).

Unless you backed her, or have a birthday on that day, it won't mean much, but if you're one of the many people who now make a living from betting on exchanges it's the day you have to thank for your current financial security.

That's the day Betfair traded their first race, matching bets totalling just £3,462. Those were small beginnings and seemingly nothing to worry about for bookmakers, but Betfair was a steamroller about to gather remarkable momentum.

In less than a year they were matching £1 million in bets per week, much less than a year after that they were matching £10m in bets, and by 2003 it was £50m.

Even figures like that are dwarfed these days and it didn't take long for traditional bookmakers to start crying foul. It was to no avail, though, as the horse had bolted and the current bookmaking landscape, in which most firms now routinely offer money-back concessions and extra places for each-way betting, can almost certainly be traced back to the birth of betting exchanges, most notably Betfair, which is by some way the market leader. They simply had to do something.

The fact they whinged so vociferously in the first place is an indication as to why – exchanges, with their incredibly low margins, offered value hitherto unheard of for punters.

We will get on to how to best use them for profit shortly, but for the uninitiated here's a brief summary of how they work.

## WHAT IS A BETTING EXCHANGE?

In the simplest terms, a betting exchange is a market place that pits punters against each other. The exchange is merely the middleman, providing the platform for wagers to be placed and then taking a small cut from whoever profits.

Betfair, now the dominant force, was not an original idea and nor was it the first betting exchange, but it was the first to adopt a stockmarket-style display, showing the prices of all possibilities and the amount of money available.

That was Betfair founder Andrew Black's 'big idea' – one that made him extremely rich – and, while it seems obvious now, it was a model that set him apart from his rivals.

The first on the market, Flutter, adopted an eBay-style system, posting bets as if they were on a billboard. There was no horseracing and placing multiple lays on the same market would cost a fortune as they didn't seem to understand that laying more than one eventuality in the same market actually reduced the total liability. Instead, if you wanted to lay four 5-1 shots for £100 in the same event they would require £2,000 of your money – Betfair would hold only £200, which is the total amount you could actually lose.

There were plenty of other mistakes made by rival exchanges, but there's no need to list them all here. Suffice to say they now all adopt the Betfair model.

Now it's time to look at how we can best utilise an exchange and the best way to do that is to discuss some of the individual markets, but first a word on laying.

## NOW WE CAN ALL BE BOOKMAKERS

This was the big elephant in the room for traditional bookmakers – the idea that anyone without a licence could suddenly become a bookmaker and, what's more, not pay any tax for the privilege.

However, opposing a single horse in a market is hardly a new idea. It was just a lot of hard work in the past as you'd have to back every rival. The problem with that was the bookmaker percentages (explained elsewhere in this book) made it really expensive to do so and if you wanted to bet against an even-money shot the chances are you'd be laying it at nearer 6-4.

Nowadays, if you don't like the look of an even-money shot you simply hit the lay button on an exchange. You will still have to lay at a slightly bigger price than the bookmakers are offering given the low margins you have to deal with on an exchange, but it will be much better value than covering the rest of the field.

*'Andrew Black's big idea made him extremely rich'*

| | |
|---|---|
| **2.44** £16 | **2.48** £49 |
| **3** £22 | **3.2** £15 |
| **8** £16 | **9** £10 |
| **14** £10 | **19** £14 |
| **23** £35 | **30** £14 |
| **42** £10 | **650** £11 |

*'Exchange betting is not an automatic route to riches'*

There will be professional traders on Betfair, Betdaq et al, but making a book is not going to be easy for the average punter, especially with books of little more than 100 per cent in most instances, but the ability to oppose individual horses, teams, humans, etc, is an incredible weapon to have in your armoury.

## THE WIN MARKET

The first and most obvious thing to say about exchange betting is that it is not an automatic route to riches.

With any form of betting you need to have done your homework. If not, you'll lose on an exchange just as surely as you will elsewhere, although you'll likely do so at a slower rate given you haven't got a big, fat bookmaker's margin against you in the first place.

We will proceed on the assumption that the homework has been done and you know what you want to back or lay.

When opening up a race market on a mobile or desktop you will be presented with the list of runners in price order, the prices being quoted in decimals. On a desktop there will be three sets of prices (two on mobile) next to each horse in blue and three in pink.

The blue one on the right will be the current best price and underneath you will see how much is available at that price to back, while the pink one on the left will be the current best price available for you to lay and the amount available at that price. Bear in mind that these are live markets and the nearer to the off you are, the more fluctuations in price you will see.

There is little more to add to this as having a win bet is nothing more than you can do with a bookmaker, but you will notice that

virtually all the prices will be bigger than the bookmakers are offering, in some cases much bigger.

At the front end of the market the price differences may not be so great, so you always have to bear in mind what commission level you are on. On Betfair, the maximum commission level is five per cent (unless you are a premium charge payer, of which more later) and the minimum two per cent.

Most punters will be on five per cent or a little less depending on how much turnover they are responsible for – it would have to be a vast amount to get anywhere near two per cent.

## THE PLACE MARKET

This is where it gets a bit more interesting as before the advent of exchanges the only option for a place-only bet was on the Tote, which has a massive profit margin and rarely offers anything approaching value.

The first thing you will notice about the place market is that the prices bear no relation to the standard each-way terms. This is because in some instances the place terms greatly favour each-way backers and in others they greatly favour the layer.

For instance, any market where a quarter the odds the first four is standard (any handicap with 16 or more runners), you will find that the place prices tend to be a fair bit shorter than a quarter of what is on offer in the win market. This is because in a near 100 per cent win book a quarter the odds the first four would be underround no matter how many runners are in the race.

Conversely, you will find that in an 11-runner race in which standard

*Place odds for handicaps on the exchanges – like the one below – bear little relation to traditional each-way betting*

○ 4-1 shot and 10-1 shot take out 29.1% of the market

○ 4-1 shot and 10-1 shot take out 42.9% of the market after being backed into 5-2 and 6-1

terms are a fifth the odds the first three, the place-only prices will often be significantly bigger than those linked to an each-way bet.

On Betfair these days, depending on the size of the field, there will be place markets for two, three, four, five and sometimes six places and these are some of my favourites to play in.

I like to find what I consider to be a bad favourite and get stuck into laying it for places and covering the stake with a win lay.

Obviously it can go very badly wrong, but so can all forms of betting.

## MARKET MOVERS

Before we get on to arguably the most important exchange innovation – in-running betting – it's worth discussing the dynamics of the Betfair market, or any other betting market to be honest.

By their nature, a lot of punters are conspiracy theorists and once a horse starts drifting in the market there is the assumption that something is wrong or the horse is a non-trier – and 99 per cent of the time it will be complete nonsense.

In any race some horses will be more fancied than others and some will attract more money than others and it's pretty much as simple as that. Those who get backed shorten and those who are not so popular drift, but on Betfair the drifts can seem incredibly large for the simple reason we are dealing with not far off a 100 per cent book on every race.

There is often more than one horse well punted for a race and, for argument's sake, we might have a 4-1 shot who comes into 5-2 and a 10-1 shot who comes into 6-1 from their opening shows.

At the opening show those two took out 29.1 per cent of the

market, but at the off they took out 42.9 per cent. That's a difference of 13.8 percentage points and that 13.8 will be reflected in drifts among the others.

One horse could easily drift from 10-1 to 20-1 (a difference of only 4.3 per cent) or 20-1 to 50-1 (just 2.8 per cent). It is market forces pure and simple.

It's a while since there has been a study of market drifters, but in 2004 Betfair looked at 2,000 races over the last six months of the year and discovered punters would have fared much better backing the drifters than backing the shorteners – the profit was 575 points on drifters against a loss of 345 points for the gambles.

A drifter was defined as a horse who moved out a minimum of 20 per cent in the market, while the reverse was true for the shorteners.

Obviously plenty of gambles are landed, but screams of "they knew" should really be replaced with "they hoped" because that's much nearer the mark.

One thing is for certain, more gambles fail than succeed and if you jump on at the lowest price on every one you are certain to lose a lot of money in the long run.

*'One thing is for certain, more gambles fail than succeed and if you jump on at the lowest price on every one you are certain to lose a lot of money in the long run'*

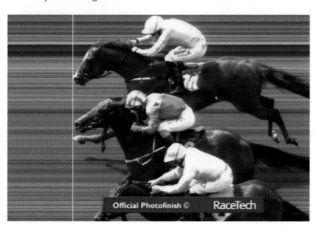

Official Photofinish © RaceTech

## IN-RUNNING BETTING TAKES OFF

In-running is where Betfair really comes into its own. The idea of being able to bet in-play was not a new one when exchanges hit the marketplace, but it was generally limited to slow-moving or long-lasting (or both) sports events – not 5f sprints at Epsom.

Betfair changed all that, and you can now bet right up until the last second of any race in Britain or Ireland (and some in Europe too).

There are many pitfalls, which we will deal with, but here's how it works. As soon as a race is off, Betfair clear all pre-race money and then the market is reopened. After that it's pretty much a free-for-all as punters and traders look to back and lay during the contest.

It is a case of fastest finger first and, because the markets are so fast-moving, if you want to snap up the best price you have to ask for a much shorter one.

That's because the shorter the price you ask for, the nearer the front of the queue you go. For instance, if punter A asks for 5-1 and presses the back button at the same time as punter B who asks for 2-1, punter B's money will sit in front of punter A's and he/she will get matched at whatever is on offer at the time as long as it's bigger than 2-1.

*Pookie Pekan (circled) trails the field at Wetherby in February 2018 before coming with a late run to win after hitting 1,000 in running*

The dynamics of this form of betting meant that pretty soon punters who wanted to get a bet on were asking for the lowest possible price, which on Betfair is 1.01 or effectively 1-100, while layers would routinely offer much bigger than was on offer (the max is 1,000, or 999-1). However, because you can cancel bets as quickly as you can place them, punters can often get a much shorter price then they hoped for or a much bigger one than they really intended to lay. Now we'll look at the different ways you can bet in-running.

## THE MONEY BUYERS AND TIME DELAYS

The first thing to say about in-running betting is that, no matter how much Betfair would like it, there is no level playing field.

If you are sitting at home in front of Racing TV, Sky Racing or ITV the pictures you are seeing are not live. Some can be as much as eight seconds behind real time and that's more than half a furlong. It's a very dangerous game to be playing when you are that far behind the action and it's no surprise there have been those willing to go the extra yard to get an edge.

Exchange shops, which have access to much faster pictures, became popular in the early years and are still in use. Quite simply, punters pay a fee to be able to sit at a computer terminal in a shop and punt on quicker pictures.

*Access to the fastest pictures is key and even drones have been used in a bid to stay one step ahead of the competition*

Even they are not at the head of the pack these days as many racecourses rent out hospitality boxes to punters who sit and watch the action live, while more recently, and much to the chagrin of racecourses, drones have been used to livestream pictures.

Those with access to the fastest pictures tend to be the ones who either bet at huge odds-on (up to 1.01) in the closing seconds of a race or lay horses who cannot possibly win.

The downsides may seem huge (£1,000 to win £10 would not appeal to most people) but there is clearly plenty of no-risk profit to be made if you are good at it or it simply wouldn't happen.

As for the speed of placing bets, if you're going to take it seriously you're going to need to upgrade to some suitable software to enable you to get your bets into the exchange as quickly as possible.

The list of trading platforms available is too long to list in a book of this nature and I wouldn't be able to tell you which ones I think are best. However, you can get details of them all at apps.betfair.com.

## MORE HOMEWORK REQUIRED

Assuming you do not have access to the fastest pictures, you're already at a big disadvantage and it would not be advisable for you to be betting entering the closing stages of a race, but it doesn't mean there are not options still available. But if you think it's just a case of firing up your computer and banging away, the chances are you are not prepared for what lies ahead.

We can all do our pre-race homework and form an idea of what is going to happen before it does, but if we're all honest we'll admit that our preconceived ideas are going to be wrong more often than not.

So you have to be prepared to change your opinion quickly during a horse race and therefore it is imperative you do your homework and understand the running styles of horses, how much they are likely to find when coming under pressure, the riding styles of jockeys on top of them and the tracks they are racing at.

Fortunately there is help out there, not least since Betfair bought Timeform in 2006. Timeform now lists the lowest and highest traded price about every horse in every race, so you can soon build up a fair profile of the sorts of horses you're looking for.

**TOP TIP**

Be prepared to change your opinion of a race once it has begun – an open mind is so important when trying to gain an edge on the exchanges

For instance, some routinely look like they're going to win, trade at odds-on and then get beaten, while others have a habit of trading at much bigger than their pre-race odds and then winning. These are the sort you can look to take advantage of without really needing super-fast pictures.

## BACKING TO LAY

If a horse has a profile of one who routinely trades shorter than its pre-race price, this is the perfect vehicle for backing to lay.

There are various ways of doing this and some simply like to put up a shorter price just to lay the stake back and have a free bet. Others will look to make money whether it wins or loses by laying more than the stake at shorter odds or even putting up several lays at various prices.

As an example, say your opening bet was £40 at 10-1. You could ask to lay £40 at 5-1, thus guaranteeing yourself £200 if it wins and no loss if it fails to do so (assuming your bet gets matched, of course). You could then put in another lay of £100 at evens and if all the bets get matched you've guaranteed yourself £100 whatever happens.

Of course, that is a very simplistic explanation and it will be a case of feeling your way but it is one of my favourite forms of in-running punting.

My own tendency would be to offer the first lay at much shorter than the 5-1 just mentioned, but the lower you go the greater the risk there is of not getting matched.

You also have to keep a clear head and try to keep emotions out of it if you are sitting over your PC while punting. I've lost count of the times I've suddenly decided the horse is going so well it will surely win this time and then cancelled all the lays, only to see it do what it does best and duck out of things.

*'You have to keep a clear head and try to keep emotions out of it if you are sitting over your PC while punting'*

Thankfully I took the potential for this to happen out of the equation when Betfair introduced their 'Keep Bet' facility as now I can put up all the intended lays before the race, change them to Keep Bet so they are entered back into the system once the race is on, and let things unfold without making any rash decisions during the race myself. I basically make sure I'm not in a position to change things. If you've got a game plan, it's best to stick to it.

## LAYING TO BACK

We all know certain horses travel really well and others make it look hard work but keep on finding for pressure, and it's the latter who can be moneyspinners for laying to back when you cotton on to them.

It's simply a case of back to lay in reverse. You lay a horse at a short price pre-race and then hope to get it matched at much bigger once they are off.

However, you have to bear in mind that the Betfair in-running punters are altogether smarter nowadays than used to be the case in the early days and once they have cottoned on to a horse with this sort of profile, the chances of getting fancy prices are reduced.

The 2019 Stayers' Hurdle winner Paisley Park is a case in point. He had looked in trouble at some point in each of his last four races over hurdles but won them all. However, while his biggest traded price for the first of those wins was 130, the second was just 14, the third 9.2 and the last 3.9.

*The diminishing price in running for Stayers' Hurdle winner Paisley Park (below) during his last four runs in the 2018-19 jumps season*

## THE PREMIUM CHARGE

We will finish with just a few words on Betfair's premium charge. Back in the old days Betfair used to trumpet themselves as the fairest option for punters and they never closed down winning accounts. Winners were welcome, they said.

That is still true, but it's also true now that if you win a shedload of money they're going to have some of it – quite a lot in fact.

This really only affects in-running punters and traders who win a lot for very little risk, but they can have to hand over up to 60 per cent of their winnings. The fact they still do so and keep coming back for more tells you it is still worth their while and is a clear indication that Betfair is the dominant force in the market. ■

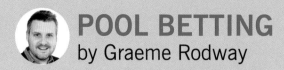

# POOL BETTING
## by Graeme Rodway

## INTRODUCTION

Pool betting is a simple concept that was introduced in Britain with the Littlewoods football pools competition back in 1923. Every player contributes a stake that goes into the pool and then makes selections on an outcome or series of outcomes. The pool, minus deductions made by the operator, is then divided among those who have made the correct selections.

Until recently the Tote was the only bookmaker licensed to provide pool betting on horseracing in Britain, but their exclusive licence expired on July 12, 2018 and since then all bookmakers have been able to provide that service subject to holding a pool betting operating licence. The Tote remains the leading provider, but there are other firms springing up to challenge with Colossus Bets among the main competitors. They offer a similar range of pool betting options on British and Irish horse racing and give the customer the opportunity to cash out after each leg of the bet, a facility that is currently not available with the Tote.

Pool betting is the only type of betting legally available in many countries with France a prime example. The Pari Mutuel is the way of placing traditional win, place and each-way bets across The Channel but, while those types of pool bets are also available on British racing, the reality is that, in the UK, the majority of those wagers are placed at fixed odds with traditional bookmakers. In Britain, pool betting is more commonly used by punters to place bets that give the chance to win a large amount of money for just a small layout. That's the big appeal.

The best examples of such bets are the Exacta (picking the first two in a race), Trifecta (first three), Jackpot/Scoop6 (picking the winner of each of the six nominated races on a single day) and arguably the most popular pool bet available at every British meeting is the Placepot (picking a horse to be placed in the first six races). In this chapter I'll aim to give you a brief rundown of my strategies and I'll also run through the ins-and-outs of the spread markets too.

Spread markets aren't quite as simple as pool betting. The bookmaker will provide two quotes to create a spread: a price at which you can buy (go higher) than their quote and a price at which you can sell (go lower) than their quote and you win or lose money according to the margin by which the value of a particular outcome varies from those quotes.

*'In Britain, pool betting is more commonly used by punters to place bets that give the chance to win a large amount of money for just a small layout. That's the big appeal'*

## PLACEPOT

This bet offers the chance to win without even backing a winner. You need to find a horse to be placed in races 1-6 on a racecard. However, it isn't as easy as it looks and the average Placepot dividend is £407 to a £1 stake. If you get really lucky, the bet has the potential for a huge payout and the record dividend stands at £91,774.50 for just a quid.

You can pick more than one horse in each race and perm up selections to give yourself a better chance. That is also the case with the Jackpot and Scoop6 although the more perms you choose, the more expensive the bet will cost, but the greater the likelihood of a win.

Beware not to play too safe, however. Small dividends are also common and if the favourite is placed in every race the bet will almost always pay less than £20, and in most cases less than £10. The best way to bolster the dividend if you fancy all the favourites is to include the unnamed favourite along with your selection. Therefore, if your original selection goes off favourite you'll double your perm. It also means that if the favourite creeps into third you'll have it covered along with your selection. Using the unnamed favourite to bolster your perms and increase the amount of winning lines makes sense on a day when the market leaders look solid.

The other way to try and bolster the dividend is to leave out the market leader in at least two of the races and the shorter price the favourite, the better. I'll often look for races in which the favourite is forecast to go off at shorter than 2-1 and then include two or maybe three against the market leader, in the hope it is unplaced. This is a risky strategy, but you don't want to be sharing the pool with everyone and fielding against the favourite is the quickest and easiest way to eliminate some of the competition. And that should be the aim of the game in a pool bet.

*If you choose two horses in every race it will equal 64 lines (2x2x2x2x2x2), but, my preferred strategy is to have at least one race in which I include just one horse, the banker. That helps keep the cost of the perm down and opens up the chance to include three, or even more runners, in another race in the bet.*

*My Placepot banker will usually be the most solid, consistent horse on the card, a horse who can be relied upon to run its race. I'll go through the form and try to find a runner who has been placed in at least 50 per cent of its races, if not more.*

## JACKPOT

This bet runs on the same races as the Placepot but requires you to pick the first six winners at a meeting nominated by the Tote. The minimum stake is £1 and multiples are allowed but at no lower than 50p. That makes it tough to keep the bet affordable if playing multiple lines.

This is another bet where I favour the approach of having at least one banker. With a minimum unit stake of 50p, perms can quickly become expensive and sticking with one banker and surrounding that selection with several well-covered legs is the way to go.

Finding the Jackpot banker is a little different to the Placepot. The Jackpot banker really needs to be the most likely winner on the card and, for all that everyone will probably be looking for the same, I'm happy to take a chance on getting a result in one of the other races in order to try and bolster the dividend, rather than taking a chance on the banker. I'll often stick with one of the shortest priced runners on the card, bank on it, and move on quickly.

If the shortest-priced horses on the card do go in then the dividend will suffer so don't be afraid to stick in a few outsiders in some of the other legs. Because only the winner counts, a massive outsider can often prove a skinner, taking out all bar a few units and leaving the potential for a massive payout. With that in mind, don't be afraid to put in four or five different horses in the more competitive races in the hope of getting the results you need.

One of the toughest of all the horse racing pool bets, the Jackpot offers the chance for a massive reward but you will probably need plenty of perms to have a realistic shot at it and even then the likelihood of success isn't high. Plenty of luck will be required along the way.

*'Because only the winner counts, a massive outsider can often prove a skinner, taking out all bar a few units and leaving the potential for a massive payout'*

## SPREAD BETTING

The financial markets and sports betting tends to be where spread betting comes into its own, but firms like Sporting Index and Spreadex offer markets on horse racing and I like to simplify the task. They are giving you a value and asking you if the result is going to be higher or lower than their quoted values. Buy and sell equals higher or lower.

Spread firms will offer an index. In races with 12 or more runners they will offer 50pts to the winner, 30pts to the runner-up, 20pts to the third and 10pts to the fourth. It's usually 50:25:10 for any other race although there are exceptions, the Grand National being the big one.

They will then give each horse a quote, so for example the favourite might be quoted at 20-23. That means you need to choose higher than 23 or lower than 20. So if you think the favourite will finish in the first two you'll be a buyer, but out of the first two you'll sell.

You then win or lose the unit stake times the difference. So if you've bought the favourite at 23 and he finishes only third and is awarded 20, you'll lose three times your unit stake. If he were to win and be awarded 50pts, you'd win 27 times your unit stake. Beware of the other side though, if he finishes out of the first four and makes up 0, you lose 23 times your stake.

There are several other options available including match bets, where one horse is pitted against another in a match, and you can buy or sell one horses supremacy over the other in lengths. Daily markets encompassing every race on a single meeting, or even day, are also on offer with any number of betting options, but you'll need to be an experienced spread punter and have a serious knowledge of figures before venturing into those murky waters. Playing the percentages is key.

*The big upsides and downsides make this way of betting not for the faint hearted, but it can be an appealing way to back outsiders. Most horses trading at double-figure prices in traditional markets will be on offer with single-figure buy quotes on the spread markets and your horse will usually need only finish in the first four to net you a profit.*

## SCOOP6

A similar bet to the Jackpot in that you are required to pick six winners. The significant difference being the six races are selected across the cards on a Saturday, usually made up of a combination of the most competitive on the day and those shown on terrestrial television.

Add to that a minimum unit stake of £2 and the bet becomes an extremely expensive one if you wish to select multiple perms, which is the only realistic way of finding six winners.

Given the high minimum unit, the best way to play it is with two bankers and coverage on the other four races. I attempt to turn the bet into a double, trying to pick two certain winners and banking on them, then filling the other four races with as many horses as my budget allows.

*(Above) The £2 Scoop6 bet that netted over £150,000 for Geraldine Hughes from Liverpool in 2014; (right centre) Agnes Haddock celebrates landing the Scoop6 bonus in 2007, winning a total of nearly £650,000*

How you find your bankers isn't easy as the races selected for this bet rarely contain short-priced favourites. But there should still be a couple of races that contain a clear favourite, so try to find the least-competitive races of the six in the bet and bank in those.

Even if all the favourites win and the results are favourable the payout is still likely to be relatively high given the competitive nature of the bet and there is a bonus pool into which all win fund winners are entered for the following week. To win a share of the bonus fund, you'll need to pick the winner of the nominated bonus race as selected by totepool.

Should you fail to find all six winners, there is also a consolation place fund which operates in the same way as a Placepot. If you have a selection placed in each of the six races you can scoop the place pool, but if you're playing this bet you're probably in it for the lottery style windfall.

## EXACTA/TRIFECTA

Two of the most popular pool bets that don't include multiple legs or races. Instead we just need to concentrate on one race and find either the first two home (Exacta) or first three past the post (Trifecta). We can use perms effectively here too by selecting several horses.

You can choose your horses in the correct order or any order and I'd usually perm my runners up to come home in any order. It's hard enough to predict the winner of each race let alone trying to come up with the second and third as well, in the correct order.

Perm them up to make it easier and I usually look to get between four and five runners on my side if the race is competitive enough to allow that approach. Four horses in a Trifecta is 24 lines, five is 60 lines, and four in an Exacta is 12 lines, while five comes out at 20. It sounds like a lot but I'll be aiming at races with between 15-20 runners in which the pool is strong. That way there is a lot of competition and the payout should cover the layout. Well in theory.

This is where we can apply some Placepot strategy. Look for consistent horses who can be relied upon to run their races and then surround them with runners who are well handicapped but less reliable. That way we have a couple of shots at a big price winner to bolster the dividend, while also putting in the more solid options alongside them with the places in mind.

We can apply this strategy to both Exacta and Trifecta but always remember the more perms you take the better the result you are going to need in order to make a profit and, like all pool bets, it doesn't pay to play it too safe. If you want to play the favourite I'd suggest perming the market leader with some of the big outsiders in the field in an attempt to boost the dividend.

## TOP TIP

Don't play it too safe – you might end up winning but there is a good chance you'll get back less than your outlay

## ❝ EXPERT VIEW

Years of experience tell me that pools can be the most fun and rewarding bets but also the most agonising. If you take this route then you're going to end up with any number of hard luck stories. I've lost count of how many times I've reached the last leg of the Jackpot or Placepot only to be denied a potentially life-changing windfall at the final obstacle. It's so frustrating.

However, when you do hit the big one it'll more than likely be enough to cover the majority of the losses and that's the great appeal of pool betting. That chance to win big money from just a small outlay

is something that generally isn't on offer with the majority of bookmakers.

Spread Betting is for the thrill-seekers but if you're going to make it pay you need an iron grip on the numbers. I've always felt this type of betting is more of a maths challenge than anything else. Can you play the percentages well enough to make it pay?

To sum up, it's hard enough to find one winner, let alone the several needed to land some of these exotic bets and you will need to be tough to survive some long losing runs. But the rewards are there if you can stick to your guns and not let the agonising losses get to you. ∎

Fun and rewarding bets

Win big money from a small outlay

Prepare yourself for long losing runs

please check your tickets

**SINGLE RACE BETS**

**tote**win

**tote**place

**tote**trifecta

**tote**exacta

**tote**swinger

**MULTI RACE BETS**

**tote**placepot

**tote**quadpot

**tote**jackpot

**tote**scoop6

# ANTE-POST
## by Tom Segal

### INTRODUCTION

There was a time when ante-post betting was a huge part of the betting industry. The Derby is named after an ante-post wager between the Earl of Derby and Sir Charles Bunbury in 1780, while one of racing's hall-of-fame trainers, Barry Hills, got his career started when landing a huge gamble on Frankincense in the 1968 Lincoln.

Many punters will remember the Nashawn story when the lads in Lambourn were queuing up to use the telephone boxes in the high street to back him for the Guineas and Derby after an incredible bit of work.

None of that was possible for a good 20 years afterwards with bookmakers wary of laying any horse for decent money and, as a result, ante-post betting went completely out of fashion.

Of course bookmakers will never allow a Nashwan situation to occur again but there is strong evidence that ante-post betting is having a bit of a resurgence and amazingly it's the bookmakers that are responsible.

If we consider an ante-post bet to a wager placed before the declarations are known then all of a sudden we are in a golden period

*Following success in the 2,000 Guineas, Nashwan wins the 1989 Derby to land a plethora of ante-post wagers*

for small-scale ante-post punters. The bookmakers are pricing up every televised race at the five-day stage and are using punters to shape the market for them. Consequently, the five-day stage is where punters can find the best value because it is there that we find the untouched market and big prices about horses that end up being backed off the boards.

Contrast that to bets placed on the morning of the race. Those punting at that time are always going to struggle to find a value bet. All the midweek punters have sorted out the overpriced horses and have backed them accordingly, while the bigger prices are out there because no one fancies them.

There is a proviso, though, why is there always a proviso? And that is staking because ante-post punters will be limited to how much they can stake. However, having a bet with five or six different bookies racks up quickly and, in the exchange era, you can quickly find yourself in a great position, whether you are a punter that likes to let things ride or one of those trading types.

Throw in non-runner no bet concessions at the Cheltenham Festival and the Grand National and it really isn't hard for a punter to beat the price these days. The problem is getting one over the line in front, but as a keen ante-post punter, I would say that now is as good a time as any to start considering betting before the declarations are known.

*'The five-day stage is where punters can find the best value because it is there that we find the untouched market and big prices'*

## FIVE WAYS TO BET SMART ANTE-POST

### 1. The price must be right

The only point to ante-post betting is securing a bigger price than you would on the day. Why risk your stake days, weeks or months before the race if you can't be sure that you are beating the market.

Consequently, in the modern age where the on-the-day bookmakers are vying for your business and tend to find their betting percentages by pushing out those at the front of the market, there is simply no point in playing at short prices ante-post. You might not beat the price and you have all the risks that come with betting ante-post.

In fact, it's best to make a rule as to what is an acceptable price for the risk involved and stick to it. I rarely bet ante-post unless the horse concerned is a double-figure price or I'm supremely confident that the market has got it wrong on a shorter priced one.

## 2. Choose right race with an opposable favourite

The big key to ante-post betting is finding the right horse for the right race. What I mean by that is we can all find a horse we like but if his/her big-race target is in a highly competitive race where there is a rock-solid favourite, then stepping in early might not be the right play.

Try to find the race where it's pretty obvious that those at the head the market are the weakest, or where you are betting into a market that hasn't been formed properly yet. Immediately you have found the value and the potential for your horse to crash in price, that in essence is the whole point of ante-post betting.

Trying to take on a Treve in the Arc or a Kauto Star in the King George was a total waste of time, effort and money. Whereas there are plenty of races where the market is made up on reputation rather than form. Assessing the strength of the opposition is a key component to a good ante-post bet – it's just as important as assessing the worth of any particular horse.

*Tiger Roll could be backed at 20-1 for a second Grand National when the weights came out*

## 3. Timing is the key

The one big advantage ante-post betting has over betting on the day is timing. On the day the bookmakers know when we are going to bet. They have all the runners – normally a lot more information than most punters – and the market is always skewed in their favour.

Ante-post betting is the opposite – bookmakers have no clue when you are going to bet or what the make-up of the field is going to be. Time is on your side and therefore make sure the timing of your bet is correct.

For example, it's rarely a great idea to back a horse ante-post in the days before he or she is due to run in a trial for the race you fancy them in. You won't be the only one to have noticed and mathematically it often makes more sense to back it in the trial and then accept a smaller price in the big race with the extra knowledge you have gleaned from it's trial run.

In terms of the big handicaps on the Flat and jumps, the day of the unveiling of the weights is often a good day to consider having a bet. For example Tiger Roll was available at 20-1 to win his second Grand National in 2019 when the weights were announced, but was 6-1 after he'd won the cross-country at the Cheltenham Festival.

However the best edge for ante-post punters is on the Tuesday and Wednesday every week. The bookmakers price up all the televised Saturday races and it is you versus an odds compiler at that stage. A one-on-one match. Come the morning of the day of the race it's you versus thousands of others who have had a look and any value that would have been there has almost inevitably gone. Of course winning is still possible but to do so you have to be less price-sensitive than used to be the case.

## 4. Put yourself in the mind of the trainers

Trainers are creatures of habit. They like to repeat processes that have worked well for them in the past and ante-post punters can take advantage by studying their methods and asking why a trainer is running a horse in a certain race.

For example John Gosden likes using trial races. He hates going into a Classic or a big race without his horse having had the ideal preparation, so when the entries come out for the Dante or the Voltiguer, for example, we can use that as a way into his mind.

That doesn't mean we back all his horses entered in those races for the Derby or the St Leger but we get a clue into how highly he rates those horses.

Similarly if he enters a three-year-old in the Cambridgeshire we can be pretty sure that he thinks they are well-handicapped potential

*'In terms of the big handicaps on both the Flat and jumps, the day of the unveiling of the weights is often a good day to consider having a bet'*

## Race Simplification

One of the biggest problems punters have when it comes to striking a bet is overcomplication. On the Flat we are all obsessed by factors like the draw, the ground, the pace, trainer form and the jockey that we often forget the crucial – and by far the most important factor – the ability of the horse concerned.

Over jumps there are less of those factors to worry about, but nevertheless, punting on the day of the race provides a much tougher mental conundrum than ante-post betting does.

Take the draw. On every Flat race there is discussion about the draw, sometimes it's worthwhile but sometimes it's not. Ante-post betting involves none of that because we don't know it. Without any of those factors punting is taken back to its basest level, trying to find the horse that runs the fastest.

However, it's not always that easy to avoid conversations on the draw, ground conditions or which trainers are in form, and consequently we have all been guilty of overcomplicating a simple puzzle.

What all those factors provide is a mind muddle. The best punters can rid themselves of all the clutter and concentrate on the factors that really matter in any race but it's not always that easy unless of course, you are betting ante-post when the mind clutter simply isn't there.

Group horses. The easy victories of Halling, Pipedreamer and Wissahickon prove that.

Furthermore, using stable tours and listening to what trainers say after and before races gives vital clues too.

It's no different over jumps. Try thinking like Willie Mullins or Nicky Henderson. Why have they chosen to run this horse in that race, have they done it before, is it the perfect time span between this race and a big target coming up.

The best trainers have a plan for their best horses and if we can cotton on to what that plan is we are not one step ahead of the game we are three, four or maybe more.

## Pedigrees are an underused betting tactic

Flat racing is all about the bloodlines – it always has been – but it still amazing how little attention is played to pedigrees when it comes to the Group 1 races on the Flat and increasingly over jumps too.

Never has it been more important than on the Flat because the whole of society is based on speed and everything happening now and quickly. Consequently the whole of the breeding industry has turned into the 'need for speed' and all anyone wants are fast, two-year-olds.

As a result not many horses stay middle-distance and we get into a situation where few horses have a chance of staying the mile and a half in the best races. Consequently the Ballydoyle team clean up year in year out and sons and daughters of Galileo are probably still underrated in the market.

The Classic races are nearly always dominated by the breeding shed and it's pretty easy to get an ante-post edge by concentrating on the guaranteed stayers in middle-distance Group 1 races.

## 5. Make sure to use all the bookmaker concessions at the Cheltenham Festival

There is no doubt that the Cheltenham Festival is now the biggest ante-post race meeting in the world and it provides a great opportunity for punters. The reason being, the non-runner no bet concession that some bookmakers start months in advance of the meeting.

The main problem with any ante-post bet, and the reason why it isn't more popular, is the worry about not getting a run for your money. That is basically taken out of the equation at Cheltenham and in races like the Grand National. Basically the non-runner no-bet provides punters the ability to back horses at big prices without that concern.

Furthermore, there are so many races at the festival in which horses hold many entries and trying to establish the one they intend to run in is a matter of guesswork. That is irrelevant with the non-runner no bet concessions because we know we can back our horse in as many races as we like.

## EXPERT VIEW

All winning bets are fun but some are more fun than others and anyone who has backed the winner of one of the big races of the season at a big price, well in advance of the day, will know what exactly what I mean.

Yes a 10-1 winner of a Thirsk handicap or a Fontwell novice hurdle pays exactly the same as a 10-1 winner of the Derby, the Ebor or the

*Muntahaa and Jim Crowley land the 2018 Ebor*

Champion Hurdle, but in terms of satisfaction and self-esteem there is no comparison.

Since the advent of exchanges the punting narrative has all been about chiselling out a profit in any way possible and that is all well and good but betting should be all about fun and there is nothing like landing a big-priced ante-post bet for that.

The point being that any ante-post bet is simply about your own personal judgement of a good horse. If like me you are a racing fan first and a punter second, then a winning ante-post bet is satisfying on both counts. It's you versus the bookmaker at the basest level – it's why we watch racing day in day out and it's our chance to make it all the thinking time we have put into the sport worthwhile.

We won't be able to set up training like Barry Hills did on the back on an ante-post coup – and getting on for any significant amount is difficult – but on-the-day betting in the exchange era can feel like a bit of a grind. Ante-post racing never does and there is nothing like a successful wager for the punting soul. ■

It's all about your view

Enjoy the ride and have fun

There's nothing quite like an ante-post win

*'If like me you are a racing fan first and a punter second then a winning ante-post bet is satisfying on both counts'*

# THE FESTIVALS
## by David Jennings

*'The most
important piece
of advice is to
work hard and
put in the hours.
Watch every
video you can
– something
you didn't have
access to a few
decades ago
– and gather
every statistic
available. It
will help point
you in the right
direction'*

## INTRODUCTION

Punters have never had it so good. Everything is on our side at the big festivals so you must take advantage.

Ante-post punting has never started so early. There was once a time when the first price you would see for the Cheltenham Gold Cup was on the morning of the race, not now. Betting at the big festivals has changed and changed utterly. Markets are often formed 12 months before the race and all 28 races at the 2019 Cheltenham Festival were priced up by the major firms at least two months before the four-day extravaganza kicked off. It gives the punters every chance to spot value.

The days of betting in cash on track on the day of the race are gradually dying out, although there is still something enjoyable about having an old-fashioned wager minutes before the off.

With 48-hour declarations for all big festivals on the Flat and for the Cheltenham Festival and the Grand National, there is plenty of time to study the final fields and there is terrific value to be snapped up on the morning of each day of the festivals. There are various offers with different bookmakers and vastly improved each-way terms compared to decades ago when it was always a quarter the odds to finish in the first three.

Make sure you take advantage of these place terms and back each-way, especially in handicaps, and don't be afraid to have two bets in the one race at the big festivals.

The most important piece of advice is to work hard and put in the hours. Watch every video you can, something you didn't have access to a few decades ago, and gather every statistic there is available. All that information will help point you in the right direction. Not always, but most of the time.

Betting at the big festivals has the potential to be a punter's paradise but you need to know the right way to go about it.

## FIVE WAYS TO BET SMART

### 1. Don't be put off by big prices

A 25-1 shot at the Cheltenham Festival or Royal Ascot has a stronger chance of winning than a 25-1 shot at Plumpton or Windsor of a Monday. The reason being that most 25-1 shots who run at the smaller tracks midweek are available at such lengthy odds because they have either shown little or are woefully out of form. There are plenty of 25-1 shots at the big festivals who have top-class back form and/or have the potential to win at the highest level.

Take Espoir D'Allen (left) for instance. The unexposed five-year-old had only been beaten once in his previous eight starts over hurdles before his 2019 Champion Hurdle victory, and had easily beaten Wicklow Brave, a Classic winner on the Flat, in his prep at Naas. He had the potential to win a Champion Hurdle but still went off at 16-1.

On the final day of the 2019 Cheltenham Festival, the average winning SP was 23-1. Croco Bay won the Grand Annual at 66-1, Albert Bartlett winner Minella Indo was 50-1 and Pentland Hills won the Triumph Hurdle at 20-1.

The opening winner at Royal Ascot in 2018 was Accidental Agent at 33-1 in the Queen Anne.

Do not be fooled into thinking big prices cannot do the business at the big festivals. They can. You just need to find the right ones.

*The average winning SPs at Cheltenham since 2010. Left is 12.678-1 in 2019*

*The average winning SPs at Royal Ascot since 2010. Left is 9.471-1 in 2019*

*'Backing each-way at the big festivals is essential. The contests have never been so competitive, and the number of places being offered by bookmakers have never been bigger'*

## 2. Back each-way

Double the cost but you are multiplying the prospect of getting something back. Backing each-way at the big festivals is essential. The contests have never been so competitive, and the number of places being offered by bookmakers have never been bigger.

The Grand National is the biggest betting event of the year and firms can offer as many as seven or eight places.

Imagine if you backed Pleasant Company in the 2018 Grand National. You knew he was being trained for the race, had the right profile and was trained by a master in Willie Mullins.

He jumps for fun, is always front rank and goes in pursuit of Tiger Roll from the elbow. He is cutting back Tiger Roll with every stride, but the winning post comes a stride too soon. If you backed him win only you are completely deflated. You have spotted an outsider at 25-1 with a live chance and you got his credentials spot on, yet you come away empty-handed. A short-head is all that had separated you and a small fortune.

At least there is some compensation if you had backed Pleasant Company each-way. A quarter the odds at 25-1 is a shade over 6-1 so you still make a nice profit.

*Pleasant Company (left) just fails to master Tiger Roll at Aintree in 2018*

## 3. Trust festival form

Yeats won four Ascot Gold Cup, Best Mate three Cheltenham Gold Cups and Istabraq three Champion Hurdles. Tiger Roll has won the last two Grand Nationals. Festival form has a habit of recurring and it is not just in the main races either and it is not just the winners who return to races and repeat the dose.

Le Prezien was an eyecatching eighth in the 2017 Grand Annual at Cheltenham and came back a year later to win the same race in impressive fashion under Barry Geraghty. Croco Bay was having his first go at the Grand Annual in 2019 and he made his fourth appearance a winning one.

The Alan Berry-trained Selhurtpark Flyer won the Wokingham in 1997 off a mark of 94 and again in 1998 off 6lb higher.

When a horse wins or runs well in a big handicap at one of the

*Form at the big meetings is a huge plus. Yeats was the Gold Cup master between 2006 and 2009, winning the Ascot marathon four times*

# BETTING GUIDE

*'When a horse wins or runs well in a big handicap at one of the most famous festivals, trainers tend to want to return for another crack'*

most famous festivals, trainers tend to want to return for another crack. They have been bitten by the bug and want to experience it again. They also know the level that's required to win the race in question.

William Henry is a good example. Nicky Henderson's charge was a close-up fourth to Bleu Berry in the 2018 Coral Cup off a mark of 151. Fast-forward 12 months and he arrives back at Cheltenham in the very same race off the very same mark. He storms home to win narrowly under Nico de Boinville *(above)*. Festival form stands the test of time.

## 4. Don't be afraid to have two bets in one race

So much value and so many options. It is ludicrous elsewhere but having two bets in the one race is not a bad idea at big festivals like Cheltenham and Royal Ascot. Indeed, it makes perfect sense.

With so many places on offer with firms in the big handicaps at the big festivals, having two bets each-way is actually a shrewd move.

If firms are offering a quarter the odds the first five places in handicaps, two each-way bets are advised. In last year's Wokingham at Royal Ascot, Dreamfield was a red-hot 2-1 favourite in a massive field of 28. The two I liked in the race were Major Jumbo, whom I backed at 25-1, and 20-1 shot Tis Marvellous.

Both ran as well as I was hoping with Major Jumbo taking third, only beaten three-quarters-of-a-length, and Tis Marvellous just a short head behind him in fourth. There was a tidy profit from both bets despite neither of them winning.

*The business end of the 2018 Wokingham at Royal Ascot, with Major Jumbo (grey) and Tis Marvellous (far left) third and fourth at decent prices*

ROYAL ASCOT

## 5. Play on the morning of the race

If you're not on at juicy prices in ante-post markets, then wait for the morning of the race. That is when the best value can be mopped up.

Al Dancer was an 11-4 shot for the 2019 Supreme Novices' Hurdle, the race that opened the Cheltenham Festival, ten days before the race following his impressive Betfair Hurdle success at Ascot. On the Tuesday morning of the race, a few different firms were offering 11-2 about him. He was then shortened a point to 9-2 joint-favourite at the off.

Al Boum Photo was as big as 16-1 on the Friday morning of the Cheltenham Gold Cup before winning the race at an SP of 12-1.

There is terrific value to be had on each morning at the big festivals and it is perhaps most important to remember that fact on Grand National morning. Everything tends to shorten in the hour before the world's most famous race so shop around for the best price you can and make sure to take the price.

*Al Boum Photo wins the Cheltenham Gold Cup at 12-1 having been 16s on the morning of the race*

### TOP TIP

Always take a price when having a bet on the morning of the Grand National

## EXPERT VIEW

As a punter, the big festivals should be your bread and butter. There are endless opportunities.

There are so many form lines, there is so much information at your fingertips and bookmakers are falling over themselves looking for your business. What's not to love.

There will be a price war among betting firms on the opening day of most big festivals, especially Cheltenham and Royal Ascot and you need to take advantage.

You need to put in the hours. Watch videos, see what the stats say and figure out where the value lies. Don't be lazy and focus on the top few in the market either. As already mentioned, the big festivals are where big prices pop up time and time again. You need to delve a little deeper at Cheltenham or Royal Ascot than you do at Taunton of a Tuesday.

In the handicaps, and often in the graded races, it is vital that you back each-way to give yourself the best possible chance of getting something back. There are some terrific place terms with certain firms during the big festivals.

Festival form tends to stand up so familiarise yourself with what happened at the previous year's festival and the year before that and perhaps even the year before that.

The most recent development of betting at the big festivals has been the value on offer on the morning of each day. You seldom see a horse shorten on the morning of the race as firms are keen to push them out to attract business.

With 48-hour declarations now in place for all the big festivals on the Flat and for Cheltenham too, you have plenty of time to study the final fields so time constraints cannot be used as an excuse.

The big festivals host the best racing with the best horses. It is the cream of the crop, so punters pride themselves on making a profit at them. ■

**You need to put in the hours**

**It's vital to back each-way**

**There is plenty of value on the day**

# PEDIGREE PUNTING
## by James Thomas

### INTRODUCTION

Profitable punting requires some understanding of the thoroughbred. You don't need to know how to saddle up or have any experience of mucking out, but it is a major advantage to have a grasp of the world of difference that can exist between one horse and another.

Much like humans, racehorses can exhibit a vast array of traits. Some are all about speed while others are suited by a test of stamina; some are precocious and will come to hand early, while others require plenty of patience; and others are destined to jump fences and stay three miles.

But where do these differences come from? More often than not, the answer can be found within a horse's pedigree.

Given that each horse's pedigree contains a wealth of information that is valuable, not just on a horse's first start but often for a good time afterwards, it would be folly to overlook the clues contained within them.

Examining pedigrees can be a daunting task, with each racehorse

hailing from a family that goes back many generations. Indeed, the entire modern thoroughbred breed traces its roots to just three founding stallions – the Byerley Turk, the Darley Arabian and the Godolphin Barb – who were imported to Britain in the early 18th century.

However, an equine history degree is not required to make sense of pedigrees, as an enormous amount can be gleaned merely by an understanding of a horse's sire (father), dam (mother) and damsire (mother's father), and these are likely to be names who have made an impact on the racecourse much more recently.

Some stallions are better than others and familiarising yourself with the big names is a useful starting point. Much like the best trainers tend to be sent the most expensive or exciting prospects or the most successful jockeys are booked to ride the most fancied runners, success also begets success in the stallion ranks.

This means those stallions perceived to be the best at producing winners will ultimately receive the best opportunities to breed the most winners by being sent the mares with the best credentials.

Understanding stallions like Dubawi and Galileo have better records – and will have therefore received better opportunities at stud and will consequently produce the winners of more races – than the likes of Multiplex and Sepoy is a basic but often underestimated fact of racing. All horses are not born equal.

'Understanding stallions like Dubawi and Galileo have better records than the likes of Multiplex and Sepoy is a basic fact of racing. All horses are not born equal'

Sadler's Wells leads his sons Galileo, Montjeu and High Chaparral at Coolmore in 2007

*O Dark Angel's progeny
have a strike-rate of 37
per cent over 5f-6f*

*O New Approach's progeny
have a strike-rate of 27
per cent over 5f-6f*

*O Dark Angel's progeny
have a strike-rate of 21
per cent over 10f-11f*

O New Approach's progeny
have a strike-rate of 32
per cent over 10f-11f

## FIVE PEDIGREE AND BREEDING ANGLES TO HELP YOU BET SMART

### 1. Sire habits

As a rudimentary rule of thumb, a stallion's progeny (sons and daughters) will tend to follow in the mould of their sire.

Sprinters tend to sire horses whose main attribute is speed, stayers tend to produce horses whose forte is stamina, while milers usually fall somewhere in between.

Pedigree may not help you predict with pinpoint accuracy a horse's optimum racing distance, but it can be a great way to compare and contrast the various runners in any given field, especially when there is limited form to go on.

If you see a three-year-old son of Galileo, himself a winner of the Derby and now the dominant sire of the modern era, lining up in a Derby trial, it would be a fair assumption that the horse would be better suited to the test at hand than one by Exceed And Excel, another hugely successful sire but one whose runners are much better known for their speed and precocity.

By the same token, a daughter of Kodiac – a record-breaking sire of two-year-old winners – is likely to be better suited by making her debut over 5f in early May than a filly by Sea The Stars, whose progeny tend to progress extremely well with age.

Admittedly the cases mentioned above are clear-cut examples, but the wider point is applicable to just about every race. In the same way as deciphering other pieces of evidence such as jockey bookings, draw stats, market moves and trainer form, a level of judgement is required when using pedigree to help assess a horse's suitability for a particular set of circumstances.

The Racing Post website features a whole host of stats on a stallion's progeny performance, and with very little effort you can quickly build up a picture of what sort of attributes a stallion is likely to pass on, making those crucial judgements easier to formulate.

For example, if you wanted to compare a son of Dark Angel against a son of New Approach, who are taking on each other in a race over 6f, the former's progeny have a strike-rate of 37 per cent over 5f-6f, whereas the latter's operate at 27 per cent. These stats would suggest that, generally speaking, the progeny of Dark Angel will be better suited by the test at hand.

However, should the two meet again next season over 1m2f, one could reasonably expect the outcome to be different, as New Approach's sons and daughters have a strike-rate of 32 per cent over 10f-11f, compared to Dark Angel's 21 per cent.

Once you are in the habit of checking such facts, you will quickly build up a picture of which stallions' progeny perform well under particular circumstances. Availing yourself of such information can be a useful tool not only in finding winners but avoiding the horses who represent bad value.

## 2. Seek out the stamina

Stamina has become something of a maligned trait in the thoroughbred, with a marked shift towards speed and precocity having taken place in the breeding world in the modern era. Thankfully that shift has not been mirrored in the race programme, so there are still plenty of races where stamina is essential.

When assessing a horse's chance as they step up in trip, their pedigree should be your first port of call. Based on a horse's breeding, primarily the distances at which his or her sire and/or dam performed best, you should be able to get a fair sense of what sort of trip will prove to be their optimum. Therefore, while a horse may have performed only to a certain level over shorter distances, his or her pedigree may point to improvement – and sometimes a lot of it – being on the cards once a stiffer test of stamina is introduced.

Take Stradivarius, for example. He is by Sea The Stars, who had the class to win over 7f at two but was at his best over 1m2f and 1m4f at three. His dam,

*'Based on a horse's breeding you should be able to get a fair sense of what sort of trip will prove to be their optimum'*

*Stradivarius – as his breeding suggested – was a massive improver at three*

Private Life, won over 1m3f at three and was placed at Listed level over 1m4f, and in turn she is by Bering, a Group 1 winner over 1m4f at three and runner-up in the Prix de l'Arc de Triomphe.

When the sum total of that lineage is taken into consideration, it was a near certainty that Stradivarius would progress as his stamina was drawn out at three. By the end of his three-year-old season he had duly improved his Racing Post Rating by a huge 39lb having won three races – over 1m2f at 9-4, 1m6f at 11-2 and 2m at 6-1. He won each time he went up in trip and those who delved into his pedigree are likely to have been richly rewarded.

Not every horse will scale the heights that Stradivarius has, but each year there are any number of horses with similar profiles who will improve beyond all recognition from two to three (and possibly beyond) once granted a sterner test of stamina.

As Stradivarius proves, such horses can win at two, but their juvenile campaigns are often about laying a foundation and learning their trade. The real fun can begin at three, an age at which they have been specifically bred to flourish, as clearly indicated by their pedigree.

*Book 1 of the Tattersalls October Yearling Sale attracts plenty of keen eyes given its status as one of the most prestigious sales of its type in Europe*

### 3. Cash is king

When it comes to racehorses, much like everything else in life, you tend to get what you pay for. Therefore it is well worth paying close attention to a horse's sales history for clues as to his or her future prospects. The biggest outlet for Flat-bred racehorses is the yearling sales, where owners, trainers and bloodstock experts source their horses as unbroken youngsters.

On the whole, these people are hugely knowledgeable and have vast experience when it comes to understanding what makes a horse fast – be it pedigree or a striking set of physical attributes – so if they are willing to pay a large sum to buy a horse at the sales it is often with good reason.

A deal of context needs to be applied, though, as all

'The biggest outlet for Flat-bred racehorses is the yearling sales, where owners, trainers and bloodstock experts source their horses as unbroken youngsters' racehorses are luxury items, so cost plenty. One way to identify the significance of purchase price is to reference a horse's cost against either the sale's or sire's average price, information that is readily available on the Racing Post website.

Objectively speaking, 100,000gns (£105,000) is a huge sum of money. But were someone to pay that for a Dubawi colt at Book 1 of the Tattersalls October Yearling Sale – traditionally the most prestigious sale of its type in Europe – you might have to question how they managed to buy the horse so cheaply, as he will have cost £250,000 (Dubawi's covering fee) to breed, and the sire's progeny are in such high demand that they averaged 750,000gns (£782,250) in 2018.

By the same token, when a horse by a relatively inexpensive sire makes a huge sum, it often pays to sit up and take notice.

There are other types of sales too, with Flat racehorses sold as foals, yearlings, unraced two-year-olds (at sales known as the breeze-ups, where horses gallop in front of prospective buyers before being sold) and once they have run as horses in training.

Plenty will appear at more than one type of sale, so it is always worth checking to see how a horse's value has changed as it progresses with age. It would be a positive sign if a horse's value has been enhanced, particularly to a significant degree, from foal to yearling or yearling to two-year-old (or in some cases both).

There will always be exceptions to the rule, however. Irish Derby winner Latrobe, for instance, cost €88,000 when bought as a foal, but his value dropped to 65,000gns when bought by Joseph O'Brien as a yearling before going on to land Group 1 laurels as a three-year-old.

By and large, though, the people who buy racehorses know what they are doing, so their expertise can become your expertise by taking note of a horse's purchase price before it runs.

## 4. Give a dam

Given they are often names we are familiar with or have the most information about, there is a tendency to focus on the impact a stallion has on a horse's profile. However, there are two sides to every pedigree, and it would be unwise to think the mare would not have just as much of a bearing on a horse's profile as the sire does.

The first thing to consider is what the mare achieved on the track herself. Was she precocious and performed to her best at two or did she take time to reach her peak? Was she a sprinter or more of a middle-distance performer? Did she like quick, summer ground or was she an all-weather specialist?

Attributes such as these tend to be heritable traits, so if a mare had a liking for a particular set of circumstances on the racecourse, the chances are her progeny will follow suit.

**TOP TIP**

Don't overlook the female side of the pedigree - this can reveal plenty of information and is just as significant as the sire profile

There is also a mare's progeny record. Like stallions, some mares produce more than their fair share of winners, instilling in their sons and daughters an inherent ability to run harder and faster than is the norm. While such mares are uncommon, their talents can be overlooked by the betting market, giving those inclined to dig a little deeper that vital extra bit of insight.

Sometimes it won't be possible to assess how a mare performed on the track as she didn't race herself, and for younger mares they may not have produced any previous runners on which to base an opinion.

However, there is still her own pedigree to provide some basis for assumption, with the mare's sire (damsire), the stallions she has been mated to or how much she herself cost – or the price of her subsequent offspring – often giving an indication as what type of progeny she is likely to produce. The same critical processes applied to stallions can be transferred almost directly to mares.

## 5. Foaling date

They say age is just a number, but when it comes to racehorses, especially two-year-olds, that is not quite true. All racehorses have their official birthday on January 1, but there can be a wide variance between their real birthdays.

The majority of Flat-bred racehorses are foaled between January and May. Given that the first juvenile races of the season are usually held in March – with the Brocklesby at Doncaster's Lincoln meeting the traditional two-year-old curtain-raiser in Britain – some horses may make their racecourse debuts well short of their actual second birthday.

Why does this matter? In simple terms, it can put them at a distinct

*'All racehorses have their official birthday on January 1, but there can be a wide variance between their real birthdays'*

developmental disadvantage. Should a horse foaled in the last week in May take on a horse foaled in the first week in January, it would have had four months less in which to grow and strengthen up. That is a significant difference, precisely the kind that can impact the outcome of a race.

Clearly things even themselves out as time progresses, but it is always worth double checking what date a horse was foaled, particularly in relation to those it is taking on during its two-year-old campaign.

As with all pieces of information you can harvest pre-race, context is still important. So if Horse A has a later foaling date than Horse B, but Horse A is bred to be particularly precocious and Horse B is bred to be a later-maturing type, the difference in age can be negated by breeding.

Another factor to consider is where the horse was bred. Those born in the US, where the summers are warmer and therefore a greater rate of physical development would seem likely, are often thought to be at something of an advantage in the early stages of their racing careers compared with their European counterparts.

## EXPERT VIEW

A question often asked about the talent of racehorses is: is it nature or nurture? In my opinion, nature very rarely comes into it. While it is true enough that the level of talent a horse inherits will come from its relatives, no two horses are mated purely by chance, as would happen in nature.

Breeding racehorses is a complex business, and one that has given rise to a multi-billion-pound industry worldwide. While the old adage of 'breed the best to the best and hope for the best' is often wheeled out, it is unlikely any breeder will allow their fortunes – quite literally in some cases given the huge sums of money involved – to rest on blind hope alone.

A blend of cutting-edge genetics, analysis of countless statistics and a wealth of experience will be called upon when most breeders decide which stallions to mate with their mares, which in short means that almost all racehorses have been precision engineered for a specific purpose.

Understanding what that purpose is – or the circumstances that will

*'A blend of cutting-edge genetics, analysis of countless statistics and a wealth of experience will be called upon when most breeders decide which stallions to send their mares to'*

best allow a horse to perform to its peak – can be key when it comes to finding winners.

To be clear, breeding and pedigrees matter, as they are at the very core of the animals we seek to understand when we look to profit from punting. Of course human factors come into play, be it the trainer, owner, jockey, clerk of the course determining the ground or anyone else who comes into contact with a racehorse, and clearly it would be unwise to back pedigrees blind, as context is vital.

But the horse's pedigree is a constant, and to understand what that tells us about each horse can help us get ahead of the crowd who rely upon racecourse form alone.

Those who are familiar with pedigrees will already understand the impact they can have on traits like speed, stamina, precocity and even outright talent. But anyone who deems pedigrees as something to be disregarded really are missing a trick.

While it's true that making sense of pedigrees and associated information is not always straightforward, even the most basic elements, such as knowing the sire of an unraced runner or being aware of a horse who cost significantly more than his or her rivals, is information well worth knowing. ∎

Great way to get ahead of crowd

Not wise to back pedigrees blind

But to ignore them is missing a trick

*Focusing on the action in the ring at the Arqana August Yearling Sale*

# INTERNATIONAL BETTING
## by Ron Wood

## MAJOR WORLD RACING EVENTS

**Dubai World Cup Carnival** *With regular meetings at Meydan from January to March, this event attracts runners from around the world and culminates in the mega-bucks Dubai World Cup, a 1m2f Group 1.*

**Royal Ascot** *One of the highlights of the British calendar, this glamorous five-day June fixture is very much international these days.*

**Prix de l'Arc de Triomphe** *Staged in Paris at Longchamp in October, this 1m4f Group 1 is considered by many to be the best race in the world. It has been dominated by the Europeans but the Japanese have been trying for years to win it.*

Racing is truly an international game and these days it's easier than ever to keep up with – and punt on – the action from around the world.

With trainers taking horses here, there and everywhere, increased television coverage and bookmakers pricing up races from all sorts of weird and wonderful venues, punters are spoilt for choice.

## DON'T CUT CORNERS

It'd be easy to get lazy when it comes to betting on foreign racing, as it might seem an impossible task – or too much like hard work – to learn the local form. But putting in the time can give you a big edge.

Whereas there are countless shrewdies to hoover up the value on the domestic racing scene, there is often less focus on international racing so bookie errors can be easier to spot and cash in on.

The Racing Post's ever-increasing database is a useful tool, and for the high-profile international races there's video aplenty on YouTube.

## FAMILIARISE YOURSELF WITH THE TRACK

It's essential to understand the course: Does it favour front runners? Is it a stiff track? What sort of going conditions can be expected? Is there a draw bias? That sort of thing. Gaining an understanding of the circuit is crucial in knowing which horses might be favoured.

## RESPECT THE HOME ADVANTAGE

When it comes to the major international meetings it's easy to fall for the exciting foreign raiders and/or those horses you're already familiar with, like an Aidan O'Brien runner at the Breeders' Cup. Favouritism towards those you know so well may creep in.

But home advantage can be huge given that the local horses don't have to acclimatise and many of them will have established themselves as the best of the best in their jurisdiction.

Delving a bit deeper, there will be certain types of races that the home team do particularly well in – think dirt races at the Breeders' Cup – and others where they are less dominant, so take a look back at past editions for any such trends.

## THE MARKETS

Most bookmakers will offer prices on major international races, often including ante-post markets, and many firms also price up the more mundane day-to-day action in a whole host of countries.

In some cases bookmakers will offer the local pool betting like France's PMU (Pari Mutuel Urbain), a state-controlled betting system.

There can be huge amounts of money in such pools for major races so visiting horses, who may not be on the radar of local bettors, can offer value.

Not all bookmakers provide this service so it can be a tiresome process trying to find a firm who'll take such bets, but it's worth the effort to make sure you get on in the market offering the best odds.

There's also often the option of the betting exchanges like Betfair. ▨

MAJOR
WORLD
RACING
EVENTS

*Spring Racing Carnival* A series of race meetings in Australia featuring a number of Group 1s, most notably the Melbourne Cup – the race that stops a nation on the first Tuesday in November.

*Breeders' Cup* Two days of top-class racing in the US at the end of October/ early November, it attracts the best domestically trained runners as well as plenty of global challengers and has produced any number of memorable clashes since its inception in 1984.

*Hong Kong International Races* Not much explanation needed with a title like that, other than to note it is four Group 1 races at Sha Tin racecourse in December. It's usually high-class and competitive.

*Cross Counter streaks home in the 2019 Melbourne Cup*

# TWO-YEAR-OLDS
## by David Baxter

Punting on races where there maybe no form to go on might seem a foolhardy betting medium, but if you do your research then getting ahead in the two-year-old division can be a profitable exercise. There are lots of different approaches you can take but here are some of the fundamentals to apply.

## FOLLOW THE MARKET

You are dealing with horses who have little to no form in almost all races. When nurseries begin there is sometimes some form to analyse but in novices and maidens there is usually a handful of newcomers or once-raced types. So if a horse has been working up a storm at home, more often than not that information will make it out to the public domain and be reflected in the betting.

*The Godolphin string stretch their legs on the gallops in Newmarket*

Have a look at how the market reacts to initial SPs the night before, it could be there is a rush of money for something at a big price. Gambles in juvenile races should always be investigated as there is a good chance people who know something are getting in early.

The same applies to market drifters. Something may have an appealing pedigree or ran well when last seen, but if it drifts alarmingly it could be it is not yet ready to do itself justice.

## KNOW YOUR PEDIGREES

Take the time to look through a horse's breeding. The Racing Post breaks down a horse's pedigree in easy-to-understand language and can help pinpoint the sort of horse can excel at two.

Concentrate on horses who have siblings who were juvenile winners and who ran over similar trips. Stallions and dams who produce lots of juvenile winners are also worth noting.

You might see a horse making his or her debut from a powerful yard but its pedigree is for later on in the season. If that is the case I will be looking for alternatives, though referring to my first pointer, if there is a lot of money for the horse, despite the pedigree concerns, it is worth bearing in mind.

## KEEP AN EYE OUT FOR PATTERNS

Have a look at the race to see if it has been won by one or two trainers on multiple occasions. If so, and they have a runner in this year's race, that could be a tip in itself.

Certain trainers like to send their better prospects to certain tracks, so if you can spot those sorts of patterns then you can make it pay. Also look at how trainers are doing with their two-year-olds for the season. Are they firing in winners or hitting the frame, or are their runners taking a start or two to get the hang of things? ■

*'Something may have an appealing pedigree or ran well when last seen, but if it drifts alarmingly it could be it is not yet ready to do itself justice'*

# RESPONSIBLE GAMBLING
## by John Cobb

What is the most important skill you can develop as a punter? It isn't learning how to read between the lines of the form book or devouring video footage of obscure football leagues to gain an edge. The answer is self-discipline, because without it you are certain to fail.

Keep a record of all your bets, big and small. There should be no such thing as a throwaway bet – every one counts and you should count every one. Don't cheat yourself by missing out some of the smaller losers.

And keep a record of how much time you spend betting – not just placing the bets but all the time spent researching too. If you are enjoying every moment that's great, but if you're betting more to recoup losses and losing track of time as well as cash then that's a big warning sign.

Another really important quality to develop is humility. Every one of us has got carried away after backing a few winners, especially when we've worked them out ourselves and we think no-one else has. Just

*Bet sensibly, keep records – and above all, enjoy your gambling*

don't believe you can do it all the time, that you are an infallible gambling god.

In fact winning is more dangerous than losing, so if you have some success thank your good fortune and put some of the winnings away. Certainly don't leave it in your bookmaker's account where its presence will tempt you to have another bet. And don't use it as a stepping stone to bigger stakes. Decide the stake that suits you and stick to it.

Also decide how much money you are prepared to lose each week and don't bet a penny more. Lose is the operative word. There will always be the scenario where everything you touch turns to excrement so be ready for those times and bet accordingly and appropriately.

Set aside a small amount for betting and don't dip into funds you had intended for saving, for purchases or even for household bills. And never bet in order to try to pay a bill. Seek proper financial advice instead.

Talk to your friends and family about your betting, including your stakes and how much you bet each week. It shouldn't be a dirty secret. If you are enjoying an activity you should want to talk about it. If you're ashamed of it then that's a sign all is not well.

Above all gamble for pleasure. If it's not pleasurable and you think you need to stop then almost certainly you do. ■

## HELP IS OUT THERE

*If you want advice or help then the place to start is by getting in touch with Gamcare at www.gamcare.org. uk and 0808 8020 133 or in Ireland contacting Dunlewey at dunlewey.net and 1800 936 725 (RoI) or 08000 886 725 (NI).*

# FOOTBALL BASICS
## by digital football editor Mark Langdon

*With help from the Racing Post's team of experts, you could also find yourself celebrating*

Football is Britain's number one sport so it makes sense for it to also be the biggest business for bookmakers.

According to the Gambling Commission figures from April 2015 to March 2018 football accounted for 45.9 per cent of total remote betting with horseracing next best on 27 per cent. Most people have an opinion on football and many of those enjoy putting their money where their mouth is with the plethora of markets available truly jaw-dropping.

Gone are the days when football punters were limited to longlist coupons and an exotic bet may well have been a scorecast on a player to score first combined with a correct-score prediction.

Now you can literally make up your own punts featuring anything from the obvious to the quite ludicrous via request-a-bet type offerings.

Both-teams-to-score betting is booming and others are getting bigger, among those are player special markets. One used to be able to bet on a player simply to score first whereas now it's how many passes he completes, shots on target or even fouls made.

It's important, therefore, to separate the wheat from the chaff and hopefully this section of the book will do exactly that, offering advice from the Racing Post's established football betting experts on what to do and, perhaps just as crucially, what not to do.

We will take you through the thought process of how to find winners for the daily grind of churning out single selections, to the smaller stakes of more speculative multiple bets.

There will be tips on how to make it pay in the rapid, fastest-finger world of in-play to the more considered approach of unlocking the tricky conundrum of finding ante-post selections to potentially land that elusive dream acca come the end of the season.

Don't miss our guide to the confusing Asian handicaps that could quite easily take your betting prowess from the EFL to Premier League because, despite what many seem to assume, there is a difference between knowing football and understanding betting on football.

Discipline is key and so too is value.

It's quite easy to predict Manchester City are favourites to win a football match, but what makes them a 1-3 shot or 1-6? Every team will have their price and even the worst teams will occasionally scupper an accumulator.

Like most forms of betting, football is a sphere of gambling where thinking outside the box often pays.

Following the crowd is a path to the poor house so don't be afraid to take contrary views to the general public – quite often it's those type of bets which will lead to value wagers.

In betting there will be many ups and downs and football is no different.

It's a low-scoring sport where luck plays a major part in short-term outcomes and to become a successful punter there needs to be an understanding on the good/bad fortune in football. A bounce of a ball makes a massive difference and to be a long-term winner it is absolutely crucial to take on board the idea that decisions rather than results will win out in the end.

Fast Eddie Felson, the character played by Paul Newman in the film The Color of Money said it best as he guided his pool young hustler.

"I've learned the lesson that the worst thing that can happen to a gambler is to let his recent losses or wins knock him off keel emotionally."

The last-minute losers will always hurt more than the joy a last-minute winner brings but if you make enough correct decisions the results will eventually look after themselves.

And hopefully this book will help you make enough right decisions.

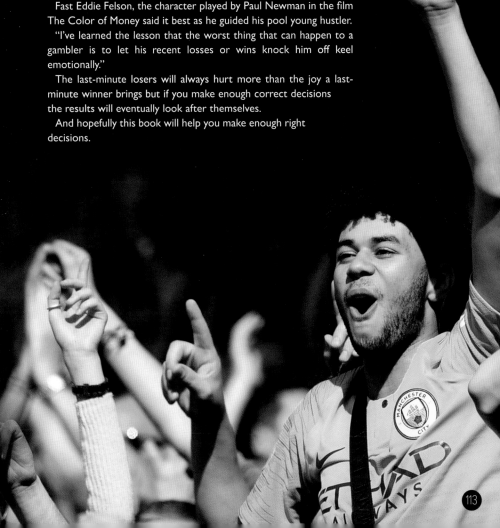

# FOOTBALL ACCUMULATORS
## by Mark Langdon

### INTRODUCTION

In most forms of betting singles are the king of the jungle.

It's hard enough picking the winner of one 16-runner handicap hurdle where it's 5-1 the field never mind another couple of horses to go with it.

The same can be said of competitive golf events and the beauty of those kind of betting heats is the opportunity to win a decent sum for a small outlay.

Football is not quite the same and as an example here is a list of the prices for the ten favourites on the final round of Premier League matches in the 2018-19 season: 2-11 Man City, 5-4 Arsenal, 9-10 Crystal Palace, 13-8 Newcastle, 29-20 Leicester, 3-10 Liverpool, 2-7 Manchester United, 4-9 Southampton, 11-10 Tottenham, 5-4 Watford.

*Ilkay Gundogan (centre) celebrates after scoring Manchester City's fourth goal against Brighton in the final match of the 2018-19 campaign*

A £10 bet on a 2-11 shot isn't going to get the pulse racing whereas the potential returns on all ten of those winning for a £10 bet is £3,706.57, so it's obviously understandable as to why accas make up the majority of football bets.

Even doubles (two bets) and trebles (three) are not greatly popular. For most recreational football bettors it's all about the Hollywood bet every Saturday and great big long lists of teams to win as they tune in to watch the scores on Sky Sports' Soccer Saturday.

There is nothing new to football accumulator betting with that effectively being commonplace from the football Pools, a bet which mainly relied on people trying to predict score draws.

It started in 1923 and was part of the football results service on BBC's Grandstand with a Pools Panel consisting of former footballers and referees adjudicating on postponed matches.

The format was different but the theory is the same then as it is now. People have liked to speculate small amounts in the hope of landing a hefty payout by predicting the outcome of football results, something that certainly happened in 1986 when Nurse Sister Margaret Francis and ten colleagues from Wilshere scooped more than a £1 million between them on the Pools.

It's different now and the variety on offer from bookmakers has seen the Pools market shrink.

The relatively recent addition of both-teams-to-score (BTTS) betting has added a new dimension to accumulators and bookmakers know it's terrible for business when they all score – which happened one midweek in December 2018.

It was a 444-1 shot that all 20 Premier League teams would notch and the popularity of the bet continues to grow, started by Betfred's original Goals Galore coupon which priced every match up as a 4-5 shot before changing due to a massive punter-friendly bias.

With both teams to score prices shortening to less attractive odds, the boom in a team to win with both teams scoring has become understandably increasingly popular.

In the example earlier of City being 2-11 to beat Brighton they were a much more backable 15-8 to win in a match where they also conceded.

As the gap between the best and the rest in football continues to grow so too will these auxiliary markets in an attempt to increase potential winnings.

Soon enough we may consider simple match betting as old fashioned as the Pools.

*Where it all began: the old-style football pools coupon*

*'Both teams to score betting has added a new dimension to accumulators and bookmakers know it's terrible for business when they all score'*

115

*'Keep it sensible otherwise you may as well buy a lottery ticket or scratchcard because it's not realistic to get up a 20-fold'*

# FIVE WAYS TO BET SMART ON ACCUMULATORS

## 1. Accas are not always for mug punters

There is often a stigma attached to those who prefer to bet accumulators with many seasoned gamblers refusing to bet doubles never mind find five or six selections. Their currency is singles and the purity involved, limiting the risk of outcomes which can go wrong.

The reasoning is simple enough and apart from anything else with every leg you have there will be a bookmakers' margin to pay each time.

Commercial departments concentrate much of their football pre-play spend on accumulators and the cynic would suggest if that is an area of betting being pushed it is because it is one where it is likely to prove profitable for them.

Accas are being boosted all over the place, although it is also true that the competitive nature of the recreational side of the industry means bookmakers need to get people through the door. The golden rule of any bet is whether you consider it to be value for money and there is an argument that if you are getting that value on more than one occasion the sensible option is to double/treble it up.

What I personally try to look for is home teams probably ranging from around 1-2 to 5-4 and there probably would not be any more than four or five across a whole weekend that would appeal.

Keep it sensible otherwise you may as well buy a lottery ticket or scratchcard because it's not realistic to get up a 20-fold. We know that draws are usually a skinner for bookmakers and yet nearly 27 per cent of matches in the EFL in the 2018-19 season finished all-square.

Football is a low-scoring sport and the draw is a big enough runner. They are difficult to avoid on trebles, never mind these dreamy wagers that involve the longest of longlists.

Bookmakers love to push stories of the person nailing a 20-team acca but in reality there is no way that many teams would be priced up incorrectly. Once you start straying into those Hollywood-style bets that is where the term mug punter begins to hit home.

## 2. Avoid the real shorties

There is a temptation to look at the absolute home bankers across the continent and decide they will all definitely win.

However, elite sides are going off at ridiculously short prices these days and there is not much mileage in boosting a bet with a load of 1-10 shots when it only takes one draw to suffer an ultimate kick in the teeth, or somewhere ever more painful.

*Facing page: Paul Pogba celebrates as Manchester United beat City in a thriller at the Etihad Stadium in April 2018*

Even when Manchester City accumulated a record-breaking 100 Premier League points in the 2017-18 season they failed to win three times at the Etihad, suffering a shock defeat to Manchester United as well as draws with Everton and Huddersfield.

Those slips against Huddersfield and Everton were at odds of 1-9 and 3-10 respectively and almost impossible to predict pre-match.

Just under 50 per cent of all Premier League matches in 2018-19 finished in home wins compared to 43 per cent in the EFL, but for accumulator purposes the real powerhouses of League One and Two can often be better for the accumulators as the price often is much closer to a shade of odds-on rather than 1-3 or lower.

Indeed, in October 2018 it was the lower leagues that did the damage to bookmakers with Coral estimating British bookmakers lost over £15m in one round of matches despite the Premier League being off the coupon due to an international break.

"This is the worst day of trading we have ever had on football over an international break weekend and the worst football results of the season so far," said Coral's Simon Clare after nearly every favourite in League One and Two did the business. "It is the last thing a bookie would expect from a supposedly quiet weekend of football betting."

Don't be afraid to move away from the elite leagues to be a successful acca backer.

○ Just under 50 per cent of all Premier League matches in 2018-19 finished in home wins

○ 43 per cent of all EFL matches in 2018-19 finished in home wins

## 3. Don't be limited to sections

More and more online bettors are becoming savvy to this but retail coupons still tempt people into betting one, two or more from each carefully selected section by bookmakers.

You probably know the drill by now. It starts with a load of easy ones.

City at home to Fulham, Liverpool against Cardiff etc and then gets slightly more tricky before the final section usually includes a load of matches which are virtually 6-4 each side with the draw massive runners in games that could go either way.

Under no circumstances should a punter limit themselves to bet on only matches bookmakers have selected for them unless there is serious compensation in way of boosted odds that make a bad bet into a value one. Even then only do it if you think it's a good bet.

It's rare to find loads of ricks outside of marketing-style offers and when they are available – such as Betfred's early Goals Galore coupons that really helped the both-teams-to-score betting take off – they swiftly disappear.

The Goals Galore loophole was eventually closed but there was a time when Betfred were betting every fixture at 4-5 for BTTS despite the true odds of some matches being around 1-2, so the old adage about bookmakers never making mistakes is far from correct.

## TOP TIP

If you fancy three legs of a four-team boost then just back the three teams in a separate treble – ignore the marketing

*Everton's Kevin
Mirallas attempts
a spectacular
shot at goal
against West
Bromwich Albion
in January 2014*

## 4. Go for goals at the end of season

My own personal betting calms down towards the end of the
campaign when different factors come into play such as motivation
and artificial odds generated by whether a team needs to win or not.
If you are determined to keep betting accumulators in the latter
stages of the campaign then goals could be a better
avenue compared to match betting.

I am indebted to Racing Post colleague Kevin
Pullein for the following information based on the
last 21 final days of the Premier and Football
Leagues ending in 2017-18.

When both teams had something to play for
the average number of goals was 2.9. When

one team had something to play for the average number of goals was 2.8. And when neither team had anything to play for the average number of goals was 2.7. The average number of goals in all games at other times in a season was 2.6.

The chance of over 2.5 goals in a match was 56 per cent *(figure 1)* when both teams had something to play for, 54 per cent when one team had something to play for and 50 per cent when neither team had anything to play for. In all games at other times in a season it was 48 per cent. *(figure 2)*.

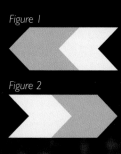

*Figure 1*

*Figure 2*

## 5. Understand related contingencies

In a perfect world, betting shop staff would alert punters to the problems of related contingencies as soon as the bet was being placed or there would be software available from all online bookmakers to make sure these issues are obsolete. But some always slip through the net.

Perhaps the most high-profile of those had nothing to do with football, but the weather.

It turned out to be snow joke for Cliff Bryant who believed he had won over £7m from a bet on a white Christmas all over Britain in 2009. Instead of the £7m Southampton-based Bryant thought he was about to collect, the actual winnings were just £31.78 on two separate £5 multiple bets of 13 and 11 legs respectively on where snow would fall on Christmas Day.

A Ladbrokes spokesman at the time said: "We have apologised to the customer for any confusion and for mistakenly accepting an accumulator bet when our own rules state that only single bets are available on a market of this nature. We are happy to void the bets and to pay the customer his winnings on the relevant singles."

Unsurprisingly, the novice punter was more concerned with trying to get his £7m rather than an apology!

Most regular bettors would understand you can't treble up snow falling in Newcastle, Durham and Darlington as the chances of it landing in one part of the North East mean it is more likely to fall in another nearby postcode. Not everyone, however, is aware of the rules.

The increase in build-a-bet type products mean it is now possible to bet on related contingencies more frequently. Just don't expect to be the true odds of all the outcomes and also take note of bookmakers' maximum payout limits in case you're due £7m but can only collect a significantly lower sum.

*Snow covers the pitch at Old Trafford in March 2018 before Manchester United's clash with Brighton & Hove Albion in the FA Cup*

## EXPERT VIEW

Chances are if you have watched enough sport down the years you will have heard the voice of the excellent Dave Farrar – he covers many sports but is arguably best known for his mic work on European football. Farrar also likes a bet and wrote a book called The Perfect Punter.

In the book Farrar describes his love of gambling, before losing half of all the money he had in a whirlwind six-month period fuelled by a girlfriend ending their relationship.

Bizarrely, it was on a trip to the bright lights of Las Vegas that Farrar saw the light after witnessing somebody blow $12,000 on half-baked

ideas around the roulette table. Farrar then entered into a more disciplined approach to trying to sort out his own betting woes with a more balanced approach combined with a strict staking plan.

"In the end, I didn't win all my money back but I was much wiser," wrote Farrar. "I realised how much gambling properly takes out of you. To be a professional, you'd have to do it to the exclusion of everything else in your life – and that just wouldn't be me."

My presumption – which is hopefully correct – is that many readers of this book see something of Farrar in themselves.

They don't want to be a professional but they want to be a better bettor and the two are different, requiring a more varied thought process.

There is a professional school of thought, for instance, that betting an accumulator across a whole weekend of football, from say the Saturday to Monday, is a dumb move unless you know the prices are about to collapse.

The idea is rather than back an acca with the last leg on the Monday it's much better to have the lot on the final selection. For most recreational football punters, however, that is unrealistic.

You can't have £100 bet on an even-money shot but you may be able to afford the £10 which gets the rolling stake up to £100.

And that's okay. Don't be ashamed of it. For the majority of football bettors an acca is used to enhance the viewing spectacle, hopefully win a few quid over the season without being overly concerned by the finer details which will often be consumed by professionals.

The key will be to not be limited by bookmakers guiding you into a coupon or marketing offer that consists of more accumulator legs than you would ideally like.

If you fancy three legs of a four-team boost then just back the three teams in a separate treble, ignore the marketing guff if it's not the bet you want to have.

Don't be stuck to golden rules such as always doing a certain amount BTTS fixtures. If there are only six you like that weekend, just stick to the six, if there's ten do ten.

It's okay to shoot for the stars but a dash of realism is also needed. Keep the stakes sensible, keep the number of selections sensible and keep a record of your acca bets so you don't kid yourself how much you are up following any decent win.

*Hit the back of the net with an acca and you could be celebrating just like Jack Grealish and Jed Steer of Aston Villa (right)*

Shoot for the stars ...

...but also try to keep it real

Don't be lured by marketing tricks

# FOOTBALL ANTE-POST
## by Mark Langdon

## INTRODUCTION

Before a domestic season begins there is a buzz of ante-post football punting with so many different betting opportunities available, particularly in the Premier League where you can predict who will win the league, finish in the top four, a market without the big six, top-half/bottom-half finish, relegation and to finish bottom.

It's also possible to bet top teams in the region, get higher or lower on seasonal points and bet on which select teams will finish in the higher league position. In terms of individual players there is betting on the top overall scorer, leading team scorers and PFA Player of the Year.

Lower down the ladder you can chuck in promotion too and it's fairly common practice for even occasional bettors to get involved in a seasonal multiple bet which offers the potential for juicy returns for a small outlay. Most bookmakers offer a cash-out facility on the main markets.

Famous gambles have been landed before and will be again, but nothing will ever compare to Leicester's astonishing Premier League title success of 2015-16 at odds of 5,000-1.

The story was one that went far beyond betting circles and to such an extent a book was published by Ron Tanner of the Leicester Mercury detailing the fabulous Foxes remarkable tale of David defeating Goliath.

*Leicester City winning the Premier League at ante-post odds of 5,000-1 has become the stuff of legend*

It was called 5,000-1 The Leicester City Story, going on to describe how they upset the odds to become the Premier League champions.

Usually, or at least in horseracing, a 5,000-1 winner would be an absolute skinner for bookmakers but football is different. There are many people who bet with their hearts rather than their heads and bookmakers were battered by Leicester with industry figures estimating the final payout was well in excess of £15 million.

*'Famous gambles have been landed before and will be again, but nothing will ever compare to Leicester's astonishing Premier League title success of 2015-16 at odds of 5,000-1'*

Sky Bet reported a £4.7m loss – their biggest ever payout at the time with a total of 128 customers taking the 5,000-1 and the largest stake was £35. This was mainly a victory for the little guy over the serious punters and Betway said it was their worst ever day as a company when it finally came to settling Leicester wagers.

At the time of writing it remains the largest ante-post priced winner, rating it the biggest upset in sports betting history, and even speculative specials rarely get to those kind of prices.

Hills reportedly laid Harry Wilson at 2,500-1 to play for Wales when he was just 18 months old but thankfully most ante-post wagers don't take 15 years to be settled.

## TOP TIP

Go for a team
that was top-half
the season before
with a strong goal
difference and
impressive shot
statistics

## FIVE WAYS TO BET SMART ANTE-POST

### 1. Shortlist teams who just missed out the season before

Football fans are a funny bunch. No matter how bad the previous season ended in May there is always fresh optimism when the new campaign starts in August. It's almost as if the summer sun goes to the head and everyone has some kind of amnesia to a whole seasons worth of evidence whether it be good or bad.

The EFL divisions tend to be wide open and even drawing a long shortlist of potential winners can be difficult, but always keep in mind those who just missed out the season before.

I will always start with those who were in the playoffs or just missed out on promotion. Pay particular focus to those with strong goal difference records and a healthy budget because generally speaking the level of form will be strong.

There is always the chance of being chinned by a team dropping down from the league above or a summer improver but those playoff losers always set a high standard of form, particularly if it is

backed up by strong key performance indicators.

Goal difference is one of those as are shot statistics – ie those teams who tend to dominate the ratio of shots and shots on targets.

One example of this came in the final standings of the League Two table of 2017-18 when Accrington surprised many by edging out Luton for the title honours.

Both went up to League One where Luton finished first on 94 points compared to Stanley's still respectable effort of 14th with 55 points.

Accy winger Sean McConville said afterwards: I'm surprised. Obviously they came up with us last year and I think we were the better team last season, as shown by us winning the league."

However, the clue was in the goal difference.

Accy went up with plus 30 and Luton's was plus 48 when they were together in League Two and in terms of EFL ante-post betting I would nearly always go for a team that was top-half the season before with a strong goal difference and impressive shot statistics which can be found match-by-match on soccerbase.com or collated on simplesoccerstats.com.

*At home with Accrington, who were promoted to League One at the end of the 2017-18 campaign*

## 2. Avoid being on the backend of gambles

Teams who just miss out and remain steady the following season tend not to be the sexy names in the ante-post lists, meaning they are often overlooked in the summer gambles.

The opposite of that – and there will be many examples at all levels – are the kind of teams who make wholesale changes. A whole new squad is brought in, the old players are kicked out and there is a feel-good factor around the club in question no matter what happened the season before.

There are two things to consider with these type of teams.

Firstly, do you trust the owners to sustain the cash flow for the whole of the campaign?

If it looks too good to be true it usually is and quite often a lavish summer spending is replaced by fans going around with buckets in bleakest winter months looking to keep the club alive. The expensive players depart as quickly as they arrived and you've done your ante-post money.

The second is how quickly you can get on the gamble.

It is one thing to take a chance on a 33-1 shot just as news hits of a takeover from a new owner promising the world; it's quite another to be on the backend of that gamble, taking 8-1 when there was 33s around just a couple of weeks ago.

In my opinion those types of teams can win and I still won't be disappointed as far more of them get chinned, sinking without trace at stupidly short odds.

For a good reason is there the old betting saying: "If you missed the wedding, don't go to the funeral."

If you have missed the good times don't get involved at the worst of it.

## 3. Premier dropouts are underpriced

In the past ten full seasons, starting with 2009-10, only twice had the Championship been won by a team at single-figure odds. On both occasions it was Newcastle.

More often than not it was won by a surprise team such as Norwich at 25-1 or Bournemouth at 25-1. Leicester and Burnley were 14-1, Reading 18-1 and so on, with relegated Premier League teams often vastly overrated.

Over the past ten seasons the average finishing position of relegated

*'Since 2009-10, only twice had the Championship been won by a team at single-figure odds. On both occasions it was Newcastle'*

Premier League teams were not even in the playoffs and the front two in the betting for the 2018-19 season (Stoke 5-1 and West Brom 8-1) failed to collect for each-way backers.

Much is made of the parachute payment advantages held by Premier League clubs and yet it is probably overstated, at least in the betting markets.

Dropping out of the elite division brings with it untold issues that often take time to rectify and it means the solid sides who just missed out the season before are often better placed to make swifter starts.

○ In the 2016-17 season Newcastle United's wage bill came in at some 16 per cent of that for the entire Championship

There will always be exceptions to the rule and Newcastle topped the second tier at odds of 15-8 in 2016-17 when they assembled a squad of expensive talents with manager Rafael Benitez, somebody who had won the Champions League, choosing the tactics.

According to Deloitte, Newcastle wage costs alone constituted 16 per cent of the Championship total, with the club spending 4.5 times the median and 82 per cent more than the second highest spender, Aston Villa.

In other words they were an abnormal case and still Newcastle needed Brighton to lose each of their last three matches to overtake them in the final moments of the season.

When building a shortlist be wary of backing Premier League teams dropping down as even the best ones can make hard work of it.

*Rafael Benitez guided Newcastle to the top of the Championship in 2016-17*

## 4. Top-scorer tussles should be avoided

This is another that applies more to the EFL and it involves the top goalscorer market - a market that should always be called the top scorer rather than Golden Boot for betting purposes, as bookmakers settle as a dead-heat in the event of a tie rather than any way the league in question attempts to adjudicate an official winner on a different criteria.

Betting is hard enough without adding more questions to the conundrum and that is exactly what happens in betting on top goalscorer markets lower down the ladder.

You need to work out who is good enough to score plenty of goals and yet not be so good that they are signed up the league pyramid during the season.

It happens often and was again highlighted during the 2018-19 season when Jayden Stockley was signed by Championship club

*'Betting is hard enough without adding more questions to the conundrum and that is exactly what happens in betting on top goalscorer markets lower down the ladder'*

Preston from League Two outfit Exeter for £750,000.

At the time of his departure, Stockley had been the highest-scoring player in England throughout the whole of 2018 and his departure allowed 40-1 shot James Norwood a nice run to the top goalscorer honours which was great news for Racing Post followers as the Tranmere hotshot had been tipped up in our pre-season supplement, The Big Kick-Off.

If you are getting involved at least do research as to which players have known release clauses – like Stockley did – as it could save a lot of heartache down the road.

Another potential issue in terms of the Football League comes in backing teams to win the division when their primary aim for the season is to gain promotion.

It can quite often be the case that once the main task for the campaign is done the side in question can lose focus with the title in sight. Don't be surprised if those final few matches matter more to you than the manager and players, who have usually been out on the town celebrating going up.

The prices are obviously skinnier but at least consider promotion rather than the title. It also gives you the option of sneaking up via the playoffs which could keep the interest in the bet running longer.

*Jayden Stockley goes for goal as Exeter take on West Bromwich Albion in an FA Cup clash in January 2018*

133

## 5. Bet during the season

This is where the term ante-post needs to be used loosely, but in football the ability to bet on outright markets lasts until the final seconds of the final matches.

And that should be taken up as quite often the best football bets will be offered in these markets compared to the 90-minute prices which will be derived from sophisticated computing models and usually involve scraping odds from the influential Asian betting markets.

Coral's former head of football Nick Goff and now professional punter explained to the Racing Post how things work and how it's possible to take advantage of the situation.

He said: "Asia drives everything on a match day. It's like a pyramid and you can't even see the prices at the top where the big syndicates bet, but there are five or six we can monitor and what happens at the summit trickles down before entering Britain.

"As a general rule by 2pm on a Saturday the price in Asia is the correct one and on a matchday you need to know what is happening in their market. We have our own ratings but it is an absolute must to take the Asian prices at the off because that information is used to formulate how Asia rates teams for future odds."

"If there is one part of the British market that is not yet mature it is ante-post and those who follow the market moves positively and negatively, can make it pay. An example came when Bournemouth didn't make a great start to the 2014-15 season despite being backed every week.

"You could see they were being rated as one of the best two teams in the division yet still available at 16-1 and I know they were that price because I kept looking but never backed it!"

Luton, winners of League One in 2019, followed a similar pattern and it is definitely worth betting on the outright markets once the season has started.

*Fans cheer as Luton head to the League One title in 2019 after a slow start*

## EXPERT VIEW

There are two schools of thought when it comes to ante-post betting.

Some believe it is the best way to get involved in football punting as it often takes the luck element out of the way.

In one game anything can happen and an incorrect refereeing decision or dodgy bounce of the ball can decide results but over an extended period the cream tends to rise to the top, even if suggestions of the league table never lying at the end of the season is pushing reality.

Prices tend to be more attractive than the day-to-day grind of betting football singles and there is a lot to be said for getting involved in longer-term markets.

Also remember the ante-post opportunities don't stop when the season starts and, quite often, there will be attractive opportunities during the season, particularly just before the each-way terms change to reflect fewer teams are likely to get involved in the final finish.

It's really not unusual for ante-post markets to be stale with bookmakers not updating quickly enough and a fine example of this comes in the FA Cup outright market.

The odds barely move until the third-round ties in January and yet by the halfway stage of the Premier League season it is often obvious which of those dark horses are superior to the rest of the middle to lower end of the pack.

Also check out which teams are getting backed every Saturday with that being a reliable guide to which sides are popular with professional syndicates. You may not be able to jump on those gambles from a value point of view but there will be chances to side with those teams in long-term markets.

All of this sounds perfectly reasonable and a potential to path to profit, so where is the second school of thought that suggests ante-post betting isn't sensible?

It mainly comes in the shape of betting funds and money being tied down for long periods. For some punters there just isn't the option to lock in money to bookmakers until May and therefore it's a waste of time, at least outside of a speculative ante-post accumulator before the season starts.

There is no doubt in my mind that ante-post football betting is one of the best ways to bet should the financial opportunities be available and, where possible, it could be a tactic to leave swap some of the weekend funds to a longer format of betting.

Think of it as a way of keeping an interest throughout the season and, while it is true bookmakers don't make many mistakes, if they do it usually comes in ante-post.

If you're not a fan now is the right time to be a convert.

'Cream rises in the long term'

'Ante-post odds often tempting'

'You can get involved all season long'

*'Prices tend to be more attractive than the day-to-day grind of betting football singles and there is a lot to be said for getting involved in longer-term markets'*

# FOOTBALL IN-PLAY
## by Mark Langdon

## INTRODUCTION

There was a time when in-play betting was such a small part of the betting industry that your only glimpse of the prices would come if you had patiently waited for the Stan James teletext pages to tick around (slowly) past the markets in which you had no interest just so that you could see what price Manchester United were to launch one of their famous comebacks under Sir Alex Ferguson, or just plain old Alex Ferguson as he was back then.

When the company migrated to Unibet in 2018 the then Racing Post editor Bruce Millington wrote: "Spreads, exchanges and the internet followed, but what Stan James did during the 1990s was ground-breaking."

Offering in-play odds for telephone customers doesn't feel too ground-breaking in the technological world we live in today, but it certainly laid the platform for what followed in the in-play boom, boosted greatly by the success of Betfair, before the real digital push of recent years with smartphones at the forefront.

At one stage you were lucky to be able to bet on a football match result after the game had started, but now there are hundreds of in-play markets available at your fingertips. Goals, team total shots, player passes, bookings, corners and cards are just some of the markets covered by bookmakers eager to offer the best in-play service where rapid turnover of next this, next that and next whatever drives punter involvement.

Bet365's financial statements from November 2018 showed the online gambling giant recorded sports and gaming turnover of £2.72 billion in the year to March 25 with operating profits rocketing to £682.2 million.

In-play performed strongly, representing 77 per cent of sports revenue, up from 72 per cent the previous year, aided by the number of streamed sporting events, which had hit 160,000 on bet365's platforms.

○ In 2018, some 77 per cent of Bet365's sports revenue came from in-play markets

Football in-play betting is basically a 24/7 365 days a year offering and bookmakers' marketing spend has been enormous. A constant stream of TV campaigns, which peaked at the World Cup, have offered punters the opportunity to have a bang on that or various bet boosts during the half-time interval.

Or at least that was the case until the Remote Gambling Association, which includes most major bookmakers, voluntarily agreed to a 'whistle-to-whistle' TV advert ban on all sports bar horseracing.

However, in-play football betting is hugely popular and is unlikely to be slowed down, with flicking through the markets a normal part of the match routine for punters.

The feeling for many is that in-play offers greater winning potential because the odds are often automated and a football fan will often feel he knows more about the game than a machine churning out odds usually derived from pre-match expectations. If only it were that simple.

Just go back to those bet365 figures – more than three-quarters of their sports revenue is in-play and their overall profit was £682.2m. It's not impossible to be profitable in-play but it's far from easy.

## FIVE WAYS TO BET SMART IN-PLAY

### 1. Stay in control

This applies to all kinds of betting but even more so in-play where the adrenaline is flowing, the opportunities are endless and there is a fastest-finger-first mentality as you desperately chase the bet you want before the price changes or the market is suspended.

It's arguably easier to lose control in-play, chasing losses with the knowledge that one more corner could in theory get you back into profit. It can sound a boring attitude but the advice is to control the craving to bet for the sake of it and wait for the right opportunities. For most people betting is about fun and there's no fun in spraying the cash around recklessly after a bad run. There will always be another match at another time and maintaining discipline is key.

Multi-billionaire Warren Buffett, the successful stock market investor, wisely once said: "The difference between successful people and really successful people is that really successful people say no to almost everything."

Often the impulse is to overreact to what you see but always be aware that what you are watching at a particular moment is rarely a reliable guide to what will happen in the future.

Don't overreact to a bad tackle, thinking there are bound to be

*'The difference between successful people and really successful people is that really successful people say no to almost everything'*

loads of bookings to follow. If it were that easy we'd all be driving flash motors and bookmakers would not be clearing profits in excess of £600m.

Here's Buffett again: "If past history was all that is needed to play the game of money, the richest people would be librarians."

It's also easy to fool yourself into believing in your own success, remembering the winners and forgetting the losers. Keep detailed records of where you are making and losing money.

*'Are certain teams more likely to strike late, maybe because of their strong substitutes' bench?'*

## 2. Goals change games

Professional punters will have their own computer models that determine in-play betting opportunities, but for those not at that level the work needs to be done pre-game as there is not enough time when a match has started.

Have a pre-game plan of what price you want to take if x, y or z happens. It is often much easier to make calculated decisions away from the buzz of the game when the clock is ticking, the markets are moving and the heart is pumping.

Are certain teams more likely to strike late, maybe because of their strong substitutes' bench, or is a manager primed to park the bus to preserve a result?

These are the kind of small details that could help, as well as fully accepting goals change games. There are fewer than three goals per game and therefore each one is greatly important.

My esteemed Racing Post colleague Kevin Pullein studied every Premier League fixture from 2006-07 to 2016-17 and found the following: home teams took 50 per cent of all corners awarded while they were leading, 57 per cent of all corners awarded while they were drawing and 62 per cent of all corners awarded while they trailing.

He also looked at seven years' worth of Premier League bookings data (10pts per yellow card, 25 points for a red) ending in 2017 and found home teams received 42 per cent of all bookings points awarded while they were winning and 48 per cent of all bookings points awarded while they were losing.

Goals change attitudes. Goals changes games.

○ *In the analysis of seven years' Premier League bookings the home teams received 42 per cent of all bookings point while they were winning*

○ *The analysis also showed home teams home teams were awarded 48 per cent of bookings points while losing*

## 3. Be prepared to take on favourites

This is much easier said than done, but bookmakers often report hefty losses if a strong pre-match odds-on favourite overturns a losing deficit to run out winning, collecting for pre-game punters, those on the jolly to win and both teams to score as well as in-play bettors too.

It's an easy trap to fall into and for many recreational punters the only time they can get to back the high-profile teams in single bets is when those elite sides are trailing.

There's something thrilling about being on the team with the star-studded players chasing goals, whether it is watching them on TV or just following the stats on the in-play consoles most bookmakers use to encourage turnover.

The numbers tick over – shots, corners, dangerous attacks – and for the other side of the coin it's horrible being financially linked to the underdogs, seeing the plucky opponents being pinned back, defending for their lives.

However, if most people want to bet the favourites in-play and I know that and you know so too do bookmakers. The value will usually be for those watching, possibly from behind the sofa, on the teams which don't possess a Messi, Ronaldo *(right)*, Mbappe or Aguero.

Former Betfair trading director Craig Mucklow, who has also worked for Ladbrokes and Paddy Power before moving to Las Vegas-based odds provider Don Best Sports told sportshandle.com:

"In 20 years I can count on one hand how many balanced books I have had. When trading in-play one can only take positions as the game state dictates, and usually it's a defensive position. For example if Golden State [successful NBA team] are down 20 points at the half then no matter what the algorithm says, every bet will be on Golden State. Mathematically they should be +300/+400 [3-1/4-1] but instead liability drives the price to be in the +150 region [6-4]."

## TOP TIP

Find those who are on penalties, particularly in these days of VAR when handballs are going to be awarded more often

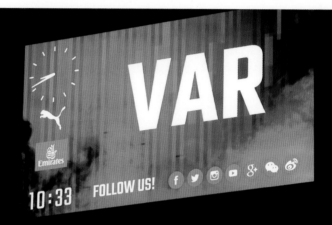

## 4: Keep an eye on stoppage time

This was something that won't have kept those Stan James traders awake in the early days, but in an era of VAR it is absolutely imperative to know how long is remaining of each half rather than the time shown by the match clock.

Like diving, stoppage time is on the increase, particularly in the second half when referees feel more obliged to add on time even outside of the relatively new phenomenon of VAR.

In the 2010 World Cup the average second-half stoppage time was 3.6 minutes, rising to 4.1 in 2014 before breaking the five-minute barrier at the 2018 finals in Russia.

More time means more goals and more pain or more joy depending on where you placed your in-play punts, with 15 per cent of all goals scored from the 90th minute onwards up until the semi-final stage of the 2018 World Cup, before the late drama quietened down.

In total 23 goals were scored at the death, which suggests VAR is having an impact on time extended at the end of each half.

Dr Seuss, the children's author, once asked the question: "How did it get late so soon?" Maybe he could have kept more of an eye on the time.

## 5. Think like a manager

This is more for player markets but there are few more frustrating outcomes for a punter than not getting a proper run for your money.

Backing a player to score next who goes down injured 20 seconds after your punt will almost certainly be filed in the unlucky column. However, backing a player to record two or more shots in the second half, only to see them subbed after 60 minutes, could be bad betting.

This is all part of the 'fail to prepare, prepare to fail' mantra.

How well do you know managers and their substitution patterns? If you don't know, you had better get to know because most coaches are creatures of habit, which makes predicting substitutions a little easier if you can find a trend.

Another smart in-play tactic is to find those who are on penalties, particularly in these days of VAR when handball spot-kicks are becoming easier to award for attacking teams.

Get a list of penalty-takers. Transfermarkt.com has penalty records for all teams and players and who is on the pens could be the difference between a fair bet and a bad bet.

For instance, at Liverpool in the 2018-19 season James Milner was the first-choice penalty taker but was not a guaranteed starter, making potential deputy Mohamed Salah *(right)* a more likely goalscorer when Milner was absent from the team sheet.

*'Backing a player to score next who goes down injured 20 seconds after your punt will almost certainly be filed in the unlucky column. However, backing a player to record two or more shots in the second half, only to see them subbed after 60 minutes, could be bad betting'*

## " EXPERT VIEW

There are certain strengths, such as discipline and control, that will stand you in good stead in all forms of betting but nowhere is that more evident than with in-play betting.

So much happens so quickly that even an otherwise clear thinker can become hazy, with the temptation to chase losses obvious and the extra panic over whether to cash out often leading to poor-value judgement calls.

A study from the University of Basque Country in late 2018 looked at Spanish bettors and found in-play betting was "especially associated with those being categorised as problem gamblers".

The analysis added: "Problem gamblers are expected to gamble more in any given circumstance, including before and during matches. However, the proportion of their gambling that they devote to in-play betting should be irrespective of their gambling participation. This is not the case.

"One interpretation could be that bettors who experience more problems with gambling also feel more inclined to consume impulsive, less planned and immediate forms of gambling such as in-play betting, in which the bet cycles are brief and the time elapsed since the placement of the bet until the reward (or lack thereof) is also shorter."

Understand the dangers of in-play impulses and setting safe limits, while doing as much of your preparation pre-game, will help, albeit in the knowledge that some things will change over 90 minutes.

The best in-running horse judges don't just bet on a whim as the race unfolds, they already have a plan of action, and it should be the same in football.

Speedy pictures are more crucial for horseracing in-running punters where every second counts, but in football it remains important to be on a device that allows you to be as up to date as possible, with some streaming services often as much as a minute behind the real action.

Be prepared to take on favourites, who tend to be over-bet in play. As we have seen, a favourite on the comeback trail should sometimes be a 3-1 shot but will be trading at 6-4 because of the way most punters focus on favourites.

It is perhaps the same in all forms of football betting, but particularly in-play where arguably the methods are not as sophisticated and many punters will simply go off gut feeling. The gut usually says the underdog can't hold out and yet it's often those uncomfortable moments that will provide superior betting.

I was lucky enough to serve my Racing Post early days under some unbelievably shrewd operators, none more so than Kevin Pullein, whose best piece of betting advice to me was this: "Just because you're standing alone, it doesn't mean you're standing in the wrong place."

Bet away from the obvious, bet away from the crowd. That maxim remains as true as ever and is particularly appropriate for those hoping to profit in-play.

Stay as up to date as you can

Take on the market leaders

Go with your gut feeling

*Don't be afraid to stand out from the crowd*

# FOOTBALL SINGLES
## by Dan Childs

## INTRODUCTION

Betting is supposed to be fun – that's what we are told – but it is a lot more enjoyable when it delivers a profit and one of the best ways to do just that is to focus on football singles.

Singles betting on non-televised football has been around only since

2002 – when the minimum trebles rule was scrapped – but it soon gave punters a fantastic opportunity to put their knowledge and decision-making powers to the test.

Betting tax had been abolished the previous year, in favour of a tax on bookmakers profits, and the developments were a godsend for football punters, who were presented with a more even playing field than had ever existed before.

Previously punters may have fancied a team at a certain price with a certain bookmaker but would have to back them alongside two other teams with the same firm, significantly diluting the chances of success and reducing value. Now they had a chance to make a precision surgical strike – poring over the coupon and selecting only the most attractive individual wagers.

The downside to single bets, when compared with multiples, is the lower prices which remove the prospect of making a big killing all in one go. However, for punters more interested in long-term prosperity and regular returns than the thrill of a big win every now and then, singles betting is the way to go. The difficult bit is how to make it pay.

Successful betting in all sports is about gaining useful information and knowing how to apply it.

When it comes to football singles some people prefer to look at statistical trends and the tools at their disposal are improving all the time.

A lot has changed since the many people selected their weekly football accumulator by taking a cursory glance at the league table and assessing the home and away records of the teams involved.

Shot statistics for the top flights of major European have been widely available since the turn of the century and, in recent seasons, more sophisticated expected goals (xG) data has been churned out.

The more sophisticated statistical tools get, the more likely they are to influence the markets. However, there will always be occasions when they do not give an accurate picture of events on the field of play.

I have always looked at football betting a different way and tried to focus on the story behind the statistics rather than the statistics themselves. It is a labour intensive approach but a necessary one.

Football is a fast-moving, unpredictable sport with individual players going from heroes to zeros and back again in a very short space of time.

Never forget that it is the players – not the clubs they represent – who decide the outcome of matches and the challenge for punters is to second guess how they will perform in the future, not simply look at the past and expect the same patterns to be replicated.

*'For punters more interested in long-term prosperity and regular returns than the thrill of a big win every now and then, singles betting is the way to go'*

*Facing page: Lucas Moura celebrates scoring Tottenham Hotspur's fourth goal against Huddersfield in April 2019*

# FIVE WAYS TO BET SMART ON SINGLES

## 1. Gathering the information

It might sound obvious but the best way to accumulate useful football knowledge is to watch as much football as possible.

The best way to do this is to be at the game in question.

There is a reason that football clubs spend large sums of money on sending scouts to watch players around the globe. It is because they get a much fuller picture of the player's performance than by watching video or television footage.

Being at the game makes it much easier to assess a player's movement off the ball and their overall impact on the contest. First-hand knowledge is hugely valuable but there are obvious limitations to how many games any individual can attend.

Watching televised matches is the next best thing and following the highlights is also useful – allowing the viewer to build up a picture of which players have affected the key moments in a game, whether positively or negatively.

Coverage of the EFL is as good as it has ever been with several Championship games screened live every week and a two-hour highlights package devoted to the weekend fixtures in the second, third and fourth tiers. Watching those highlights each weekend helps to build a picture of the teams I regularly take a view on. However, any football fan would recognise that highlights can be deceptive so it is important to try to fill in the gaps and get an even clearer picture.

Reading post-match reports can be a worthwhile exercise although the ones on club websites are unlikely to go into detail about individual players. Local newspapers will be more opinionated and the views on supporter message boards will be even more forthright.

Supporters often have a wide range of views and some of them, quite frankly, will talk utter rubbish. However, many of them will have had first hand knowledge of the games (remember how valuable that is) and some watch their team week-in, week-out.

And, if the majority are saying the same thing about a certain player, they are probably making a salient point that is worth listening to.

*With so much information out there, studying as much as possible can reap substantial rewards.*

## 2. Assessing the players

For those attracted to the idea of understanding the story behind the statistics it is important to limit the number of leagues you focus on.

Punters basing their wagering decisions solely on shot statistics and expected goals can consider bets from a large pool of matches from a variety of different countries. But when your strategy relies on gaining an awareness of the strengths and weaknesses of individual players, it becomes more difficult to cast the net too far afield.

Some players are more important than others but the value of their contributions are not always easy to discern. Goalscorers always attract the most attention and their value is demonstrated by the huge fees they command on the transfer market.

Few football fans would disagree that Lionel Messi and Cristiano Ronaldo are the most talented footballers of the modern generation, but their attributes are known around the globe and their inclusion or omission from any starting line up will have a major impact on the match prices for any game their clubs, or nations are involved in.

The same criteria applies to key players much further down the pyramid.

For example, Tranmere striker James Norwood, scorer of 29 of the Sky Bet League Two side's 63 goals this season, is of obvious value to the team.

It is worth remembering that football is a team sport and there are plenty of clubs who struggle with a prolific scorer in the side and others who flourish despite the absence of a star individual. But it doesn't take a genius to establish that Ronaldo, Messi and Norwood are of huge value to the teams they represent.

A more valuable skill is to identify individuals playing a crucial role in their team's success but failing to show up towards the top of the goalscoring charts or the assists table.

Every good team needs a platform to play their football and that means doing the ugly stuff - keeping defensive mistakes to a minimum and winning midfield battles.

Look at Liverpool in their remarkable 2019 Champions League

*James Norwood proved of huge value to Tranmere in the 2018-19 season, scoring 29 of the side's 63 goals*

# BETTING GUIDE

*Georginio Wijnaldum scores Liverpool's second goal as they beat Barcelona 4-0 at Anfield in the 2019 UEFA Champions League semi-final second leg*

semi-final success over Barcelona. They were 3-0 down from the first leg and went into the return game without two of their famed front three – Roberto Firmino and Mohamed Salah. But they blew Barcelona away at Anfield, thanks largely to the intensity of their play which was too much for the Catalans to handle.

Gini Wijnaldum and Divock Origi grabbed two goals each and hogged the headlines but it was the energy of midfielders Fabinho and Jordan Henderson that drove Liverpool on from start to finish. Neither of them featured heavily in the seasonal assist or scoring statistics but their value to Liverpool that night was clear to anyone who witnessed the drama.

## 3. Get your timing right

Timing can be a crucial factor in making singles betting pay a long-term dividend. Match prices will fluctuate in the days before a game and punters must take a decision over when to make their move.

The disadvantages to getting on early are that even fairly small wagers can nudge the betting in a certain direction. However, there will be occasions when you look at the early price about a team and think it is unlikely to be anywhere near as attractive by the time match day arrives.

Maybe you have recently seen a performance that makes you significantly upgrade or downgrade your opinion of a certain team. Or perhaps you have seen a key player pick up an injury that will not attract wider attention until later in the week.

There will also be instances when you want to side with a team that you feel the market will be against and, in those cases, it is worth playing a waiting game.

Maybe a team has not been performing well on the shots or the xG statistics (these teams tend to be well-backed) but you feel there are grounds to expect a future improvement in performance.

Every weekend there are teams who play better or worse than expected but there are usually underlying reasons and a shrewd punter gets ahead of the curve.

There are usually three different stages when I consider placing a bet.

Early wagers come under consideration after an assessment of the previous round of matches. Further bets are considered once the pre-match team news filters through – usually between one and two days before the game.

And final wagers are added within the last hour before kick-off when team line-ups are revealed.

Every weekend there will be some surprise inclusions or omissions on the team sheets and the shrewd punter will have amassed sufficient knowledge to digest the news quickly and act on it accordingly.

## 4. Get to know your managers

Football is not simply about having the best players. Top-class managers can make a huge difference to a club's fortunes while less talented ones can waste the talent at their disposal. However, like players, managers fortunes can go up and down and there will be certain environments they are better suited to than others.

As a punter interested in singles betting, it is the short-term impact of managers that should be of interest.

Why is it that some managers have an immediately positive impact, while others take a long time to get their ideas across?

Ole Gunnar Solksjaer (left) fits perfectly into the first category. He inherited a team that had won two of the previous eight games and led them to eight consecutive victories in his first five weeks at the helm.

Given the stories of discontent coming out of the Old Trafford dressing room towards the end of Jose Mourinho's reign, it was perhaps understandable that results initially improved. However, it is always far easier to be wise after the event.

The key for any successful singles punter was to anticipate an upsurge in performance at the time of Mourinho's sacking and start getting the Red Devils on side.

Different managers have different priorities and there is money to be made by paying attention to how they make their team selections.

Some managers like to rotate players and others prefer to stick with the same ones even when fixtures are coming thick and fast.

Knowing those habits can give punters a better idea of what to expect when the team sheets are handed in.

Managers also have different priorities when it comes to assessing various competitions. Some will make wholesale changes for the cups – especially in the early rounds – while others will go all out for glory.

However, it is worth bearing in mind that some teams possess deep squads with fringe players, who are not much worse than the first team regulars.

Watford manager Javi Gracia made 11 changes for an FA Cup fourth-round tie at Newcastle in January but his team posted a comfortable 2-0 victory and went on to reach the final for only the second time in the club's history.

*'Emotion needs to be taken out of the equation. Dumping a bet that goes on to win is extremely frustrating, perhaps more so than sticking with one that loses. But if Saturday afternoon arrives and the principle reasons behind the wager have vanished it makes perfect sense to walk away – even if the market has moved and you have to take a slight loss'*

## 5. Know when to pull the plug

The most hectic time of the week for a singles punter specialising in English football is between two and three o'clock on a Saturday.

This is when late decisions must be made with regard to adding to the betting portfolio but it is also the time when previous wagers need to be re-examined.

Bets would originally be placed according to a careful assessment of the strengths and weaknesses of both teams.

But all of that could suddenly fly out of the window if players are unexpectedly absent from the starting eleven or others return from injury ahead of schedule. In that case it is time to make a decision and make it quick because the market will not take very long to react. Emotion needs to be taken out of the equation.

Dumping a bet that goes on to win is extremely frustrating – perhaps more so than sticking with one that loses – but if Saturday afternoon arrives and the principle reasons behind the wager have vanished it makes perfect sense to walk away – even if the market has moved and you have to take a slight loss.

It is important to wait for both line-ups of a particular match to be revealed before making an assessment.

There will be times when the team you have backed are indeed weaker than you might have expected or hoped for. But the bad news could soon be cancelled out if their opponents are denied the services of important personnel.

Unfortunately decisions either way – whether to add bets or remove them - will often be finely balanced, but if you have an in-depth knowledge of the clubs and players involved, you will be in the best possible position to make them.

## " EXPERT VIEW

There is no real secret to successful football singles betting but, like many things in life, the more work put into it, the better chance you will have of turning a profit.

Singles betting relates to taking a short-term snapshot of where two teams are at a certain moment and making a call that the market prices are simply wrong.

Due to the wealth of information and the increased awareness of punters in general, it is probably true that football markets are more mature than they have ever been.

However, the masses are still capable of getting it wrong and there remains scope for the most knowledgeable punters to take advantage.

Nonetheless, making money over the long-term is tough and, to maximise your chances, it makes sense to follow some basic rules.

Firstly, keep a note of every bet you place and monitor long-term performance.

*'The masses are still capable of getting it wrong and there remains scope for the most knowledgeable punters to take advantage'*

There is no need to panic after a short-term losing run. Even professional punters will go through periods when they feel the whole world is against them. Plenty of good bets make a loss, while lots of bad bets will be successful. The important thing is to assess the game not the outcome.

If your strategy has been generally successful for months or even years, it makes no sense to ditch it suddenly because of a few disappointing weekends. However, the landscape of football singles betting has changed and will continue to change so be prepared to re-assess and adapt if long-term results do not bear fruit.

In the early years of singles betting it was possible to look at the shots statistics and bet accordingly because the markets appeared to pay little attention to them.

That has all changed and it means having to work harder to gain that edge everybody football punter seeks but few manage to find.

Speaking to other football punters, many feel more comfortable to wager on the big games in the biggest competitions because they are much easier to assess.

There can also be a reluctance to bet on cup games, especially the early rounds when managers are more likely to make changes, or matches at the start of a new season when there is less recent form in the book.

However, in an era when it is more difficult than ever to gain an advantage, I would argue that chaos can be a punters' friend.

When opinions vary and markets are at their most volatile there are always opportunities for those with the knowledge and inclination to back it.

Once the season gets going and the transfer window shuts, I often find it more difficult.

It soon becomes apparent which teams have improved and which have regressed over the summer months and, as a consequence, the matchday value dries up. Then the challenge is to react quickly to any key moments which take place during a season.

Injuries and suspensions will always occur and when they do, an opportunity may arise to back a team at an inflated price. However, only place a bet when the moment is right and not as a force of habit.

It might feel comfortable to place a similar number of bets each week but it is not the right way to operate. Some weekends there may be lots of opportunities while on other occasions the landscape could be very different.

Last, you will have a much better chance of success if football is your absolute passion.

Successful gambling is usually labour intensive and it helps if you enjoy doing the research required.

Keep a note of all your bets

Chaos can be used to your benefit

Be set to react quickly to secure value

## TOP TIP

Go to as many games as possible. Being at the game makes it much easier to assess a player's movement off the ball and their overall impact on the contest

# ASIAN HANDICAPS
## by Kevin Pullein

## INTRODUCTION

Asian handicap betting originated, as you might have guessed, in Asia. To be more specific, in Indonesia. It has been around for almost 30 years.

Visanu Vongsinsirikul, a lecturer in economics at Dhurakij Pundit University in Bangkok, Thailand, says: "The Asian handicap system was invented in Indonesia after the 1990 World Cup, when football betting really began to become popular in Asia."

It was known there as hang cheng betting. The term Asian handicap was coined in 1998 by Joe Saumarez Smith, once a contributor to the Racing Post.

Today Asian handicaps are traded around the globe.

As in other forms of handicap betting, one competitor gives up a start and the other competitor receives a start. The competitor giving up a start is denoted by a minus sign before the handicap – for example, -0.5. The competitor receiving a start is denoted by a plus sign before the handicap – for example, +0.5.

*A colourful scene during a 2015 friendly at the Karno Stadium in Jakarta, Indonesia, where Asian handicaps originated in 1990*

There are three types of Asian handicap: whole-ball, half-ball and quarter-ball.

Half-ball handicaps are the most straightforward. Every bet must either win or lose. Examples of half-ball handicaps are 0.5, 1.5 and 2.5. If you back a football team -1.5 goals you will win if they score at least two goals more than their opponents. Otherwise you will lose. If you back a football team +1.5 goals you will lose if they concede at least two goals more than their opponents. Otherwise you will win.

With whole-ball handicaps there is the possibility of a tie, which is called a push. When a push occurs all bets are off and all stakes are refunded. Examples of whole-ball handicaps are 0, 1 and 2.

If you back a football team -2 goals you will win if they score at least three goals more than their opponents. If they score two goals more your stake will be returned. And if anything else happens you will lose.

If you back a football team +2 goals you will lose if they concede at least three goals more than their opponents. If they concede two goals more your stake will be returned. If anything else happens you will win.

Quarter-ball handicaps are really two markets, with stakes split equally between the nearest half- and whole-ball handicaps. For example, if you back a football team -1.75 goals your stake will be divided evenly with half going on that team -1.5 goals and the other half going on that team -2 goals. (This will sometimes be made explicit with a quarter-ball handicap written as -1.5, -2 or -1.5 & -2).

'As in other forms of handicap betting, one competitor gives up a start and the other competitor receives a start'

## FIVE WAYS TO BET SMART ON ASIAN HANDICAPS

### 1. Bet on the unpopular side of the line

The original purpose of Asian handicaps was to provide lines with similar odds on both sides. This does not mean that bookmakers take a similar number of bets on both sides. Usually one side is much more popular than the other.

You should bet on the unpopular side. Not always, not sometimes, just now and then. Every now and then the odds on the unpopular side will be bigger than they should be. They will understate the prospect of a payout.

The key to profitable betting of any type is to bet selectively against the things that most people bet for.

Even if you do not speak to other bettors, or ask a bookmaker, you will be able to work out which side of an Asian handicap is going to be the most popular. It is the side on which there are the most powerful-sounding arguments. These tend to involve the best-supported teams, with better-known players, especially if things have been going well for them.

The most powerful-sounding arguments are right less often than their backers need them to be. Between October 2017 and September 2018, according to the Gambling Commission, British bookmakers won nearly £4 billion from bets on horses, dogs and sports. That means their customers lost nearly £4bn. To have any hope of betting profitably you have got to bet the other way to most people.

**TOP TIP**

To have any hope of betting profitability you have got to bet the other way to most people

156

## 2. Bet low

Actually there are two types of Asian betting line – handicap and total. They work in the same way. A total line can be whole-ball, half-ball or quarter-ball, just like a handicap line. The best-known example of a total line in football is over/under 2.5 goals.

On a total line there will be a popular side and an unpopular side. Just as there is on a handicap line. On a total line, as on a handicap line, you should bet discerningly on the unpopular side. It is under.

A senior football trader for a British-origin bookmaker with a global reach says: "We never take a bean on under."

Most people prefer to bet on things happening. Unfortunately for them, not as many things happen in football matches as they need to – whether they bet high on goals, corners, bookings or whatever. In some matches there is a high total, but not in enough.

One of the reasons most people prefer to bet high is that they like to watch their bet and it is much more fun to watch if you have bet high than if you have bet low. In fact, it can be agony to watch if you have bet low.

Say you bet low on goals. You want the ball to stay near the halfway line and feel anxious whenever it moves toward one of the goals, worse when a player shapes to shoot. If you bet high you can win before the match is over. And even if there has been no score near the end, you can still hope there will be a sudden rush of goals.

If you bet low you cannot win until the final whistle. If you bet high you cannot lose until the final whistle. But what matters is the total at the final whistle. Most people bet high and most people lose over time. Judiciously, bet low.

*Heading to the half-way line – just where you want the ball to be if you've bet low on goals*

## 3. Bet on whole-ball handicaps

In theory, every market on a contest is related properly to every other. If the odds in one market are right – that is to say, right for the bookmaker, wrong for you – so will they be in every other. And in practice this nearly always happens. But once in a while it does not. In particular, you will find odds can be too big on the unpopular side of a whole-ball handicap.

The distinguishing feature of a whole-ball handicap is that if there is a tie all bets are cancelled and stakes refunded. So what counts is the chance that the outcome will be on the unpopular side of the line relative to the chance that the outcome will be on the popular side of the line.

The greater the possibility of a tie, you will find, the greater the possibility that the odds for the unpopular side of that whole-ball handicap are too big. It still does not happen frequently, but it does happen now and again.

One example.

A football team playing away to stronger opponents are the least likely to score the most goals. But if the home team do score the most goals they might score only one more goal. Fairly often on one-goal handicaps stakes are refunded.

Bookmakers can misjudge the other options – underestimating the chance of the away team winning or drawing relative to the chance of the home team winning by two or more goals. In other words, quoting odds that are bigger than they should be for an away team with the Asian handicap of +1 goals.

*'The feature of a whole-ball handicap is that if there is a tie all bets are cancelled and stakes refunded'*

| Asian Handicap | | Newcastle | | Goal Line | | Over |
|---|---|---|---|---|---|---|
| Burnley | | 0.0 1.740 | | 2.0, 2.5 | | 2.080 |
| 0.0 2.210 | | | | Alternative Goal Line | | Over |
| Alternative Asian Handicap | | Newcastle | | 0.5, 1.0 | | 1.105 |
| Burnley | | +1.5 1.105 | | 1.0 | | 1.125 |
| -1.5 6.800 | | +1.0, +1.5 1.120 | | 1.0, 1.5 | | 1.275 |
| -1.0, -1.5 6.250 | | +1.0 1.140 | | 1.5 | | 1.425 |
| -1.0 5.750 | | +0.5, +1.0 1.260 | | 1.5, 2.0 | | 1.525 |
| -0.5, -1.0 3.700 | | +0.5 1.375 | | 2.0 | | 1.725 |
| -0.5 3.000 | | 0.0, +0.5 1.500 | | 2.5 | | 2.300 |
| 0.0, -0.5 2.500 | | | | | | |

## 4. Bet with less volatility

This can be helpful, but only for a small number of people.

The initial spur for Asian handicap betting, as already mentioned, was to provide lines with similar odds on each side. Nowadays some bookmakers offer a range of alternatives, with progressively more lopsided pairs of odds. Nonetheless most Asian handicap backers still bet most of the time at around evens.

If you bet regularly around evens you will win more often than if you bet regularly around, say, 10-1. Your results will be less volatile. Over any given number of bets what you get is more likely to be close to what you deserve.

This is a good thing only if what you deserve is a profit – if you are genuinely able to identify odds that understate the chance of incidents occurring. As we have seen, nearly all gamblers bet at odds that are bad for them and lose money in the long run. There are not many of the other sort. If you are one of them, or become one of them, you should benefit from the lower volatility in Asian handicap betting.

## 5. Bet against a smaller bookmaker edge

There are fewer opportunities to do this than there used to be – though for a good reason – but there are still some. The edge that bookmakers try to give themselves on other forms of betting is not always as thick as it used to be. Bookmakers want to make a profit. Almost always they do. Not on every market, but on most markets.

They work out what they think the odds should be then offer you worse odds. They lop a bit off what they think the odds should be.

Suppose they reckon that something is as likely to happen as not happen. They do not quote evens that it will happen and evens that it will not happen. They might offer, say, 9-10 that it does happen and 9-10 that it does not happen. Or less.

If the event is repeated over and over again and you bet every time, they would expect you to win as often as you lose. But every time you won they would give you a bit less than you gave them every time you lost. They would expect to make a profit out of you, and everyone else who took the same bets.

The smaller the edge that a bookmaker builds into their odds the smaller the amount by which their assessment must be wrong before those odds stop representing value for money to them and start representing value for money to you.

Traditionally bookmakers gave themselves a thinner edge on Asian handicaps than other betting styles. Over the years they shaved the edge on several other products. Even so, Asian handicaps are still lower margin than some ways of betting on the same or a similar eventuality.

*'Nearly all gamblers bet at odds that are bad for them and lose money in the long run. There are not many of the other sort. If you are one of them you should benefit from lower volatility in Asian handicap betting'*

odds in
your
favour

Look for
bets that are
a hard sell

Aim to
return a
long-term
profit

The principles of betting successfully on Asian handicaps are the same as the principles of betting successfully on anything else. To have any rational hope of making a profit over time, you have got to be able to identify events that are more likely than the odds imply.

You will find them on Asian handicaps in the same sort of places as you will find them in other forms of betting. You will find them in the places that most other people do not want to go. On the things that hardly anyone wants to back.

When bookmakers set odds they do two things. First, they consider what they think the odds should be, after which they knock a bit off with the aim of giving themselves an advantage. Then they shuffle those odds around a bit to reflect what they know from experience about how people will bet. They might shorten even more the odds for bets that they know many people will take anyway, and lengthen a little the odds for bets that they know few if any people will take.

Go to a shop, any shop on any street or in any mall. On what goods are you likely to be offered the best deal? The goods that are selling as fast as the shopkeeper can replenish the shelves? Or the goods that have been gathering dust in a corner? You will get the best price on the goods that shopkeepers find hardest to sell. And you will get the best odds on the bets that bookmakers find hardest to sell.

Every now and then – not always, not sometimes, just now and then – you will be offered odds about an unpopular proposition that are not slightly bad for you but actually good for you: odds that underestimate the prospect of a payout, odds that could contribute toward a long-term profit. Every now and then is enough.

# FIRST GOALSCORER
## by Mark Langdon

*Liverpool players celebrate their success in the 2019 Champions League*

First goalscorer betting used to be seen as the ultimate mug's game in terms of football punting but it's a more competitive market these days with bookmakers feeling the need to push the boat out and there are some professionals who believe there can be a tidy edge.

## EACH-WAY IS VALUE

The availability of each-way from some bookmakers has been a tremendous boost for punters, particularly in a one-sided contest.

Gone are the days when layers offered half the odds for a placed goal – the true short glory days of this market – but as bizarre as it sounds strong favourites around the 3-1 mark re often worth perming up with the evens for a placed goal with a third the odds for a place.

## TEAM NEWS IS MASSIVE

Following on from that area to attack is focusing on these heavy favourites, particularly when the main striker is rested/injured with his back-up playing as the central striker.

The odds don't change anywhere near as swiftly as they should. Get yourself on the internet an hour before the match starts and that is even more important for early rounds of cup ties.

## PENALTY TAKERS

It sounds obvious but penalty takers are worth keeping onside and that is even more the case now the handball laws have changed. The two biggest matches of the season are the Champions League final and World Cup final and both saw handballs awarded that a couple of years ago would never have been given.

Expect that trend to continue as the laws move even more in favour of the attacking team and also keep an eye out for those referees who are ultra-keen to point to the spot.

## SET-PIECE TEAMS

If you are looking to get with bigger-priced players then focus on the defenders of renowned set-piece masters.

Liverpool topped the set-piece goals in the 2018-19 Premier League with 20 but as a percentage that was just 22 per cent. Brighton had 40 per cent of their goals from set-pieces with centre-backs Shane Duffy and Lewis Dunk scoring seven times between them.

## NO GOALSCORER

Most bookies offer the same price for 0-0 and no goalscorer and the majority of those payout on no goalscorer if any goals in the game are own goals.

It won't collect often but if the price for no goalscorer and 0-0 is the same always head to the no goalscorer option just in case.

# CASHING OUT
## by Mark Langdon

Cash out has been one of the relatively new betting innovations in recent years and opinion is split on its merits. The fact nearly every bookmaker offers it tells you it is popular and for the skeptical punter it only goes to highlight bookies tend to push things which are good for them.

For many they offer bad value.

*'On most occasions you would be better off letting the bet ride or look to layoff in a different way, maybe on Betfair when there is the chance of laying a particular outcome (s)'*

You are betting against the bookmakers' margin for a second time and the offers of cash out are rarely considered excellent value. Sometimes they are genuinely terrible.

On most occasions you would be better off letting the bet ride or look to layoff in a different way, maybe on Betfair when there is the chance of laying a particular outcome (s).

Against that, however, is it's all well and good when punters refuse to lay off and are full of bravado proclaiming the only place for a hedge is in the garden but if it is the difference between maybe a family holiday at Pontins or Disney World who is anyone to tell that person to stick with the bet?

And the person in question may not have the funds to have a separate bet to start laying, so at least you don't need to reinvest with cash out. There's also the added convenience of the speed at which you can cash out, or in many cashes now, partially cash out bets.

Just be fully aware of the pros and cons of cashing out – it's bad because the value is not usually great and it's good because it you don't need to find additional funds to lay off.

# WIN TO NIL
## by Dan Childs

### INTRODUCTION

Building from the back used to be the ethos of most successful sides but times are changing and that may lead to a reduction in the attractiveness of win-to-nil betting.

More and more teams are happy to accept greater risks by playing an attacking style of football (think Norwich, who won the Sky Bet Championship in 2018-19 while shipping 57 goals) but there are exceptions with certain managers still placing a high emphasis on keeping clean sheets.

### FAVOURITES TO AVOID

*Norwich City fans celebrate during a campaign to remember in which Teemu Pukki (facing page) played a major role with 29 league goals*

Win-to-nil betting is often a method used to bump up the price when a short-priced favourite takes on a lowly opponent but a massive gulf in class can breed complacency, leading to opportunities for consolation goals.

No country is more synonymous with cautious tactics and no nonsense defending than Italy but many Serie A sides are changing their approach, leading to more goals, fewer clean sheets and fewer win-to-nil opportunities.

Juventus have dominated the league – winning eight successive titles – but are becoming far more interested in scoring lots of goals than racking up shutouts.

The Old Lady cruised to the title last term – finishing 11 points clear of second-placed Napoli – but they conceded 30 goals, their highest since 2010-11, and won-to-nil in just 16 of their 38 matches.

A similar story has unfolded in Spain where champions Barcelona conceded 36 goals – the highest of any La La winner since they triumphed in 2012-13 (conceding 40 times).

They won-to-nil on 15 occasions last term.

## BUCKING THE TREND

Some managers still savour a 1-0 win and perhaps the most famous in club football is Atletico Madrid's Diego Simeone.

Atleti have had the best defensive record in La Liga for four successive seasons and have long been the friends of win-to-nil punters.

In the 2018-19 season they kept clean sheets in 19 of their 22 league victories and their status as a tough team to play against is unlikely to change while Simeone remains at the helm.

At the time of writing Liverpool and Manchester City have become clean sheet kings in the Premier League thanks to stout defences and their Brazilian goalkeepers, Alisson and Ederson, who achieved Premier League shutout tallies of 21 and 20.

However, City had the edge with win-to-nil outcomes – leading Liverpool 19 to 18.

*'At the time of writing Liverpool and Manchester City have become clean sheet kings in the Premier League thanks to stout defences and their Brazilian goalkeepers'*

167

# HALF-TIME FULL-TIME
## by Dan Childs

## INTRODUCTION

With elite clubs getting richer and stronger and others often trailing in their wake there can be a proliferation one-sided betting heats on the coupon.

One way to approach these matches is to ignore them. Another is to be creative and half-time full-time betting is one of the more useful ways of finding a more attractively priced wager.

However, punters need to be careful because there are nine different outcomes and the most obvious one (a hot favourite leading at the break and going onto victory) is not necessarily an easy short-cut to better odds.

## IDENTIFYING THE WINNING TRENDS

Usually the market leader in a half-time full-time bet will be the match favourite to lead at half-time and take the points.

It makes sense to target teams which start games quickly. Take Manchester City's 2018-19 title-winning side for example. They led at half-time and went on to win in 24 of 38 league games (63 per cent), making a tidy profit over the course of the season.

Conversely, it is sensible to oppose teams who struggle defensively, making them vulnerable against an early onslaught.

In the same season Fulham had the worst defensive record in the top flight last season and had the worst half-time full-time outcomes – trailing at the break and losing in 20 of 38 games.

Other teams have a habit of slowly building up a head of steam and doing their best work in the second half.

Arsenal were famously slow starters in 2018-19 and did not hold a half-time lead until December 22 when going on to defeat Burnley 3-1.

The half-time draw, full-time Arsenal selection copped in 11 of their 38 games and may be a popular pick in 2019-20.

O *Manchester City led at half-time and went on to win 63 per cent of their 38 league games in 2018-19*

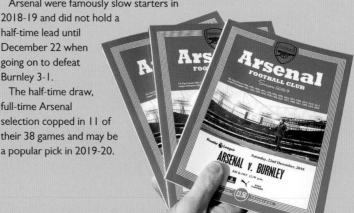

# THE DANGER OF BEING ADVENTUROUS

The largest prices on offer are for teams to be losing at half-time and winning at full-time or vice versa (winning at the break and losing on the final whistle) but it doesn't happen on a regular basis.

Of the 380 2018-19 Premier League results, there were only 17 occasions when the result flipped between half-time and full-time. That works out at an average of one in every 22.35 matches. Within those 17 occasions, there were only four times when the home team led at the break and lost the game.

So for punters drawn in by the bigger prices, it is vital to acknowledge how rare it is for a half-time result to be reversed. When it does happen it tends to stick in the memory.

The most famous example in the 2018-19 season was when Tottenham came from 2-0 down away to Ajax and won the game 3-2. But Spurs achieved the feat just once in 38 Premier League games and no top flight side did it more than twice.

*Lucas Moura scored three times in the 2019 Uefa Champions League semi-final second leg to put Tottenham Hotspur into the final*

169

# NON-LEAGUE
## by Andrew Wilsher

### INTRODUCTION

Finding a niche in betting is one of the key ways to stay one step ahead of the bookmaker, but that doesn't mean you have to become an expert in Brazilian futsal. Non-league football offers a happy medium where plenty of information is available to punters, while being one that often slips under the traders' noses.

### DO YOUR HOMEWORK

You will occasionally find odds which offer incredible value, with the first or anytime goalscorer one recent example of this. The prices hardly ever change for players each week no matter how in form they are or the level of opposition they are playing.

   If you do a bit of homework, you might find that a midfielder who has notched a couple in the past few weeks and has been shooting regularly is available at a hefty price to score, or that a team has been deadly on corners and, as expected, their centre-backs are among the rank outsiders to notch.

   That was the case for 2018-19 National League winners Leyton Orient, whose third and fourth top goalscorers were centre-back pairing Josh Coulson and Marvin Ekpiteta. Despite scoring the opener

*National League champions Leyton Orient were 33-1 to triumph for much of the 2018-19 season*

in six matches, they continued to be priced around 33-1 for the majority of the season.

Another area worth identifying is set pieces. Some clubs have defenders taking penalties – much like David Unsworth used to do for Everton – and this is not always taken into account when they are priced up.

Following non-league team's social media pages, fanzines and podcasts offer invaluable information regarding about the day-to-day operations of football clubs and can give you an edge when looking to place a bet. Stats sites Transfermarkt and Soccerbase are very handy.

## IT PAYS TO STAY CLUED UP

Money plays an enormous part in the fortunes of non-league football teams, and it is worth staying on top of all the news and updates regarding a side's financial position.

Teams in financial turmoil can understandably start the season in very poor form, but their price regularly remains unchanged following a takeover or the signing of new players.

League positions have arguably too much of an impact on prices, and if you can find a particular trend, such as top teams starting slow and regularly scoring more in the second half than the first, then that too can pay dividends.

There is no better way to get an edge in non-league betting than actually watching the games. The National League airs more matches on television than League One and League Two each season, giving a great opportunity to understand how teams set up and operate.

*'Money plays an enormous part in the fortunes of non-league football teams, and it is well worth staying on top of all the news and updates regarding a side's financial position'*

# GOLF
## by Steve Palmer

*'The occasions you get it right are hugely rewarding and provide riches that no other sports betting can match'*

## INTRODUCTION

The grand game of golf has been played for centuries – an impossible-to-perfect pursuit that has made many a grown man weep from the Middle Ages onwards. And for the last few decades, bookmakers have been laying bets on professional golf tournaments, allowing punters to feel the ups and downs of this crazy sport without having to swing a club themselves.

The typical 20-handicapper at a golf club will make several bogeys every time they step on the course – the majority of their day will be mediocre – but one birdie, or even just one good shot, will provide such a thrill that the hardy hacker will come back for more.

The life of folk in the golf betting community, even those like me who consider themselves a semi-professional punter, is similar to that of the plucky weekend club golfer. The odds are always against you –

normal tournaments feature 156 runners in the field – and picking a handful of competitors you think might have a chance of lifting the trophy means you still have 150 or so adversaries.

But the occasions you get it right – the moments when, to continue the analogy with actual golf, you flush an eight-iron from 150 yards and your ball nestles into the cup – are usually hugely rewarding and provide riches that no other sports betting can match. The odds on golfers, given how many go to post, are always full of juice. Back a winner and your return should be extremely healthy – a few successful tournaments can leave you in profit, more than covering the inevitably long losing streaks in between the sporadic triumphs.

Golf betting was more straightforward in the late-90s and most of the noughties – the odds remained relatively static from opening show to tee-off time and Tiger Woods *(right)* was often a winning short-price favourite – but times have changed. There is a frenzy of early betting activity as soon as prices are issued on Mondays – the markets rapidly mature – and the era of Tiger dominance is long gone. There is enormous strength in depth, particularly on the US Tour.

Bookmakers have shown mercy to the modern golf punter by enhancing their each-way terms – five places used to be the maximum available, but as many as ten can be offered for the super-competitive Majors, and eight is becoming widespread weekly for the US Tour. Place money can keep the golf punter ticking over nicely, as he waits, patiently as ever, for that eight-iron to hit the sweetspot.

## TEN WAYS TO BET SMART ON GOLF

### 1. Open as many betting accounts as possible

The most common error the casual golf punter makes is to limit their horizons to only one or just a handful of bookmakers. I have friends, who take the betting game far less seriously than me, who bet with a single firm on their mobile. If they go to back a golfer, whatever the price is with this particular bookmaker is the one they will take, regardless of what is available elsewhere.

I know other characters who will bet only in cash, trotting to the betting shop closest to their house, oblivious to the fact that the bookmaker another 100 yards down the road would return an extra £80 on their tenner wager.

The price differences in golf are wider and more consequential than in any other sport. In the example above, 25-1 might

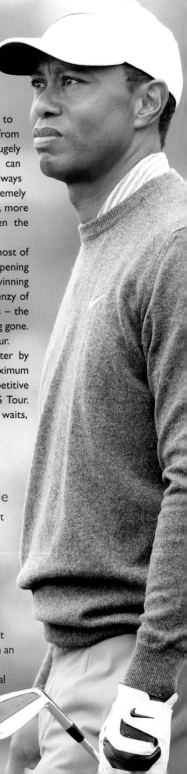

be the odds of a player in a Paddy Power shop, while 33-1 is on offer in the Ladbrokes nearby. Surely it is worth the extra few steps to access the superior odds?

Price comparison is essential to the success of the modern golf punter, especially ones just starting out in the game. Use Oddschecker to see where the best prices are, then attack accordingly. Sometimes a golfer will be 50-1 with one firm and 100-1 with another. The bigger the price, the greater the potential for disparity – a 250-1 chance may be 500-1 elsewhere. This hunt for value is the essence of effective betting.

Sensible punters will open online accounts with every reputable bookmaker they can find, leaving themselves free to easily access the best price in the marketplace.

Consistently successful betting will probably bring stake restrictions, and eventually account closures, so punters winning big over the long-term can find their account options narrow to an infuriating extent. Newcomers should take advantage of their freedom while they have it and get their betting careers off to a flyer.

## 2. Work from the full-field list and do not be put off by big prices

It can be difficult for golf-betting virgins, especially those who have been brought up on a diet of horse racing and greyhound racing, to see three-figure prices against the name of a player and take that option seriously.

A 100-1 chance in horseracing can be quickly dismissed from your punting plans. The poor prancer will probably be out of puff before it even reaches the start-line. A 100-1 chance in a greyhound race is likely to hobble to the traps with a missing leg. Animals at that sort of price just do not win – or only once in the proverbial blue moon – but humans, or more specifically golfers, triumph at three-figure prices on a regular basis.

The strength in depth on the professional golf circuit these days is incredible. Most of the players competing on the Korn Ferry Tour – the grade below the US Tour – are good enough to win top-flight events if they get an opportunity. It was much easier to draw a line through 'makeweights' in decades gone by, but almost everyone in the fields on the European and US Tour nowadays have some hope of victory. You have to be extremely good just to get a chance to tee up.

This means no stone can be left unturned. There are no shortcuts to successful long-term golf betting. You need to do the hard yards, that means you start with a list of every golfer in the field, without any prices alongside them. And assess the merits of each candidate from there.

I tipped Thomas Bjorn to win the 2011 Qatar Masters at 200-1 in the Racing Post. If I had done what most golf punters do before tournaments, I would probably not even have considered Bjorn. A casual golf punter decides who to bet by going straight to the odds, working from the favourite down, making a few selections. They don't bother with the rank outsiders – they just hastily back one of the more fancied market principals, assuming the massive-price runners have no chance.

But they do have a chance. No sport serves up more 'shock' winners than golf. Whittle down the full field without worrying about odds, then, once you have reduced your list to ten or so names you think might contend, write down what odds you would be prepared to accept about each player. The greater the positive disparity between your odds and those on offer – for example, if you make Bjorn 40-1 and 200-1 is available – then the more reason you have for including them in your staking plan.

## 3. Be quick if you want maximum value

In the olden days bookmakers slowly but surely trickled golf prices out, and tournaments would be looming large by the time every layer had issued their odds. In the last few years, though, aided by advancements in technology and the range of information on the internet, odds compilers are able to rapidly fire their opening shows. The complexion of the golf-betting week has changed dramatically.

Mondays have become manic. The first shows of the week will arrive around noon, with other firms soon following, and by dinnertime almost every bookmaker has got at least one, and usually two, tournaments priced up. All the while, early-bird punters are gobbling stand-out prices almost as soon as they appear, seizing upon any obvious errors.

Matthew Wolff, for example, was chalked up at 250-1 by William Hill for the 2019 Travelers Championship. The amateur superstar was bound to be a popular selection on his

**Next best**
▶▶Thomas Bjorn 200-1
Another former Dubai Desert Classic champion has been discounted too easily as well. Thomas Bjorn saw off the challenge of Tiger Woods in a famous eyeball-to-eyeball duel for that title in 2001 and the Dane loves the challenge of a windy desert layout.
Bjorn, who won the Portuguese Open last June to prove he is still a force at the age of 39 and was fifth in the Valderrama Masters at the end of October, has finished in the top ten at Doha in two of his last four starts there. And having finished strongly in Bahrain last week – he went ten under par for his final three rounds having finally shaken off the close-season rust – he could threaten again.

*Thomas Bjorn savours the moment after winning the Qatar Masters in 2011 after being tipped up at 200-1 by Steve Palmer in the Racing Post (above)*

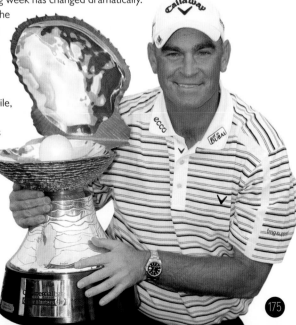

*'Sundays are typically a day of rest but if you have the time and inclination to get your research done for the following week's events, you can hit the ground running on the Monday afternoon and hoover up the best possible prices before they disappear'*

professional debut and the Monday-afternoon army quickly feasted on the price. Less than 48 hours later, with still another 24 hours to go until the tournament started, Hills were laying Wolff at 80-1, their liability skewed by punting wolves who had hunted in a pack, forcing price cuts, as soon as they could.

Sundays are typically a day of rest for most people – and golf tournaments will be reaching their conclusion – but if you have the time and inclination to get your research done for the following week's events, allied to the range of online betting accounts mentioned earlier, you can hit the ground running on the Monday afternoon and hoover up the best possible prices before they disappear forever.

An early bird can truly catch the worm, although bookmakers tend to restrict stakes more often earlier in the week, before accepting bigger bets closer to the start time, once the market has been knocked into a more solid shape by punters taking advantage of the most distinctive prices.

## 4. Be patient if you want investment security

The negative flip-side to being one of the Monday wolves, tearing eagerly into fleshy prices, is that you will be having your wager three days before the action starts. Three days is enough time in the life of a human for them to turn from an obvious title contender into a complete no-hoper.

Obviously, transformations as dramatic as that are rare and unlikely, but they happen, so there is always an element of risk attached to backing your golfers early. Injury information can be revealed during the Monday, Tuesday or Wednesday, that was not common knowledge prior, or your player may get crocked during practice for the event.

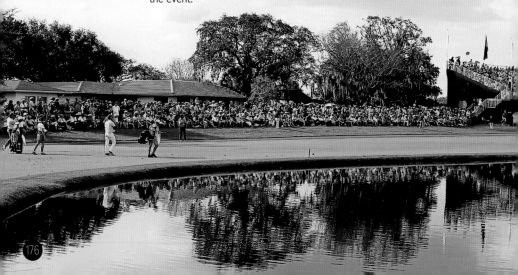

More likely is they fall ill and weaken. Illness can hit a player suddenly and strongly, rendering them lame ducks for the tournament. You may have been delighted with all the fancy prices you claimed on the Monday afternoon for the Indian Open, but come tee-off time, your selections are all labouring with Delhi belly.

This is a balancing act the golf punter must play. If you are going to be investing heavily, it is wise to leave your bet as late as possible, allowing you the chance to check, and check over and over, on the health of your fancies. The internet is crammed with golfing news and the pgatour.com website screens live media conferences before tournaments, where the biggest names are grilled on their title aspirations.

Jason Day was well fancied for the 2019 Arnold Palmer Invitational at a Bay Hill course where he triumphed in 2016. Punters chunked on early and the Australian went off a well-backed 14-1 chance, then he withdrew after just six holes with a back injury he had picked up the Sunday prior. His backers had done their dough only a couple of hours after the tournament had started.

In this case Day, scandalously in the eyes of many, did not reveal his health problems to anyone until he was hobbling back to the clubhouse during round one. But he was the exception to the rule – players will typically use conferences or press interviews to reveal any fresh niggles – bringing punters up to speed.

Small-stake punters may prefer to be quick out the blocks with their wagers to get bigger odds, but it is always safer to wait if you are risking a significant sum. You may need a higher stake if the odds have shortened, but in return you are getting almost a guarantee of full fitness, as well as access to the tee-times and latest weather forecasts.

*Jason Day might have got his hands on the trophy (below) in 2016, but he pulled out of the 2019 Arnold Palmer Invitational at Bay Hill (main picture)*

## 5. Different tactics can be applied for Majors

The four most prestigious tournaments on the golfing calendar – the Majors – provide a slightly different puzzle for punters. The Masters, the US PGA Championship, the US Open and the Open Championship all give you the option of betting ante-post a long way from tee-off time.

Horseracing fans love to identify runners that may flourish at the Cheltenham Festival several months in advance of the annual National Hunt highlight and golf lovers can do something similar with the Majors. Most bookmakers will have prices for Majors running permanently and they often neglect to update the markets each week. They can be extremely vulnerable to on-the-ball punters.

My personal ante-post strategy is to have a four-fold on the winners of the following year's four Majors around Christmas time – an ambitious accumulator that will return a retirement-clinching total if successful. For 2019, I had an £11.87 each-way four-fold with bet365 on Jon Rahm for the Masters (22-1), Brooks Koepka for the US PGA (14-1), Dustin Johnson for the US Open (10-1) and Tiger Woods for the Open (10-1), that could have returned £499,766.31. My race was run when Rahm finished ninth in the Masters, and I was cheesed off when I gained nothing from Koepka winning the US PGA, but I had lost only a small stake for the potential of life-changing success.

More cautious and more sensible characters, with more time on their hands, use the ante-post markets in a more consistently lucrative fashion. The bookmakers, like myself, have a million-and-one other things to be worrying about on a weekly basis and do not pay much attention to their ante-post books. A lively

*Patrick Reed slips into the Green Jacket after winning the 2018 Masters having been 66-1 with Ladbrokes*

*'Bookmakers will have prices for Majors running permanently and often neglect to update the markets each week. They can be extremely vulnerable to on-the-ball punters'*

candidate for the Masters, for example, may be finding some form in the early months of the year, yet his price remains unchanged in the Augusta betting.

With so many ante-post prices left dormant for long periods by lacklustre layers, punters with long-range Major plans and an eager eye on the formbook should be able to get several players they fancy onside early at larger prices than they could get in the week of the tournament.

Busy odds compilers often leave absolute howlers, particularly early in the year. The average golf punter is also too busy with the here-and-now to worry about the next Major, but those who focus on the four main events can build strong positions. Even during the April-July Majors season, errors remain in the ante-post betting. Brandt Snedeker, for example, was 175-1 for the US Open just three weeks prior – an event at a Pebble Beach course where he had twice been victorious. He had found form, but bookies failed to react, then come US Open week no bigger than 50-1 was available.

Less than two weeks before the 2018 Masters, Patrick Reed was a stand-out 66-1 with Ladbrokes and I was able to give my friend Mark Ashby an excellent birthday present with £10 ante-post on the feisty Texan. A short while later, the general pre-tournament 50-1 chance was slipping into the Green Jacket.

## 6. Be fluid with how many selections you have and obsess with your staking plan

How many players you back in each tournament is not an exact science. Firstly, the field size will influence your strategy – 240 players go to post for the South African Open, but only 18 for the Hero World Challenge. You may decide you need an army for South Africa, but only a couple for the World Challenge.

For me, the overriding factor in how many selections I have is how many likely title contenders I can identify and how many of them are available at value prices (bigger odds than they should be). Then I determine whether backing all of them is viable – could the average working man or woman afford to include them all in their staking plan – or is further reduction of the shortlist required?

If there are too many short-priced players in your staking plan, it can be difficult to make significant profit. The punter must decide what their profit targets are – they could back 20 or so players and look to grind a tiny yield, or load all their stake money on just one or two, seeking larger returns.

The punter must also decide whether win-only bets or each-way investments are the best policy. Again, this is down to

*'Busy odds compilers often leave absolute howlers. The average golf punter is also too busy with the here-and-now to worry about the next Major, but those who focus on the four main events can build strong positions'*

**TOP TIP**

Don't be put off from having several runners carrying your cash. It is an increasingly competitive golf-betting landscape and spreading your stake money is very sensible

personal preference, based on ambition and profit targets. Each-way bets – particularly if you can access the increasingly available terms of a fifth the odds the first eight places – generally represent better value for money. Bookmakers typically have a huge, ugly overround on their golf win prices, but offer a much fairer package to each-way punters.

The betting exchanges – headlined by Betfair – offer an alternative route. The Betfair Exchange win prices are usually better than what is available with bookmakers. And the Betfair Exchange top-ten market becomes a useful tool when liquidity increases for Majors.

I have between one and seven selections for each event. I start with the full field, then use an X Factor-style process to whittle the field down to a shortlist of ten or so names, then I continue, using as many variables as possible, including prices of course, to decide who qualifies for the all-important staking plan.

I usually have between three and five selections. I have had seven only once in my betting career – for the 2019 BMW International – and critics argued I had "tipped half the field". I had, in fact, tipped less than 4.5 percent of the 156-runner field, the shortest-priced selection was 25-1, five were 50-1 or bigger, and one was 300-1, so fundamental mathematics still gave me precious little hope of success. Do not be put off from having several runners in an increasingly competitive golf-betting landscape, spreading your stake money.

I had only four selections for the 2019 Masters – had I had six, I would have enjoyed having Tiger Woods as a 20-1 pre-tournament winner. I had only five selections for the 2019 Memorial – had I had six, I would have had Patrick Cantlay as a 16-1 pre-tournament winner. There is no feeling more painful for the golf punter than the last name you have axed from your shortlist going on to win the tournament. If in doubt, have more, not less.

## 7. Research the course as much as possible and identify the type of player who could succeed

Golf courses change over time, whether it be a total redesign at the cost of millions of pounds or a slight revision to one or two holes, so punters studying course form need to do more than just access the results from previous tournaments at the venue. Has the course stayed the same through the years? Were the weather conditions dramatically different for previous editions, altering the style of play required for success?

The best source of course information – and the most considered advice on which players to back – is found each week on racingpost.com from 8pm on Tuesdays and in the Racing Post the following day. Those who do not want to wait until then should study europeantour.com and pgatour.com for course clues, as well as the website of the actual golf clubs in question. There are also specialist course-review websites – designed for club players looking for somewhere to golf – where titbits can be gleaned from contributors who have recently tackled the track.

Generally, accurate, tidy players thrive at tight, tree-lined venues, whereas powerful, aggressive players prefer wide-open layouts. Strong ball-strikers are favoured by tough tee-to-green tests, while good putters prefer easy courses where a premium is on who holes the most putts. Some play well in certain countries, some putt well on certain types of grass, some like fast greens, some like slow. The websites previously mentioned host reams of statistics for punters to learn player attributes.

Be wary of backing course debutants, particularly at well-established venues that many of the field know well. An Augusta debutant, for example, has not won the Masters since 1979.

On other occasions, though, if a course has just undergone a heavy redesign, changing its characteristics, debutants may represent value for money. Players with experience of the old course may employ old habits and target-lines, which are no longer beneficial, so coming in fresh can be an advantage.

Look out for players who have performed well at a course despite arriving there in poor current form. That indicates extreme affection for the layout.

## 8. Appreciate that current form is more important than anything else

The historical course-form study is essential, but the most important factor in determining selections is how well they are currently playing. Who is swinging well? Who is putting well? A player can win anywhere if they are in possession of their A-game.

Progressive, unexposed types represent the best value – who is better than they have previously shown? Youngsters who have excelled at amateur level have the scope for rapid strides when they make the switch to the pro ranks.

Viktor Hovland finished 32nd in the 2019 Masters and 12th in the 2019 US Open when still an amateur. The 21-year-old Norwegian has a frightening amount of potential and provided a conundrum for bookmakers in his first event as a professional – the 2019 Travelers Championship. Just how good is he? One firm opened up at 100-1 for the Travelers, another went 40-1.

Always being on players who are better than bookmakers think they are is a passport to profit. Much like with horseracing, you need to

**MASTERS WINNERS**

| Year | Winner |
|---|---|
| 2019 | Tiger Woods |
| 2018 | Patrick Reed |
| 2017 | Sergio Garcia |
| 2016 | Danny Willett |
| 2015 | Jordan Spieth |
| 2014 | Bubba Watson |
| 2013 | Adam Scott |
| 2012 | Bubba Watson |
| 2011 | Charl Schwartzel |
| 2010 | Phil Mickelson |
| 2009 | Angel Cabrera |
| 2008 | Trevor Immelman |
| 2007 | Zach Johnson |
| 2006 | Phil Mickelson |
| 2005 | Tiger Woods |
| 2004 | Phil Mickelson |
| 2003 | Mike Weir |
| 2002 | Tiger Woods |
| 2001 | Tiger Woods |
| 2000 | Vijay Singh |
| 1999 | Jose Maria Olazabal |
| 1998 | Mark O'Meara |
| 1997 | Tiger Woods |
| 1996 | Nick Faldo |
| 1995 | Ben Crenshaw |
| 1994 | Jose Maria Olazabal |
| 1993 | Bernhard Langer |
| 1992 | Fred Couples |
| 1991 | Ian Woosnam |
| 1990 | Nick Faldo |
| 1989 | Nick Faldo |
| 1988 | Sandy Lyle |
| 1987 | Larry Mize |
| 1986 | Jack Nicklaus |
| 1985 | Bernhard Langer |
| 1984 | Ben Crenshaw |
| 1983 | Seve Ballesteros |
| 1982 | Craig Stadler |
| 1981 | Tom Watson |
| 1980 | Seve Ballesteros |
| 1979 | Fuzzy Zoeller |
| 1978 | Gary Player |
| 1977 | Tom Watson |

judge who has the strongest form. The status of the tournaments is the most obvious indicator in this regard – a player who has just finished second in, for example, the Players Championship (arguably the deepest field of the year) has better form than a player who has just finished second in a low-grade affair like the John Deere Classic.

Potential inspiration is another factor for punters to consider. Players from the same country can egg each other on – one winning can spark compatriots into life. And even players from the same age group can do the same – a veteran success can convince other round-bellies that they can still cut the mustard.

The famous 'nappy factor' is something else for punters to note. Players often see a spike in form after becoming a father for the first time, particularly if their off-spring is a son, gaining a subconscious performance boost. Danny Willett won the Masters days after becoming a dad.

The opposite to any potential inspiration when assessing form figures is mental fatigue. Players may have a series of impressive results just behind them, but have they got anything left in the tank? Is this their fifth tournament in a row without a break? Have they been globetrotting through lots of different time zones? Players need to be fresh enough to produce their best golf.

## 9. Use social media to gain often vital clues

Watching as much golf as possible is crucial to success. Often Sky Sports Golf will be showing live golf all day and all night, with the European Tour coverage followed by the US Tour, on Thursday, Friday, Saturday and Sunday. Watch as much as you can without neglecting your other responsibilities in life. You pick up bits of information and see how everyone is swinging.

But, in addition to constantly

*Danny Willett heads to victory in the 2016 Masters having become a father just a few days earlier*

gawping at the gogglebox, the modern golf punter has to also spend time studying social media. Golfers are relentlessly tweeting on Twitter and posting photographs on Instagram, so punters should be stalking them, attempting to find out about their whereabouts, well-being, etc.

When did they arrive at the tournament? How did the journey go? Any news from the practice rounds? Preparation going well? Do they seem cheerful? Or knackered? Or distracted by something? Have they got some new equipment in the bag?

Pablo Larrazabal provided a good example of the power of social media in the lead-up to the 2019 BMW International. The Spaniard was a two-time course winner who had finished eighth and fourth in two events prior to withdrawing during the Belgian Knockout last time out with a wrist injury. Despite his course credentials, most early-bird punters were ruling Larrazabal out of their staking plans on the strength of fitness concerns. But then, he responded to a question on Twitter by reporting: "The wrist is great!"

A Larrazabal gamble followed as soon as the Twitterati spotted the positive health bulletin.

## 10. Always chance a win-double when possible

Profit targets have been discussed in a previous section, but it is difficult to think of a sound reason for denying yourself the chance of the ultimate rewards. Having an outright double on the two main tournaments of the week typically affords the opportunity of an enormous payout. A small stake for the potential of a large return.

I have won fortunes betting on golf since I started in the mid-90s – it has been betting rather than wages which have allowed me to buy a house, a car, etc – and the most profitable wagers of all have been winning doubles.

Most 'professional punters' shy away from golf doubles – too optimistic and foolish they insist – but they are wrong. There is no easier or more sensible way of a small-stake punter giving themselves the chance to win big.

You can pair your No. 1 selection from each tournament in a double – like I do every week – or you can do every available double from all of your selections. Get the winner of both tournaments and you are in clover. Each-way doubles are more sensible and you have more chance of regular returns – even a place double can yield an extremely healthy amount.

I have nailed doubles to about the same total as there are Red Arrows. And, trust me, they make you soar with joy. Reach for the skies, comrades. Be brave, be ambitious. Ambition is not a dirty word!

*'Golfers are relentlessly tweeting on Twitter and posting photographs on Instagram, so punters should be stalking them, attempting to find out about their whereabouts, well-being, etc'*

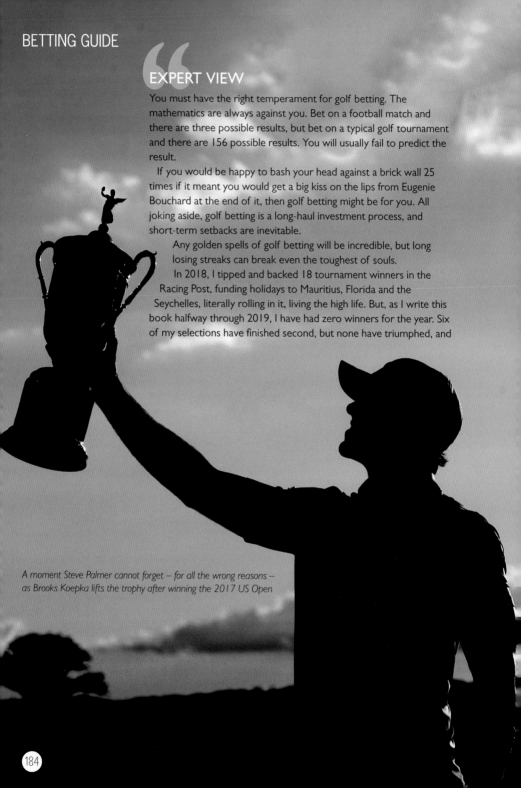

## ❝ EXPERT VIEW

You must have the right temperament for golf betting. The mathematics are always against you. Bet on a football match and there are three possible results, but bet on a typical golf tournament and there are 156 possible results. You will usually fail to predict the result.

If you would be happy to bash your head against a brick wall 25 times if it meant you would get a big kiss on the lips from Eugenie Bouchard at the end of it, then golf betting might be for you. All joking aside, golf betting is a long-haul investment process, and short-term setbacks are inevitable.

Any golden spells of golf betting will be incredible, but long losing streaks can break even the toughest of souls.

In 2018, I tipped and backed 18 tournament winners in the Racing Post, funding holidays to Mauritius, Florida and the Seychelles, literally rolling in it, living the high life. But, as I write this book halfway through 2019, I have had zero winners for the year. Six of my selections have finished second, but none have triumphed, and

*A moment Steve Palmer cannot forget – for all the wrong reasons – as Brooks Koepka lifts the trophy after winning the 2017 US Open*

Sandy Balls (New Forest) will probably be the most lavish destination I can afford this summer. To tickle some old betting parlance, I have very much done my sandy balls.

The golf punter needs to be able to handle long stretches without any respite, as well as mentally deal with the wafer-thin margins between success and failure. First, the margins are fine before the tournament starts, as you whittle down your shortlist. You can axe one last name from your list, then watch in horror as he romps to victory.

Current form and course form will always be the most important ingredients in determining selections, but there are a multitude of other reasons for fancying a golfer – and you can narrowly miss a key nugget. For example, I have still not got over – and probably never will – failing to tip and back Brooks Koepka at 50-1 for the 2017 US Open at a course (Erin Hills, Wisconsin) which was a perfect fit for him.

Koepka was the last name I removed from my shortlist – because I did not put enough stock into Whistling Straits form. That was the previous Wisconsin course used for a Major and full of similarities to Erin Hills. I did not think Erin Hills would play as easy as Whistling Straits did in the 2015 US PGA (Jason Day won at 20 under par), but in the end it was not far short (Koepka reached 16 under at Erin Hills). Koepka finished fifth in the 2015 US PGA – that should have been enough for me to get over the line with picking Koepka in my Koepka versus Billy Horschel final-selection toss-up – and I hate myself for not taking the hint.

I will take that failure to back Koepka at 50-1 to my grave and these are the battle scars that the golf punter accrues over time.

Second, you must overcome the fine margins of the actual event. Lady Luck often has a role to play, particularly with regards to the weather in which your selections get to compete, and no other form of fixed-odds sports betting provides such an intense mental examination as the four-day golfing marathon. From the moment you wake up on Thursday morning to the moment you go to bed on Sunday night, the golf punter can be living through leaderboards. You need to be in a sound and stable condition. Golf punting is not for the faint-hearted.

I have been golf punting for about 23 years and it has served me well financially. Whether it has served me well physically is another matter entirely! Stake to a level which will not put too much pressure on your heart – because golf tournaments are the ultimate emotional rollercoasters. The rewards for success are enormous, but over a long period you will need bundles of patience and fortitude if you are to prosper.

Scope for huge profit

But potential also for big losses

Prepare for the long haul

Tough mental attitude crucial

*'The rewards for success are enormous, but over a long period you will need bundles of patience and fortitude if you are to prosper'*

185

# GOLF IN-PLAY
## by Ian Wilkerson

## INTRODUCTION

So, the first ball has been struck off the first tee and the golf tournament is under way. What now?

In-play betting has become an integral element of the punting landscape in the last ten years and the opportunities have been embraced in golf as much as they have in virtually every other sport.

But there are some ways in which it is different. The majority of tournaments take place over four days so wagering during the course of a contest is not as much of an instantaneous experience as it is in other sports.

If Tottenham are holding on to a 1-0 lead with ten minutes to go and Arsenal are peppering efforts on the Spurs' goal in the hope of an equaliser, the football bettor needs to make a call there and then.

In golf, there is no such urgency. You can literally sleep on it and it should pay to use the extra time wisely to analyse potential opponents, watch the post-round interviews, cram the statistics and check that all-important weather forecast.

There really is no excuse for being lazy and a bountiful harvest of benefits are there to be reaped. But that points to issues about discipline as well.

In some instances there could be as many as 15 players who are in with a shout of winning before the start of play on the final day, so it is easy to get carried away and react to every marginal change on the leaderboard.

It is all a lot to take in, but there are some fundamentals to consider which should enable the golf punter to avoid some potentially deep pitfalls.

# FIVE WAYS TO BET SMART IN-PLAY

## 1. Don't fall into the technological trap

When betting in-play on a golf tournament, it is unwise to make instant reactions to what you see on your television.

The chances are that you will have been too late.

All sport you watch on your TV is behind actual time to a certain degree. If you use a satellite system, the pictures at the venue have to be recorded, beamed up to space and then back to that box you keep in the cupboard under your telly.

The phenomena of courtsiding has been in the headlines as some punters attempt to circumvent this.

By placing a spectator at an event, they relay information to a bettor that has not been broadcast to the viewer at home.

In a tennis match, where the system has been used and left the authorities with their knickers in a twist, bettors with contacts at the venue are able to know the result of a point before TV viewers and take advantage in the in-play markets.

I know from being at darts tournaments that sometimes TV pictures are four or five arrers behind the live action.

Information can be relayed from the course but there is a huge difference in coverage between a camera focusing on an individual football or tennis match and the pictures of a golf tournament that flit from hole to hole, on a track covering hundreds of hectares.

Common sense tells us that they cannot be everywhere in the heat of battle so rather than being a few seconds behind actual time like a darts or tennis match, it can be several minutes before a golf shot is shown.

It is not uncommon for them to stretch across commercial breaks. Just take ten minutes to watch an outright golf market on a betting exchange during the last nine holes on a Sunday and you'll be able to tell what's going on.

Unless you've got the required technology, it is better to give the hole-by-hole betting a big swerve. It won't be your pocket you're filling but someone else's.

*'Unless you've got the required technology, it is better to give the hole-by-hole betting a big swerve. It won't be your pocket you're filling but someone else's'*

*A plea for silence on the first tee at the Italian Open in 2018; (facing page) a lone spectator watches the action during the final round of the 147th Open at Carnoustie*

SHHH!
SHOW
IN
ACTION!

75° OPEN
D'ITALIA

*'Often players who performed well on Thursdays are priced up shorter than those who didn't as their showing in that round is given superior influence to their own ability'*

## 2. Don't ignore the supplementary markets

While it is difficult to bet during the action, the beauty of punting on golf during tournaments is that there is scope to take your time, which should increase the likelihood of you coming to sensible conclusions and provide you with enough time to do any relevant research.

However, spending your Thursday night or Friday morning attempting a forensic analysis of the first rounds of all 156 runners in a tournament is an unrealistic pursuit.

Key to successful punting on any sport is not to cast your net too widely. The two most important words, in my opinion, are specialisation and discipline and, in in-play golf betting, that means cutting down on the number of players you are analysing.

The saying goes that no one ever won a golf tournament on a Thursday but plenty have lost one. Of course, at this stage a chunk of the field can be dismissed from your outright calculations, but the prospect of others coming through the pack means it is sometimes too early to draw solid conclusions with regard to who will be lifting a trophy three days later.

So a sensible approach at this stage is to look at the threeball markets for the second round of play, ie which of the three players in each group will shoot the lowest score in their 18 holes.

In conventional tournaments, players will play alongside the same two opponents for the opening two rounds and there are a host of considerations that can be made.

First, keep a close eye on the prices. Often players who performed well on Thursdays are priced up shorter than those who didn't as their showing in that round is given superior influence to their own ability. Revisit the course form and recent form statistics. Is there a decent chance that there was a blip? These sorts of things have to be taken into account.

Second, consider a player's motivation. These can come into play especially in the weeks before Major tournaments or other big events like the Ryder Cup.

If it looks like a player is in danger of missing the cut, he may take his eye off the ball if he faces a trip across the Atlantic to Scotland to play in the Open Championship. Maybe he should have gone over a week early to get in some links practice and perhaps there is a flight leaving Friday night that would provide the opportunity for a couple of days of extra preparation.

Or perhaps it is the week before the tournament they won last year, or the one they are hosting when they have to shake hands with dignitaries and sponsors while trying to concentrate on their own game. Is everything going to plan?

Of course, it happens the other round as well. Qualification for these big tournaments is a huge prize for some of the game's lesser-known players and the lure of teeing off in them should not be underestimated.

So while the tournament is in progress, don't just think about who is going to win it. Threeball winners at around 3-1 often come in and it is far easier to concentrate on half-a-dozen golfers rather than analysing the whole field.

## 3. Keep an eye on the strokes-gained statistics

One piece of advice many give about punting is that you should believe your own eyes.

Some folks make a living from watching how horses perform – when they look tired, when they appear to be acting on their optimum ground and whether they are happier going right or left-handed. This is information they can use the next time the beast in question is in action.

During a football match, you can observe a defender who takes up prominent positions at set-pieces, put that in your memory bank and utilise it in the goalscorer markets on future occasions when they are up against a team who struggle against free-kicks and corners.

*Phil Mickelson is one of the few names you can easily keep track of – the same can't be said of all players*

With golf, though, we are often not afforded that luxury.

If you have backed Tiger Woods or Phil Mickelson it is likely that you will be able to catch the vast majority of the 280-ish shots they shoot over four days, whether they are in contention for honours or not.

Otherwise, it is a mixed bag. If your selection is one of the more low-profile players on the circuit, you may not get to see a single shot he hits in the first three days and they had better stay in contention until the last few holes on Sunday or they will disappear off the radar.

So this presents a problem. How can you tell

*Brandt Snedeker lines up a putt on the 17th green during the final round of the Players Championship at Sawgrass in 2019*

how well a player is performing when the TV cameras are focused elsewhere?

An 18-hole round score may not tell the full story but the development of strokes-gained statistics do.

How the figures are compiled is a complex process, but essentially they demonstrate how well a player is performing in various components of the game in comparison to the average of the field.

For instance – and this is an incredibly basic example but it demonstrates the point – if a player faces a 20-foot putt, the average number of shots to get the ball in the hole may be two. So, if Brandt Snedeker stands over the ball and knocks it straight into the cup, he has gained one shot on the field. Conversely, if Jason Dufner takes three shots to get the ball in the hole, he has lost a shot on the field.

Boffins are able to analyse all sorts of situations where shots are won and lost, but to make it easier it is probably best to concentrate on strokes-gained tee to green and strokes-gained putting. Otherwise your head might explode.

Where these statistics are helpful are that they offer potential for comparison.

Season-long figures for players are available on the PGA Tour (pgatour.com) and the European Tour (europeantour.com) websites which provide a more solid indication of a player's ability in a particular aspect of the game than how they do in a single round.

The Americans are ahead of the game in this and the excellent website datagolf.ca should have individual round statistics available by the time you wake up after watching the previous night's play.

So, if during an opening round of 68 at Pebble Beach, Matt Kuchar gained 0.98 shots on the field between tee to green, that would be a good performance if his season-long figure was 0.48 but a poor one if his regular mark was 1.58.

Unusual performances can be highlighted and puts meat on the bones of a round scoreline.

However, there are two issues.

Firstly, the European Tour is a little behind so figures for individual rounds are difficult to find and, secondly, not all courses embrace the technology needed to compile the figures. This is why you cannot find them for The Masters at Augusta National.

But, if they are available, you should find them useful when looking at who might become a factor in the closing rounds of a tournament.

*'The winner of a golf tournament has to perform at their optimum level for a 24-hour period over four days. And that's just on the course'*

## 4. Be careful of jumping on bandwagons

Generally in betting, it is not a bad idea to adopt a contrarian approach and golf provides plenty of opportunities for taking the opposite view when your fellow spectators and gamblers are getting carried away by the slightest things.

Brooks Koepka toyed with the field during his 2019 US PGA Championship success. He tore Bethpage Black apart in the opening round when he carded a 63 and even a closing 74 and a bit of a late wobble could not stop him from claiming a two-shot victory.

However, at the time of writing, that was only the sixth time since 2002 that a player who led the field at the end of the first round in a Major championship went on to triumph. It is a supremely difficult thing to do and demands incredible levels of concentration and consistency in your technical ability.

The winner of a golf tournament has to perform at their optimum level for a 24-hour period over four days. And that's just on the course. That doesn't include the time when his coach, his putting guru, his psychologist and members of his family are invading the space between his ears. He has to sleep between rounds as well and deal with his own thoughts on the situation.

So within this mammoth task, it is easy to react wildly when it appears players are on streaks.

In the 2019 Travelers Championship, Bubba Watson made a charge in the second round, which was good news for those who put their faith in him after three previous victories at River Highlands.

He sank five successive birdies in his second round and looked to be on the charge, but those who took a step back from the excitement were rewarded. He finished tied for 54th.

At time of writing, there have been ten times on the PGA Tour when a play broke 60 for his round. On only five of those occasions did the player in question go on to win the tournament.

It is very easy to get carried away and, as is often the case in punting, it can be worth swimming against the tide and if that seems a courageous approach that you would rather not engage in then sitting still and seeing what happens is a perfectly acceptable tactic too.

*Bubba Watson led the early charge for the 2019 Travelers Championship*

## 5. Don't rush back in

The final piece of advice is really a staple element of any responsible gambling manual.

The time to be punting during the course of a golf tournament is when you have identified a particular angle. Where you can see something others may have missed and your bet is the result of research that has been diligently undertaken and stones have not been left unturned.

It is not the time to be backing the bloke who hit 66 in the first round because all four of your selections look like they are going to miss the cut and you need to have a punting interest.

There is not really a close season in golf. Sure, there are times when folks like Justin Rose or Rory McIlroy decide to put their feet up once the game's big prizes have been decided – autumn is a great time to keep an eye on the rising stars of the subsidiary Korn Ferry and Challenge Tours, by the way, as they are full of young bucks anxious to prove themselves and often capable of doing so.

But if you cannot identify a fresh punting angle, take in the action and look for potential pointers that could help you in the following few weeks. Or swot up on what sort of demands will be needed for next week and try and identify a few potential openings there.

It is a difficult task to back the winner of a golf tournament, so don't go chasing your losses. Next Thursday is never that far away.

**TOP TIP**
Try not to get seduced by a player who is seemingly on a roll – and don't be afraid to swim against the tide and go with your own instinct

## EXPERT VIEW

The time it takes for a golf tournament to be completed allows plenty of time for conclusions to be drawn and analysed. Statistics and analysis is so thorough that it is not essential to watch every cough and spit of the action and there is the potential for profit if you bark up the right trees.

Patterns may emerge and, like everything, the more experienced you become in identifying them the better positioned you will be to take advantage of any things that the average viewer and bettor may not spot.

One of the reasons why betting on golf is so popular is that big-priced golfers win. The prizes are there for small investors and three or four winners in the course of a year can potentially mean you can yield a profit from your golf punting. But that means you have to be patient. Opportunities do not come along regular and you cannot expect to be winning every week. However, there are opportunities to chip away during tournaments, whether it is in the threeball markets before the weekend or twoballs on Saturdays and Sundays, or in the outright market in the closing stages.

And you will learn more about the game and betting on it the more you analyse the markets and take in the TV coverage, which is no bad thing.

# GOLF SPECIALS
## by Joe Champion

*Teeing off at the Players Championship at Sawgrass*

## INTRODUCTION

Special bets can offer an interesting accompaniment to outright punting, and some bettors may even wish to prioritise these markets, many of which allow you to concentrate on a smaller number of competitors without the need to look through the bulk of the field – a necessary but laborious process in outright betting.

As betting on golf has moved into the digital age, more and more bookmakers are offering a number of alternative markets that can enhance the golf punting experience. Many of those betting options, particularly before the opening round of a traditional strokeplay event, will mirror the outright prices, but some layers are happy to take an alternative view on occasion.

Several of these markets were, at one stage, primarily chalked up for Major championships but, such was their appeal to punters, they

are now a fixture on a week-by-week basis for both the PGA and European Tours, although coverage is often dictated by the prestige of each tournament.

Picking the winner of a 156-runner tournament might not be simple, but 72-hole match betting, for example, that pits two golfers against each other, renders the other 154 players irrelevant for the purpose of that particular bet.

Other markets, such as first-round leader, are easily explained but far from the easiest punting medium, while spread betting others a different dynamic for those looking for four rounds of entertainment, hopefully with a profitable outcome on Sunday evening.

Some spread markets are variants of fixed-odds outright markets but others offer something different which can only be done by the medium of spread betting.

While the focus for most punters will always be on outright success, there is cash to be made in special markets and, with most leading bookmakers willing to price them up in some form or another – and most firms have their specific rules in each market – they are worth paying attention to because the layers aren't always going to get them spot on.

*'While the focus for most punters will always be on outright success, there is cash to be made in special markets'*

*Jordan Spieth in action at Pebble Beach during the second round of the 2019 US Open – a contest he won in 2015*

## FIRST-ROUND LEADER

First-round leader betting is one which, like outright betting, can offer big profit from a comparatively small outlay.

Typically the market leaders in the tournament betting will be mirrored in the first-round leader betting. These are the best players in the field, after all, and if they are to justify favouritism and win the event a fast start affords them a significant advantage.

But, these players are the best because they tend to perform consistently over four rounds. Any professional golfer worth his salt is able to shoot a low round on the opening day but may not have the ability or the courage to replicate that performance over the following three days. The trick is in finding that player.

There is nothing wrong with targeting the top of the market on occasion. Sometimes that is just the best way to play it. Jordan Spieth, for example, led the Masters after round one on three occasions between 2015 and 2019. He was in the top three of the betting on each occasion.

Spieth is the ultimate Augusta form horse. He was an easy first-round leader to find, but many events are tougher and often less familiar names can emerge from the pack on the opening day, often at huge prices but not necessarily without reason.

For most first-round leader bettors, there are certain signs worth looking out for which can dictate how a round develops. Like certain racecourses, the draw can be crucial to the likelihood of nailing a big-priced winner.

Depending on the tournament, opening-round tee off times can be anywhere from first thing in the morning to midway through the afternoon. While the players are playing the same course, the weather can have a significant bearing on in conditions and should be a primary consideration in first-round leader punting.

It is important, therefore, to pay close attention to the forecast. If a golfer starts early on a winding, rainy morning, he is unlikely to fare as well as someone who tees off in the afternoon in dry weather with minimal wind and a soft golf course to attack.

This can work either way, sometimes the early-morning starters have the best luck with the draw and at other times it is the afternoon players who can make hay while conditions are best.

---

## TOP TIP

Pay close attention to the weather. If a golfer starts early on a windy, rainy morning, he is unlikely to fare as well as someone who tees off in the afternoon in dry weather

## 72-HOLE MATCH BETTING

Match betting may not be the most exciting punting medium in the sport – winners will rarely be bigger than a shade of odds-against – but they allow the punter to narrow the focus down to two competitors who are pitted against each other for betting purposes and still offer profit potential on a smaller scale.

In regular strokeplay action, most bookmakers will pick around ten fairly even 'matches', usually involving the main tournament protagonists. These will mirror the outright prices so if Golfer A is 20-1 and Golfer B is 22-1 outright, then Golfer A may be 5-6 to beat Golfer B who is an even-money chance. Some bookmakers include a price for the tie, usually 16-1, while others will refund stakes in the event of a dead heat.

*Matt Kuchar is often a solid option in Major championships having regularly hit the top ten*

As is the case in many markets across many sports, the importance of shopping around for the best bets should not be underestimated. Unlike in outright betting, bookmakers will make a decision as to what matches to offer and the markets will not be the same from bookie to bookie, so it is useful to take a look at what every firm has to offer before having a bet.

When picking a punt, consider both players in the equation. One may be a consistent performer who looks certain to make the cut but unlikely to win, while the other may be an up-and-down performer who is more likely to deliver when in contention but also more likely to go home on Friday evening. US Tour man Matt Kuchar springs to mind as a man who has regularly churned out top-ten finishes in Major championships without winning them. He often rates a solid option in a market where you do not have to win a tournament, or even contend, to take the spoils.

Also consider whether a player is the wrong price in the outright market. They could be in poor form but priced up on reputation – bookmakers are rarely keen to give certain golfers away at too big a price for fear of getting their fingers burnt.

Like form, fitness is another important angle. Golfers who have been playing well can always be feared but an energy-sapping schedule will eventually take its toll and many top players often only tee up in certain weeks to meet contractual obligations. They can be taken on with fresher opponents.

# TOP ENGLISHMAN, AMERICAN OR ELSEWHERE

The winner of a golf tournament is hard to find and sometimes it is just easier to nail the best player in a smaller group. That could be a group of Englishmen, Americans, Europeans or even left-handers.

Known as 'top' markets, the field in these betting heats can either be huge, as is the case with the Top American market in any US-based Major championship, or can be limited to just two – Bernhard Langer and Martin Kaymer have often battled to be the top German at the Masters in recent years.

That makes for plenty of variety and punters can get involved in the top American market if they wish, but they tend to dominate the field in any events held on US soil and, if you fancy someone to go close in that market, it's probably worth supporting them outright instead.

That is not always the case, or course. There is always a strong challenge from the rest of the world in Major championships but, for punting purposes, it is probably best to focus on smaller fields when weighing up a prudent punt in these markets.

Depending on the make-up of the group, one or two top players can dominante these markets. Henrik Stenson, for example, is a mainstay as favourite to be top Swede while Jason Day and Adam Scott have tended to lead the way in the race to be top Australian in recent years.

Unlike the USA and, in Europe, England, these nations only have a few representatives on both main tours in any given tournament and there tends to be a Stenson or Day making the market ahead of a main group of rivals and a few also-rans.

Sometimes it is wise to admit that the Major champion and favourite is bombproof. Depending on your betting style, you can take short odds about them if you think they are a value bet, but more often than not there is an alternative in a market where bookmakers tend to offer each-way places when there are enough runners.

Part of the skill is in finding a vulnerability in the market leader. They may be the best golfer, but have they always shown their best form at the course? Have they been carrying an injury?

Alternatively, consider whether an underdog has been underestimated and remember they do not have to contend to take the spoils in this market – a solid, consistent performer can fill an each-way place and even the best golfers miss the cut from time to time.

*Henrik Stenson often proves a wise call for top Swedish player*

## SPREAD BETTING

Spread betting tends to be popular in golf with the major spread firms happy to offer a number of markets for the week-to-week events on both the European and PGA Tours including the leaderboard index, tournament finishing positions, match bets and various specials.

In a sport where there are usually more than 150 contenders, it is possible to make good money in spread betting but equally possible to make costly errors, so it is important to tread carefully when planning a golf spread punt.

The leaderboard index is comparable to a fixed-odds outright market and typically makes up 60 for a win, 40 for second place and pays a return all the way down to eighth place. As it is possible to both buy and sell on the index, punters can take a stance by supporting or opposing as they see fit.

Those who plan to buy on the leaderboard index should consider whether a spread punt is the right option. Due to the generous each-way terms on offer, sometimes it is advisable to back a selection with fixed-odds firms, while at other times a spread bet is the perfect play, particularly in low-risk scenarios where buying at a low quote – 1.5-2 for example – can yield a serious profit.

Finishing positions are fairly unique to spread betting and can be bought or sold relative to confidence in a golfers performance. If golfer A's FP is quoted at 19-22, then sellers can only make a profit if they finish in the top 18, while a buyers can churn out a larger profit for every position that Golfer A finishes outside of the top 22.

Spread bettors can choose to take a view on whether a particular golfer will play better of worse than the spread suggests, and this can

sometimes prove profitable, particularly if there are vulnerabilities in a market leader.

Consider whether they are inconsistent, do they have history at the course or are they making their first appearance at the track, and will they have their eyes on other targets in future weeks.

Buying the finishing position of a big name can often turn a big profit, and the same is true in reverse. Sometimes the lesser lights can play better than the spread suggests and, in a market that makes up 70 in full-field tournaments, there is plenty of room for a less likely name to make a run at the leaderboard.

Take note of players who have been playing solid golf without contending. If they tend to make the cut most weeks, they could be on the verge of a profit-making performance.

## TO MAKE/MISS THE CUT

Some golf markets are binary, there are only two outcomes: yes or no. This applies to a few scenarios and one that has grown in popularity in recent years is backing a player to either make or miss the cut.

Backing an elite player to miss the weekend, or backing a lesser known player to make it, can often be a rewarding bet. That type of wager is mainly available to bet at Major championships, but some bookmakers have taken to pricing up a select few players to make/ miss the cut on a weekly basis.

Elite golfers are brilliant, but they are not infallible when it comes to making the weekend. At the 2017 US Open the world's top three – Dustin Johnson, Rory McIlroy and Jason Day – all missed the cut at

*Even the likes of Rory McIlroy – pictured during the 2019 Scottish Open – are far. from infallible*

*'Even the best of the best have off days, and not all courses are perfect fits. Take into account the type of player likely to thrive at that particular course and ask if it is a perfect fit for a market leader'*

generous odds for those who were brave enough to oppose them.

Even the best of the best have off days, and not all courses are perfect fits. Take into account the type of player likely to thrive at that particular course and ask if it is a perfect fit for a market leader. They are at the head of the betting because bookies fear them, but they are not certain to bring their A-game every week, even in Major championships.

Sergio Garcia won the 2017 Masters but went on a run of seven consecutive missed cuts at Majors, and it's important to consider who is likely to grind their way to the weekend and who is unlikely to believe they can get back into the contest.

Making the cut is different, and usually the best bets can be on unheralded pros, youngsters, and old hands who still have something to give – they will be attractively priced in comparison to the market leaders.

Look again at course form and course correlation with other tracks, while recent form can be particularly important when assessing whether a lesser known player is capable of making the weekend. If they have been playing well without going close, chances are they will continue to do so.

*Sergio Garcia went on a run of seven missed cuts after his 2017 Masters win at Augusta*

## " EXPERT VIEW

Golf betting is not easy. There are so many competitors for outright bettors to focus on and that can be daunting for recreational punters who haven't got hours and hours to put into studying the formbook.

That is where specials come into their own. They can allow the field to be narrowed considerably, giving the punter an opportunity to focus on players of which they have plenty of knowledge.

Like most golf punters, outright betting is my primary focus but it is always worth looking at what else is on offer because the same is also true for bookmakers – for whom the lion's share of their liabilities remain in outright markets – and there tends to be some undiscovered gems available for those who are willing to look for them.

Going back to the days of the famed Hole-in-One Gang – a duo who famously collected a huge sum by betting on an ace being recorded in five different tournaments at hugely inflated odds – there has been a battle between golf punters and bookies that extends beyond the realms of outright betting.

Layers are more careful these days, but there will always be savvy punters on the lookout for the latest niche and these rapidly growing golf markets are well worth taking advantage of when a profitable opportunity presents itself.

**Endless study not needed**

**Often attractive bets to be found**

**Specials markets growing rapidly**

*With so many markets to choose from, the time has never been better for golf fans to get involved in the specials markets*

# NATIONAL FOOTBALL LEAGUE by Phil Agius

## INTRODUCTION

On any given Sunday, any team in the NFL can beat any other. That famous phrase was coined by former NFL Commissioner Bert Bell in 1958 after the Pittsburgh Steelers beat the Chicago Bears for the first time in 14 meetings.

The NFL is different from many other sports in that Bell, and his successors at NFL headquarters, have embraced the concept of parity – the attempt to give every team an equal opportunity to be successful.

Do not make the mistake of thinking that means all teams are equally successful, though. Measures such as a salary cap, fixtures determined by the previous year's results and allowing the worst-performing teams to select first in the following year's draft of the top college players, all even up the competition and teams can't buy their way to the title in the way a big-spending football team can. But those who appoint the best general managers and coaches and acquire the best players will still rise to the top.

For punters, the challenge is to spot the opportunities when the

stronger teams will have an off-day and when the weaker outfits may just have a chance to shine.

Everyone loses sometimes, even the mighty New England Patriots, who would be many people's first argument against the effectiveness of the parity measures.

At the time of writing, the Patriots have appeared in the Super Bowl nine times in the 18 years that started with the first victory of head coach Bill Belichick and quarterback Tom Brady after the 2001 season.

They got closer than anyone to a perfect season, winning their first 18 games in 2007, only to lose the New York Giants in the Super Bowl. In the six years the greatest team of the modern era have won the Vince Lombardi Trophy, they lost five, two, two, four, two and five games – so there are times when it pays to oppose even the best team around. In their 2019 Super Bowl-winning season, they let down their handicap backers seven times in 19 outings.

It's the same at the other end of the scale. In the 16-game regular season era, two teams have lost all of their games, but Detroit Lions covered the handicap in seven, or 43.75 per cent, of their games even in the worst NFL season on record, while Cleveland Browns rewarded their handicap backers four times in their winless 2017 campaign.

The trick for punters is to identify the better days of the weaker outfits and the off-days for the top teams. Ony any given Sunday (or Monday, Thursday or Saturday in the modern era) any team can defy the odds.

*'Teams can't buy their way to the title in the way a big-spending football team can. But those who appoint the best general managers and coaches and acquire the best players will still rise to the top'*

## TOP TIP

Always consider the underdog on the handicap. There are no benefits for the better side winning by a wider margin

# FIVE WAYS TO BET SMARTER ON THE NFL

## 1. Remember the players are only trying to win by one

The most crucial concept for NFL punters to remember is that the players are not trying to help you win your handicap bets.

The players are only interested in winning the match whatever the margin and one point will be enough. That is not tremendously comforting news if you have backed a team to successfully concede a start of 1.5 or 2.5 points, but it can regularly lead to nightmare scenarios.

For example, imagine your initial excitement if you have backed a team to win by seven points and, leading by five with just over a minute left, they intercept a pass or regain possession on downs inside the 20-yard line. Under normal circumstances they would be in great shape to have a shot at scoring another touchdown to lead by 12 or kicking a field goal to go eight points ahead. Then imagine your sinking spirits when you realised that the trailing team had no

timeouts left and all your team have to do to seal the victory is for the quarterback to kneel down three times and jog off the pitch.

There are no benefits to winning by a wider margin. Running further offensive plays increases the risk of losing possession again through an interception or fumble, as well as unnecessarily risking injuries to players who have already done enough.

The irrelevance of winning margins is also a factor in the practice of 'running up the score' (teams who already have the game in the bag continuing to go all out to pile up more points) being frowned upon in America. Regardless of the ethics, there's no sense in a team who are already over the line reaching deep into their bag of trick plays or exposing more offensive concepts to their future opponents than they need to when some basic runs from the first page of the playbook will eat up the remaining time and get them on the plane home earlier.

The 'backdoor cover' is a situation where underdogs, who have never been in the game, steal the handicap money with a pointless late score that does not affect the result of the match, but can do great damage to the pockets of punters. A classic example came in the first NFL regular-season game played at Wembley Stadium in London in 2007. The New York Giants were strong 7.5-point favourites against Miami, who had lost seven straight games, and dominated the match. The Dolphins trailed 13-3 inside the final two minutes when they scored a touchdown that reduced the margin of defeat to three and left favourite-backers empty-handed, One option for punters who can't stand the heartbreak of a backdoor cover is to bet on the first-half-handicap instead.

*Odell Beckham Jr in action for the New York Giants at Twickenham*

## 2. Every dog has its day

More favourites win NFL games than underdogs – that's not a surprise as bookmakers and punters alike have tons of information available to help them identify the stronger side of each pair. In the 2018-19 season, favourites won almost two-thirds of the 267 NFL games (256 regular-season contents and 11 playoff games) – 66.04 per cent to be precise. That's 175 favourites coming in with only 90 underdogs winning and two ties (after overtime).

However, the results when it comes to covering the handicap were quite different.

Remembering that bookmakers are aiming to set the points spread for each match as close as they can to the outcome, they do a fantastic job. In 2018-19 favourites won for handicap backers in 45.95 per cent of games but more handicap underdogs came in – landing the money in 140 matches compared to 119 favourites and eight handicap ties (eg a team are three-point favourites and won by three).

Recent Super Bowl results have also swung towards the underdogs recently. New England's victory over the LA Rams in 2019 was only the third time in the last 12 years that backing the favourites in the biggest game of the year had paid off.

Regular examples of why it can be smart to give plenty of thought to backing the underdog can be seen in the various US websites that chart the weekly fancies of the general public versus the bigger-staking professional punters (often known as Pros v Joes) based on reports from Las Vegas Sportsbooks. Very often the most popular picks of the smaller-stakes bettors will be the big teams who are on winning runs, while the 'sharp' money is more often on an underdog who might not be quite as bad as the prices suggest.

Remember, that strategy is open to everyone, however big your betting bank.

## 3. Match-ups matter

Not all teams are created the same. Their approach to winning games will differ depending on the football philosophy of the coach and the players available to them – some are more defensively or offensively minded/ some like to run the ball, some prefer the aerial approach.

For that reason, it's wise not to have too firm an opinion in your head about which teams are good or poor or somewhere in between – they will all be seen to better effect playing against the teams that match up well for them and not so well against others.

For example, if a team has made a strong start to the season using an effective running game are up against a team with a worse record, but who happen to have a strong pair of defensive tackles and some talented linebackers, it could pay to take them on, may not in the match markets but perhaps by taking the under on their team points.

Individual match-ups matter just as much. If a team has begun to show a weakness, such as defending tight ends near the goal-line, or being susceptible to long-pass plays, that sort of thing is likely to happen again unless they make a personnel move or get a better players back from injury in that position. These kind of factors can be particularly helpful when assessing the total points market – good pass defences can be effective slowing down even the best wide receivers and even elite running backs can do little damage if their offensive linemen are being pushed back by a strong defensive line. Learn as much as you can about each unit's strength in every team and you will begin to see a bigger picture.

## 4. Fantasy can become reality

The tide finally looks set to turn as regards legal sports betting in the United States, but that doesn't mean there is a lack of information that would be useful to NFL punters around, far from it.

Most Americans are still unable to bet online, or in person outside of a casino, but they have found other ways to have a legal interest in NFL matches and that's where there is a mine of useful information to be found.

Fantasy NFL games are huge in the States and the supporting resources are fantastic for punters who can bet on games to use. Every pulled hamstring, tweaked groin and off-field indiscretion is pored over on countless fantasy football sites, ostensibly to enable people to decide who to release from their teams, add to their rosters or bench for that week's games. But knowing all the ins and outs is a huge help for punters. If you see that a rookie receiver has been gaining more reps in practice and is set to gain a bigger role in the offence with one of the regular starters struggling with an injury, maybe you should pick him up for your fantasy team – but you can also check his odds to score at any time in the next match and see if his individual receiving yards might be worth taking the overs on.

*Above and facing page: celebrations at the Mercedes-Benz Stadium in Atlanta after New England Patriots' defeat of the LA Rams in February 2019*

## 5. In-play can be the smart way

Every play brings the in-play punter information the pre-match bettor did not have. Exact knowledge of the weather, a proper idea of the crowd noise, exact team news rather than an estimate that may have involved some massaging of the truth by the teams – in every way, the in-play punter is armed with better information than those betting before the game.

So if there's a match where you consider one player's injury status to be crucial to your betting plans, or where you were thinking of a total points play but were concerned about a possible snow storm, remember you have the option to bet even after kick-off.

From the first two drives, you will be able to make an instant assessment of how the coaches are approaching the game and get an early look at whether the other team are likely to be able to deal with it or not.

Some coaching staffs are much better at making in-game adjustments to their gameplans than others, who either never learn or don't have the flexibility in personnel to be able to change what they're trying to do.

It's not so easy when the game is part of the Sunday 6pm slot to keep track of everything – even with the wonderful resource of the NFL RedZone service, which whizzes viewers to the best action in every game. But there are plenty of standalone primetime games to which you can give your full attention and you no longer have to be committed to your original thinking if it is not borne out by events. The cash-out option offered by many bookmakers also enables punters to avoid the horrors of a late handicap loss by closing out the bet early.

# A GUIDE TO THE MARKETS

## 1. Ante-post betting

Super Bowl betting can sometimes a little dispiriting. There are 32 teams to choose from and it's perfectly possible to correctly identify one of the 12 who makes it through 16 regular-season games to reach the playoffs only to find they are a bigger price than they were in September.

For example, in the 2018-19 season, champions New England were 13-2 favourites at the start of the season, and, after they had won the AFC East as the playoffs began, they were 7-1 fourth favourites, so Patriots backers could have got a better price without having to risk them bombing out in the regular season or having their cash tied up for four months.

It was worth having an early interest for those who picked the Philadelphia Eagles the year before however, as they were 50-1 in pre-season and only 12-1 when the playoffs came around.

There are other ante-post markets that can be better betting propositions, though. Backing divisional favourites is rarely an exciting prospect - four of the eight sectional market leaders were odds-on prices in 2018 and backing second favourites proved more profitable with winners at 4-1, 2-1, 3-1 and 7-2, while Chicago won the NFC North despite being 8-1 outsiders, so that's an area where it can pay to step away from the crowd. Over/under prices are also available for the number of games each team wins and many bookmakers offer prices on each team's finishing position in their division, which is a welcome addition, enabling punters to back a view on an outsider doing better than expected without necessarily winning the section or being able to oppose an overrated favourite.

The prices at the start of a season often appear to assume that the previous season's top teams will be strong again, but typically around half of the 12 playoff qualifiers will be different from the year before.

In 2018-19, six teams were different to the year before's qualifiers, while in 2016-17 eight of the previous year's 12 qualifiers failed to return, with five of the six NFC post-season teams being different.

Super Bowl winners do tend to be teams who were in the

*Alshon Jeffery in action for the Philadelphia Eagles who could be backed at 50-1 pre-season in 2018-19*

playoffs the previous season though – only three teams in the last decade (Philadelphia, New York Giants and New Orleans) have lifted the VInce Lombardi having not qualified for the playoffs the year before.

New England, in 2019, were the only Super Bowl runners-up to go one better the next season, with losers from the preceding conference championship games and divisional playoffs faring best the following season.

A last word on pre-season bets is not to get carried away by the addition of rookies. NFL playbooks are complicated to learn and few youngsters are ready to make a major contribution to a top team in their first season. The exception is in positions that are less complex to learn and rely more on pure athletic ability, such as running backs – even undrafted rookie rushers have been able to step in and contribute right away.

## 2. Handicaps

If you've ever had a bet on an NFL game it will most likely have been on the handicap. Bookmakers offer one of the teams with a start of a certain number of points, if the underdogs win or lose by fewer points than the handicap, you win. If you back the favourites, they need to win by more than the line for you to collect. Handicaps are often framed with half-point lines, to avoid the possibility of a tie (eg Dallas +3.5 wins if they win or lose by three or fewer points) but when full-point lines are offered, ties are generally declared a push and voided (three-way handicaps including a tie price are also available).

o In 2018 New Orleans converted only 86.5 per cent of their extra point attempts

An early handicap line, the Vegas line, is posted based on prices from the US casinos as soon as the previous week's games are finished, and the consensus line can change by a point or two through the week as the latest injury and weather news and the early money influences the price.

The magic numbers on handicap betting remain three and seven — the points gained from a converted field goal and a touchdown converted by a kick. Taking +2.5 when +3 is available is never wise as three points are going to be a common winning margin, and similarly if you can back favourites giving up only 6.5 points rather than seven that will be well worth it.

o In 2002 no team kicked worse than 94.1 per cent of the PATs

Recent rule changes that have made PATs harder to kick (by increasing the distance) and led to teams opting to attempt more (and often fail to convert) two-point conversions have changed the traditional dynamic slightly – New Orleans converted only 86.5 per cent of their extra point attempts in 2018, for example, while in 2002, no team kicked worse than 94.1 per cent of their PATs.

Sometimes when assessing a match you can have a fair idea about whether it will be high-scoring or low-scoring, but not such a strong opinion about which team will win. In those cases a bet on the total points may be for you.

Bookmakers give their assessment of how many points the teams will score between them and you bet higher (over) or lower (under).

The figure can vary by a fair amount – the early points lines posted for week one of the 2019-20 season varied from 38.5 points to 53.5 points, which a typical line pitched in the mid-40s.

Factors include the weather (bad weather tends towards fewer points, fine conditions and indoor stadiums produce higher make-ups), the strength of the offences and defences, and the playing styles of the teams will be taken into account, along with their track record as the season progresses.

Potentially extreme games between two high-scoring teams or two strong defensive teams, are often hard for bookmakers to set an accurate mark for. A prime example of this came in the 2018 season when the league's two highest-scoring offences, Kansas City Chiefs and LA Rams, clashed on a memorable Monday night in California. Bookmakers reported that the points line of 63.5 points was the highest they had ever set – and they were only wrong by 41.5 ponts! The gung-ho teams combined for 105 points as the Rams won 54-51 in the third-highest game of all time.

The match-up – both sets of offence v defence – is the key factor in total points assessments, A strong defence will be hard for even the best offences to score against, but even usually mediocre offences will find ways to score against bad defences.

More proof that the match-up matters is shown by the three Super Bowls from 2017-2019 featuring 62, 74 and 16 points respectively despite the largely similar New England team featuring in all three games.

*If you have a good idea of how much scoring there is likely to be in a match then total points betting may be the way to go*

The frustrating part of the first touchdown scorer market is that you can have lost before your player has even set foot on the field – if the other team gets the ball first and score. Those who want to avoid that annoyance can instead plump for the first team touchdown scorer market, which is only settled when your player's team scores first. As in football, to score a touchdown at any time markets are increasingly popular.

## 4. Touchdown scorers

The first touchdown scorer market is an easy one to understand. You pick the player you think will score the game's first touchdown. Running backs are usually the favourites, ahead of the teams' leading wide receivers with tight ends generally a big price except for regular red-zone targets such as Travis Kelce of Kansas City or the recently retired Rob Gronkowski of New England.

This is an area where advanced knowledge of match-ups and team tendencies can be a huge help, as bookmakers prices tend not to vary too much from week to week but players can be much more likely to feature in the game plan in some matches than others. For example, wide receivers will have a much better chance of scoring in games against teams who have cornerbacks who are poor in coverage – check which players scored against a team in other matches – if teams have trouble keeping track of tight ends near the goalline, for example, make your move. This is a smart area in which to react to team news too. If you think a team's third receiver might be playing a more prominent role, get on early.

## 5. Performance markets

Player performance markets are offered by an increasing number of bookmakers and offer a chance to support a player to have a good, or bad, game whether or not you think they will score a touchdown or win the game.

Layers offer over/under prices on individual players total receiving yards (for wide receivers, tight ends and some running backs, passing

*The LA Rams offence huddles during a pre-season clash with the Dallas Cowboys*

yards for quarterbacks, rushing yards for running backs, and often combined rushing and receiving yards for multi-purpose running backs. There are also longest reception, longest run, longest successful field goal for the kickers and so on. There are even opportunities to support the forgotten folk of NFL betting – defensive players, with lines on the number of interceptions, sacks and tackles a particular player makes. The thing to remember with the defensive markets is that players from teams who are up against it will often do well in this market. If you think one team will have plenty of joy running the ball, then taking one of the other team's linebackers to make a high number of tackles could pay off, similarly if you think a team will do well with their passing game, then look for the corner-backs and safeties to be charged with bringing them down more frequently. It's another area where knowledge of the individual match-ups can pay off.

Emerging rookies are often worth a look in these markets as bookmakers can be slow to latch on to players who have shown they are worth bigger roles in the offence as their first seasons progress.

## " EXPERT VIEW

Things can change quickly in the NFL and if you think your assessment is more valid than those the prices are based on, trust yourself.

One exercise that is well worth doing is writing out your own estimate of the handicap lines for each weeks fixtures before you have seen the prices, Sometimes you will find your figures are more or less the same. Sometimes you might be way off but later realise the reason why the figures are different and that your number should be nearer theirs. But if you think you can see why their number differs from yours and that yours is the right one, that's the time to bet. Be selective - you don't have to bet on all 16 games every week.

Every few weeks it is worth going back to reassess the results of earlier matches. What might have looked like a solid benchmark game after week one could end up looking like an outlier a month later.

Personally when looking at a game, I prefer to start looking at the game trying to make a case for backing the underdogs and only switch to the favourites in the face of overwhelming evidence.

NFL lends itself to betting superbly well with its host of team and individual statistics that can be assessed and argued with, and a plethora of breaks in play in which to reassess, think things over and bet as events unfold. Find an area that suits your style and stick with it whether it's a pre-match acca, some total points plays or some player performance plays.

Trust your judgment

Keep your own figures

Use the stats available to your benefit

# TENNIS
## by Adrian Humphries

### INTRODUCTION

Tennis offers punters plenty of opportunity to show profits, but bettors are only going to get out of the subject what they put in.

Having information at your disposal is of paramount importance. But even if punters are armed to the hilt with knowledge, he or she still needs to decide correctly about the best way and time to bet.

Former Racing Post tennis correspondent Paul Kealy knew this when he lumped on three-time Wimbledon runner-up Goran Ivanisevic, who had been a 500-1 wild-card to win the grass-court major after losing in the first round at the Queen's Club to little-known Italian Cristiano Caratti, at big-value two-figure odds prior to the last 16.

Since Ivanisevic defeated Pat Rafter in the 2001 All England Club final, tennis grew to be the second biggest sport for in-play punters, with most trade seen on the online betting exchanges.

*Goran Ivanisevic goes full stretch at Wimbledon in 2004. He won the title three years earlier when his odds had been as big as 500-1*

*'Having information at your disposal is of paramount importance. But even if punters are armed to the hilt with knowledge, he or she still needs to decide correctly about the best way and time to bet'*

But while that area of expertise can still prove hugely profitable for those who approach it scientifically, in this chapter we are going to stick to the basics of successful tennis betting, which hopefully will prove helpful to experienced and novice punters alike.

Bettor confidence has been tested down the years by a number of high-profile match-fixing allegations, many of which were poorly policed by authorities prior to the Tennis Integrity Unit being set up.

But while the lower end of a sport in which many competitors find it difficult to make a living still sees numerous instances of unusual betting patterns and oddsmakers taking down markets early, thankfully tennis's upper echelons can for much of the time be relied on to serve up high-quality sport.

And with US markets opening up fast, it is up to tennis's rulers, who in recent years have welcomed bookmakers as sponsors of a number of tournaments, to show more understanding and appreciation of the rapidly growing betting industry.

## FIVE WAYS TO BET SMART ON TENNIS

### 1. Don't shy away from taking big prices in the smaller tournaments

Amazingly, there are still plenty of people out there who think the tennis season comprises four majors or Grand Slam tournaments and nothing else.

What do you mean the players travel to places other than London, New York, Paris and Melbourne? Well it's true, they do. And most of the time there is much better value to be gleaned from the regular ATP 250 Series and WTA International tournaments than their big, more famous brothers and sisters.

These meat-and-drink events are usually limited to fields of 32 players, sometimes fewer when the top seeds have opening-round byes, yet a lot of bookmakers regularly issue title betting on Sundays and Mondays for these week-long competitions. In these outright markets most players in ATP 250 Series events have to win only four matches for an each-way return.

Of course, oddsmakers will be only too keen to offer pre-match player-to-win quotes, but they are often a lot less comfortable accommodating punter requests to place bets on big two-figure or three-figure outright fancies. And if punting is done sensibly, one generously priced outright winner can virtually pay for an entire year's betting, not that the idea is to give all of the profits straight back from whence they came.

## TOP TIP

Search for the
betting market
that suits you
best – and
remember
specials
are often
anything
but

## 2. Scour the markets for the best way to bet

Outright betting, the preferred punting
medium in this chapter, often involves just
one or two ways of trying to show a
profit, but these days staking on individual
matches usually offers backers the chance
to play on a variety of markets.

The original player-to-win markets can
still be handy for daily punters, but often
there are better opportunities to be had
backing, say, one of the two players
contesting a singles match to win at least
one set.

The vast majority of tournaments
matches will be over the best of three
sets, but the men's Grand Slam events
are a best of five sets. Other decent ways
to bet can be total games and sets
handicaps and total games over/under
markets. Paddy Power traditionally quote
over/under odds on each player winning
a specified number of games in a match,
a bespoke market which can also offer
decent punting opportunities.

In these days of faster betting and
austere times for many, of course it's
necessary to speculate in order to
accumulate but bettors
should also try their
utmost to minimise losses.
Punt selectively and be
patient with your betting
– legendary horseracing
punter Alex Bird often
maintained he used to have
about five bets a year.
Punters should be well aware
that the vast majority of
betting options will be losers,
so it's hugely important to try
to identify markets which
could be profitable.

*Rafael Nadal lifts
the trophy after
winning the 2019
French Open*

And therein lies a clue as to why being a successful punter seldom comes easy. Finding a suitable betting market needs a good deal of thought, consideration and judgement, even before the option you settle on has to win. Don't forget also that specially contrived specials from bookmakers are often not that special.

## 3. Women's tennis often throws up better punting opportunities

With the likes of Roger Federer, Rafael Nadal and Novak Djokovic (oh, go on then, let's add Andy Murray to the list) monopolising the majors since the Noughties, in recent times there have usually been better, more open betting heats in women's Grand Slam tournaments than in the men's majors.

Obviously, if you are happy betting on short-priced favourites, then as a rule of thumb Nadal will probably do for you in clay-court tournaments while Djokovic may well be the answer to many fast-court events.

However, with the Williams sisters Serena and Venus in the twilight of their stunningly successful careers and not quite as dominant as they once were, it has been open house on the WTA Tour and in the Slams since Serena became a mother for the first time in late 2017. In the 21 months since she held the world number one ranking for the eighth time in her career in May 2017 until early 2019, the top slot changed hands on a whopping seven different occasions.

Women's tennis has seldom been in a healthier state and while it can be annoying for punters when WTA Tour authorities tinker willy-nilly with tournament main draws when seeded players withdraw from events, there remain some seriously good betting opportunities for those who keep up to date with the news.

## 4. Use trends and results

Many successful traders use statistics to their advantage and that approach, allied to a decent dose of intuition, makes sound sense. The general advice is to keep as much sporting data as possible, but for most regular punters perhaps the most salient point is that the information used in the search for winners should be relevant.

Outright bettors should be aware of the age of finalists of tournaments, while knowing the best title prices of players contesting trophy matches from previous years can also provide helpful benchmarks.

A knowledge of courts and their speeds and which terrain players are likely to appreciate more can be invaluable. For example, in recent years, prior to Monte Carlo reportedly speeding up their clay courts

*'Women's tennis has seldom been in a healthier state and there remain some seriously good betting opportunities for those who keep up to date with the news'*

219

in recent seasons, the fastest of the slower red courts on the circuit have tended to be in Madrid, the second highest capital city in Europe at an altitude of 667m above sea level.

And so it has been less surprising to see fast-court specialists fare slightly better in Spain's premier clay tournament than, say, in the French Open.

As regards the high-quality hard-court tournaments, the fastest surfaces are often seen in the Shanghai Masters, so lower-ranked competitors who regularly ply their trade on clay courts tend to struggle more in the Chinese city.

The slowest of the superior hard-court events in recent years has been Indian Wells, the California desert venue which is no stranger to high winds.

Finally, even though golden generations tend to have long stints in the limelight, with the standard of pretty much all sports generally rising over time, punters would do well to remember that even the most amazing records get broken.

## 5. Keep up with the latest news

Successful punters should aim to be as well informed as possible and that means regularly checking the latest news. Try to read between the lines as regards certain injury-prone players. Rafael Nadal, for example, often takes out a huge percentage of outright tournament books so given his less-than-impressive record of not starting events he is due to compete in, it can sometimes be worth taking on the Spaniard with considerably bigger-priced title contenders, whether in his half of the draw or not.

*Novak Djokovic in action on the clay at La Caja Magica during the 2019 Madrid Open*

*'The fastest of the slower red courts on the circuit has tended to be in Madrid, the second highest capital city in Europe at an altitude of 667m above sea level'*

Early on in the tennis week it's often well worth monitoring the qualifiers who win through to the main draw. Qualifiers well known to the oddsmakers are often introduced at shorter prices than some unfancied performers already in the last 32, but those competitors whose names are new to market-makers occasionally take the compilers by surprise. There are sometimes big discrepancies between the prices of qualifiers, but only by monitoring the quotes of bookmakers who take the time to add the lower-ranked players to outright lists on Sunday, Monday or Tuesday will punters be able to avail themselves of the occasional each-way plunder.

A change of coaching staff can be hugely significant. There's no golden rule as regards the quality of coaches, but sometimes talented players employ the services of former professionals who were inferior performers to themselves. Fallow periods often ensue, but when the relationship ends and a new coach is appointed the change in performance levels can sometimes be startling.

Punters should be aware of the bookmakers' rules before betting on tennis. Some oddsmakers ask that just one set is completed before they pay out on whichever player progresses in the draw, while others ask that the entire match be completed. Certain bookmakers, for example William Hill, tailor their prices around players with high rates of retirement during matches and so punters should look out for the signs and assess the options before deciding which betting avenue to go down.

Social media can be hugely informative and punters should get a feel for knowing which posters on Twitter, for example, are dispensing useful material. And while keeping a check on daily results is an absolute must, there's nothing to beat actually watching as much tennis as possible if time allows.

## " EXPERT VIEW

*A packed house watches the action unfold on centre court at Wimbledon*

So what does all this mean for someone who wants to be a successful tennis punter?

Well, in a nutshell he or she has to beat the bookmakers at their own game and that's not easy. The oddsmakers are good and seldom

make mistakes. But fortunately for punters, there has to be winners of tournaments and matches and so it's just about finding them.

If the price of a tennis player is big enough and many of the necessary criteria are met as regards the bet potentially realising a profit, then yes, go for it. Shorter-priced punting may not be for everyone, but it's important to understand that if a 4-6 shot should really be a 4-9 chance, then the bet is probably worth having.

But let's get back to more familiar territory, that of bigger odds. One of the most annoying things for punters these days is bookmakers quoting best prices in tournament outright markets but not laying them. However, if you find a bookie who will accommodate your request for a decent bet on a big-priced outsider, then make a day out of it and enjoy it. Racing Post betting guru Paul Kealy's mantra is the bigger the price, the bigger the bet.

Clearly, those players in the bottom half of outright lists aren't always going to oblige – many are down in the nether regions for a reason – but once in a while your ship could sail in and the net profits could make it all worth it.

4-6 can be a price worth taking

If the odds are value then go for it

The bigger the price, the bigger the bet

# CRICKET
## by James Milton

### THE BACKGROUND

Cricket's reputation for complexity is entirely justified. Even committed fans of other sports can find themselves baffled by its arcane laws, technical details and variety of formats.

*'This is, after all, a sport in which a match can last for five days and still end in a draw'*

This is, after all, a sport in which a match can last for five days and still end in a draw. Little wonder it has never quite caught on in the USA.

And that's before we get to the bizarre vocabulary of cricket where teams are skittled on a raging bunsen and a batsman might be caught at silly point attempting to paddle-sweep a well-disguised flipper. Still with me?

If you're a complete cricket novice then it's probably wise to keep your money in your pocket. However, punters with a feel for the game and a sound understanding of gambling can make it pay and you don't necessarily need to know your fly-slip from your deep fine leg in order to turn a profit.

The cricketing landscape has changed dramatically since the start of the 21st century as the popular Twenty20 format now provides a high-octane alternative to the five-day Test match.

The sport's development, coupled with the rise of online bookmakers, is reflected by the array of betting options now available to punters.

When Australia players Dennis Lillee and Rodney Marsh decided to back England at 500-1 in-play to win the 1981 Ashes Test at Headingley, they had to send the driver of the team coach into the Ladbrokes marquee at the ground to place the famous wager.

Nowadays, punters can get involved in matches all around the world, often watching live streams on bookmakers' websites, and betting on which side will win a particular game is just the starting point.

Traditionalists can still back a team to win the County Championship in April, enjoying months of ups and downs, heatwaves, rain delays, packed lunches and cream teas before their bet is settled in September.

But punters whose attention spans don't stretch quite so far may prefer to focus on Twenty20 games, where each team bats for a maximum of 20 overs and matches are completed in around three hours.

The in-play markets reflect the frenetic, aggressive nature of the T20 format with bookies offering odds on which team will score more runs in the Powerplay period or whether or not a six will be hit in the next over.

The sheer volume of markets available, particularly on televised matches, can be daunting and those ever-generous bookmakers even offer 10-11 about your chosen team winning the pre-match toss.

The laws of probability suggest punters will struggle to make long-term profits on the toss market but there are plenty of other betting opportunities for those bidding to solve cricket's glorious, idiosyncratic puzzle.

# FIVE WAYS TO BET SMART ON CRICKET

## 1. Assess the conditions

*Jos Buttler celebrates during England's 2019 World Cup victory over New Zealand*

Few sports are as heavily influenced by external conditions as cricket. Footballers may struggle to do it on a wet Wednesday night in Stoke and thoroughbred racehorses are notoriously picky about what kind of ground they prefer.

For cricketers, though, the ability to weigh up the quirks of a venue, the weather conditions, and the state of the pitch are as important as remembering to don an abdominal protector before going out to bat.

Batting on a chilly, overcast April morning at Headingley is a totally different challenge to facing spinners on a turning wicket as the mercury creeps towards 40C in Nagpur or Mohali.

Captains and coaches are understandably obsessed with how a pitch is likely to play and punters should be equally diligent about their pre-game preparations.

Pitch and weather conditions have a bearing on every betting market. There's no point backing an opening batsman to be top runscorer at 3-1 if he should be that price just to survive the first couple

227

of overs against James Anderson and Stuart Broad when the new ball is swinging and seaming all over the place.

Conversely, on England's 2018 tour of Sri Lanka, spin-friendly pitches nullified Anderson and Broad's threat. The two most successful Test bowlers in their nation's history took just one wicket between them as England's spinners bowled them to a 3-0 series victory.

Remember that assessing conditions is not an exact science. Eoin Morgan told The Cricketer magazine that reading pitches is "actually impossible" even for his father, who worked as a groundsman at Trinity College Dublin. "Unless he gets down and takes a soil sample, he hasn't got a clue," Morgan explained.

*The scoreboard tells a story during a rain delay in the First Test match between New Zealand and Sri Lanka in 2018*

Due to heightened security at sporting venues, attempting to obtain soil samples before a Test match is not advisable but it's well worth scouring the internet for pre-match quotes from the groundstaff or tweets from journalists at the venue.

Checking the weather forecast is vital – as is researching trends or anomalies from past games at the ground. Even the dimensions of the playing area – whether there are short straight boundaries, for example – can provide an edge when betting on team runs or total sixes.

A cricket punter who neglects to consider the conditions is just as exposed as a batsman who forgets his box.

## 2. Don't just rely on the score

Neville Cardus, the doyen of 20th-century cricket journalists, wrote: "There ought to be some other means of reckoning quality in this, the best and loveliest of games; the scoreboard is an ass."

Cardus's disdain for the bare statistics of a cricket match should be shared by punters. Perhaps only baseball throws up more reams of stats than cricket but the numbers are valuable only when they are removed from the scorecard, analysed through the lens of the action out on the field, and put into their proper context.

If a spectator arrives at a ground to see the batting team struggling at 30-3, they may well assume that the pitch and overhead conditions are favouring the bowlers.

But there might not be anything wrong with the pitch at all. The wickets may have been due to a blinding catch, a shocking lbw decision and a shambolic run-out, and if the remaining batsmen keep calm and knuckle down, their side could easily end the day on 320-5.

Equally, a team who are 50 for no wicket might have been terrorised by the opening bowlers, scoring most of their runs in lucky boundaries nicked through the slip cordon.

As with expected-goals figures in football, more nuanced statistics are being developed in cricket. These allow punters to see what percentage of a batsman's shots have been played with total control or to compare the value of an innings of 70 against a brilliant bowling attack in treacherous conditions with a double-century on a flat pitch against a team of pie-chuckers.

This rule applies to in-play betting too. Don't assume that a team who have scored 70 off the first six overs of a Twenty20 game will continue at that rate.

Is there an ace spinner in the opposition ranks yet to be unleashed? Will the runs dry up once the fielding restrictions are relaxed? Does the batting side have a history of middle-order collapses?

**TOP TIP**

Checking the weather forecast is vital – as is researching trends from past games at the ground. Even the dimensions of the playing area can provide an edge when betting on team runs or total sixes

The scorecard only scratches the surface of the story of a match; you have to dig deeper to unearth the punting gems.

## 3. Avoid instinctively backing the batting side

Like backing over 2.5 goals in a football match, it is easy to get sucked into siding with the batting team, especially when they are going well in-play.

The old cricketing adage about adding two wickets to the score to get a better sense of the balance of power is a useful thought experiment for punters.

Before placing a bet on a team to score over 350.5 runs, consider the worst-case scenario. Would you be confident they could recover if they immediately lost a couple of wickets or would the bet suddenly look like horrific value?

There is a dangerous kind of recency bias at play when you're watching two set batsmen making serene progress and scoring runs freely. Remember that wickets beget wickets – it only takes one good ball or, one poor shot, to bring in a new batsman, changing the complexion of the innings.

Also consider the match conditions as the market often overrates the chances of teams chasing in the fourth innings of a game.

Punters' eyes light up when they see tempting odds about a team chasing a modest victory target but scoring 200 or 220 can be a difficult task in a high-pressure situation on a deteriorating day-five pitch.

## 4. Shop around for the value

A general principle of successful betting is to give yourself the best chance of winning by ensuring you're on at the most competitive odds.

Check out which bookmakers offer a comprehensive cricket-betting service and use an odds-comparison website for pre-match bets.

Most firms now dangle promotional odds boosts for televised matches and getting 7-2 rather than the general 11-4 about a top runscorer is an offer worth taking.

Equally, when betting in-play it makes sense to monitor two or three bookmakers' websites to check for price discrepancies or differences of opinion.

Player and team runs lines can vary significantly, especially at the start of an innings, and it's worth looking at different brackets for the team totals. Backing a side at 6-4 to reach 300 might be more attractive than the 5-6 or 10-11 that they pass 275.

*South Africa's Rassie van der Dussen in action during the 2019 Cricket World Cup*

## 5. Pick your battles

Each punter has their own individual temperament so, depending on your betting style, it is wise to focus on the format or markets that fit your personality.

If you enjoy betting on golf tournaments or building up ante-post football portfolios, you'll probably relish the slow-burning challenge of in-play trading a five-day Test.

If your stock-in-trade is greyhound racing, sprint handicaps or in-play football then your cricket-betting appetite could be sated by the all-action Twenty20 format.

More patient punters might find T20 – dismissed as 'hit and giggle' by some snooty critics – too frenetic for their taste while those who prefer an instant hit may be frustrated by the slower pace of Test cricket, making poor betting decisions as a consequence.

It's often said that the 'leave' is the most important shot in a batsman's armoury and the same applied to cricket punters.

If the weather forecast is dodgy, there is little course form to go on at a new venue, the match prices look accurate, or you simply don't have a strong opinion on the teams involved, then keep your powder dry.

The packed cricket calendar means you won't have to wait long for a more attractive betting opportunity.

*Running out to bat during day three of the Fourth Test match between England and India at Southampton's Ageas Bowl in 2018*

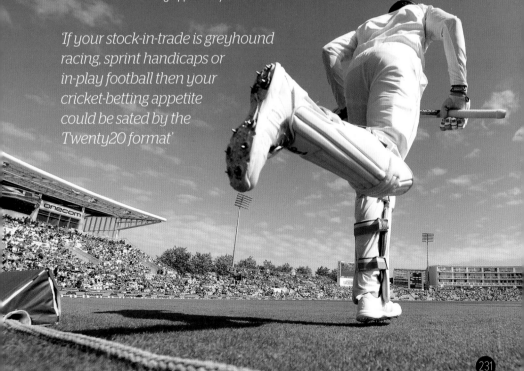

*'If your stock-in-trade is greyhound racing, sprint handicaps or in-play football then your cricket-betting appetite could be sated by the Twenty20 format'*

231

*'One way to
approach the
pre-toss market
is to weigh up
both teams'
batting units and
bowling attacks.
How will they
be suited by
conditions?
Are there any
players who are
consistently
underrated by
bookmakers?'*

## A GUIDE TO THE MARKETS

### 1. Match betting

First things first: make sure you know exactly what you're betting on.

In Test cricket the match-betting market includes the draw while match prices on County Championship games are usually draw no bet, meaning stakes are returned if it ends in a stalemate.

Dead-heat rules apply if a one-day or Twenty20 game ends in a tie, unless there is a Super Over to decide the winner.

One way to approach the pre-toss market is to weigh up both teams' batting units and bowling attacks. How will they be suited by conditions? Are there any players who are consistently underrated by bookmakers?

Home advantage has become increasingly significant in Test cricket as touring teams have fewer warm-up games in which to acclimatise.

It is very difficult to fluke a Test victory – as any grumpy old bowler will testify, taking 20 wickets in a match is hard work – so underdog triumphs away from home are rare occurrences.

One-day and Twenty20 matches, however, can be decided by a single inspired innings or a brilliant spell of bowling so punters should be wary of backing short-priced favourites in those formats.

That is particularly true of 20-over matches when the in-play betting often fluctuates wildly. A team may look down and out but as long as they have players who can hit 50 off 20 balls or take two or three quick wickets then punters shouldn't be afraid of backing them at big prices.

England's Ben Stokes won't need reminding of the volatile nature of T20 cricket. Stokes bowled the final over of the World Twenty20 final in 2016 when the West Indies, needing 19 runs to win, were 16-1 in-play.

Four balls and four sixes later, batsman Carlos Brathwaite – and in-play punters who kept faith in the Windies – were celebrating a remarkable victory.

### 2. Batting markets

One of the most popular betting heats on a cricket match is the top runscorer market, in which punters must identify which batsman will score the most runs in their team's innings.

It can be frustrating when a value selection is going along nicely only to be scuppered by a brain-freeze or the ball of the century (which occurs roughly every six months in cricket). However, it is a satisfying market to crack, especially when you find a winner at a big price.

Most cricket fans can pick out a team's star batsman but it often pays to avoid the obvious selections.

Even the best players in the world will struggle to return a profit for punters if they go off at odds of 5-2 or 11-4 to top-score and lower-order batsmen are far more competent these days.

In Test cricket, the new ball tends to cause plenty of damage, especially in England, New Zealand and South Africa, so opposing the openers in the top runscorer market is advisable.

Opening the batting in Tests is a tough job – after Andrew Strauss retired in 2012, England spent years searching for a reliable replacement at the top of the order – whereas it's easier to bat against a softer ball sent down by weary bowlers.

Don't be put off by a player's position in the batting order. More and more regularly, Test batsmen are top-scoring or making fifties and centuries from numbers six, seven or eight.

When looking at top runscorer prices, it's helpful to imagine how the innings might unfold. How many early wickets need to fall for a 20-1 shot coming in at number seven to become a serious contender? How likely is that scenario given the strength of the opposition, the weather and the venue's history?

When a team has a star-studded batting line-up it often makes more sense to back your selection to score a fifty or a century rather than top-score as you're not reliant on other players' failures.

Otherwise you'll just have to accept the odd hard-luck story. Shai Hope of the West Indies, for example, scored 170 in a 2019 ODI against Ireland yet Hope's top runscorer backers were denied by his fellow opener John Campbell, who made 179.

A more conservative way to support or oppose individual players is on the batsman runs line market with bookmakers offering 5-6 or 10-11 about a player scoring over or under, say, 36.5 runs.

A high strike-rate of winners is obviously required when betting at odds-on in this market but it can be a profitable way to support consistent accumulators of runs who tend to take fewer risks early in their innings.

*Australia's Steve Smith of lifts the Ashes Trophy during day five of the Fifth Test match in the 2017-18 Ashes Series between Australia and England*

'When a team has a star-studded batting line-up it often makes more sense to back your selection to score a fifty or a century rather than top-score' failures'

## 3. Bowling markets

The main bowler-related market is betting on which player will be the top wicket-taker for his team in an innings.

In Test matches, this market relates to each team's first innings and if two or more bowlers take the same number of wickets, dead-heat rules apply with most bookmakers. In the case of a tie in a limited-overs game some firms will settle the bowler who concedes fewer runs as the winner.

*Pakistan fans get vocal during the 2019 World Cup*

Whatever the format, some lateral thinking is required in the top wicket-taker market. Look for bowlers who are likely to get the best of the conditions – taking the new ball (and the second new ball, available after 80 overs) in Test matches or bowling at the end of the innings in one-day and Twenty20 games.

Bowling in the death overs is a huge positive as batsmen are forced to throw caution to the wind later in the innings and lower-order players come in swinging the bat from ball one.

Again, it is important to consider conditions. If the forecast is for a

damp, overcast day then the fast bowlers are likely to do most of the damage while spinners will find it hard to grip and control the ball.

Also think about the depth of competition to be a team's top wicket-taker. Some sides have one or two outstanding bowlers before a steep drop in quality to the rest of the attack so better value could be to back the star man to take over 2.5 wickets or claim a five-wicket haul in the innings.

## 4. Specials & spread betting

The disparity in talent between the best and worst teams in international cricket means the match betting can often be a one-sided affair.

However, it is possible to find an edge in the special markets available with most bookmakers.

These markets offer a chance to support a hot favourite at a decent price or back underdogs who are unlikely to win the game but might prove stronger in one specific department or period of the match.

A Twenty20 team whose key batsmen are openers and best bowlers take the new ball can be value to make the higher score in the first six overs even if you don't fancy their chances of winning the game.

Players who have been focusing on white-ball cricket may be underprepared for the first Test of a series so backing the other team to claim a first-innings lead is a bet to consider.

And depending on the personnel, backing the outsiders in the match

*'Players who have been focusing on white-ball cricket may be underprepared for the first Test of a series so backing the other team to claim a first-innings lead is a bet to consider'*

235

*'Cricket is well suited to spread betting but it is vital to use a consistent staking plan as you could be buying match run-outs at 1.5 or getting long of a team's runs at 425'*

betting to hit more sixes than the favourites can prove profitable.

If the game goes to form, the underdogs have to take more risks than a more accomplished team who are coasting to victory – Afghanistan were well beaten by Australia at the 2019 World Cup yet they hit seven sixes to the Aussies' four.

One interesting in-play market is the method of next dismissal – how the next batsman will be out. 'Caught' is usually a short-priced favourite in this market but it can be worth opposing in spin-friendly conditions with slow bowlers at both ends bringing 'lbw' and even 'stumped' into play.

'Run-out' is also worth a punt at big prices towards the end of a one-day innings or if you've noticed that a particular pair of batsmen struggle to judge quick singles.

Cricket is well suited to spread betting but it is vital to use a consistent staking plan as you could be buying match run-outs at 1.5 or getting long of a team's runs at 425.

The fixed-odds advice outlined in this chapter also applies to trading the spreads: evaluate conditions, look for teams or players who are underrated, and be wary of getting carried away if the batting side starts well.

Player performances are a popular spread market, with points awarded for each run, wicket, catch or stumping. Don't overlook the value of catches in this market – a Test player who has a safe pair of hands at slip or a dynamic Twenty20 boundary fielder can easily pick up a couple of catches in an innings, providing a useful boost to their batting or bowling performance points tally.

## 5. Ante-post betting

Big event such as an Ashes Test series or a Cricket World Cup are often priced up months or years in advance so punters should be alert to pounce on any stale prices.

Bookmakers and other bettors based in Britain may be slow to react to results and performances in a low-profile series on the other side of the world that should have more of an impact on ante-post markets.

Keep an eye on contests in the UAE, Bangladesh or Zimbabwe

which may go under the radar – a struggling team might be getting their act together while the wheels could be coming off another side who are rated too highly in the long-term markets.

Star overseas players hog the headlines in the global Twenty20 leagues but it is crucial to assess the strength of each franchise's domestic players before having an ante-post bet.

In the Indian Premier League, four overseas stars are permitted in the playing 11 while the Big Bash allows only two non-Australians per side so it is vital to do your homework on the squad members who are not household names. Most will be competent journeymen but some could be potential superstars.

## " EXPERT VIEW

The contest between cricket punter and bookmakers is similar to the battle between batsman and bowler.

Just as a bowler aims to induce a rash shot from a batsman, bookies want their customers to place ill-considered bets.

A batsman won't be successful unless his technique is sound and cricket bettors also need solid foundations: discipline, an understanding of the game, and a keen eye for value.

The best batsmen are those who are able to adapt to different conditions and formats, appraising the situation of the match and making the right decision even when they have only a fraction of a second to react.

Facing a 95mph fast bowler on an uneven pitch is marginally more stressful than trading an IPL game in-play but in both situations you need to keep a cool head, shut out the distractions, and focus on selecting the right shot to play or bet to place.

Cricket players come in all shapes and sizes and cricket betting is also a broad church, welcoming casual punters, cold-eyed statistical analysts, and patient traders aiming to grind out a profit over five days.

Find out what formats and strategies suit your betting temperament, watch as much cricket as you can, and hopefully you'll end up hitting the bookies for six more often than they have you stumped.

**Watch plenty of cricket**

**A keen eye for value is essential**

**Keep a cool head and sharp focus**

*James Anderson and England and team-mates appeal for the wicket of Cheteshwar Pujara of India during day four of the Fourth Test match in 2018*

# RUGBY UNION
## by Graham Woods

*'If you enjoy the game and have at least a basic understanding of its dynamics, betting on rugby can bring enjoyment and rewards so long as you put the work in and follow the rules'*

## INTRODUCTION

Royalty and working folk alike have been betting on horseracing for centuries, gamblers and grannies have played the football pools for the best part of a hundred years, but betting on rugby union is a relatively shallow-rooted and niche area in the worldwide betting market.

It was not until 1987 that the first league structure for English clubs was set up, while in that same year the first Rugby World Cup was held in New Zealand.

In the following 30 years professionalism and Sky Sports – then later BT Sport – have been the huge factors in growing the sport, but betting on the rugby still doesn't have the same popular following as racing, football or golf.

Why should that be? Well, one reason is that there aren't that many matches to bet on. Outside the three big club competitions in Europe – the Premiership, Pro14 and Top 14, plus the European Cups and Super Rugby in the southern hemisphere – coverage is sparse. Many bookmakers will bet on lower divisions but information is hard to get hold of and semi-pro level sport brings all kinds of inconsistencies that punters seek to avoid.

Short prices put off a lot of prospective bets. Draws are pretty rare so a rugby match is effectively a two-horse race and home advantage counts for a lot. Of course, handicap betting is the response to that. Rather than just offer the home team at, say, 1-5 and the visitors at 9-2, they'll give the underdogs a 12-point start and bet 10-11 each of

two. But you're still betting at odds-on and taking on an odds-compiler who has spent his week working out the figure which, in his judgement, renders the two teams inseparable.

Equally off-putting for many are the seemingly complex laws of the game. Give a horseracing novice a tenner to put on his fancy and he doesn't have to know too much to be able to cheer it over the line. But think of the frustration when you've backed a team to win a rugby match and they're pounding away at the tryline for ages then suddenly give away an inexplicable penalty and it's all for nothing.

You've even got a funny-shaped ball that bounces this way or that seemingly at a whim. The frustrations can be immense.

But if you're thinking it's not worth bothering with, don't. If you enjoy the game and have at least a basic understanding of its dynamics, betting on rugby can bring enjoyment and rewards so long as you put the work in and follow the rules.

# FIVE WAYS TO BET SMART ON RUGBY

## 1. Check who's playing

The beauty of rugby union from a punter's perspective is that unlike football with its fluid formations, teams always line up with the same positions and each player has a specific job to do. And on top of that, the line-ups are announced at least the day before, 48 hours before kick off in the case of international matches. This is vital information that you simply can't bet without.

The key position is fly-half – as significant as a quarter-back in American football or pitcher in baseball – who will be the playmaker. But in any position look out for unfamiliar names or inexperienced players stepping in. Look for mismatches, especially in key areas such as the front row. And look at the bench – all teams have eight replacements, usually five forwards and three backs because of the greater attritional toll that forwards suffer. Sometimes, though, you'll see a six and two split which tells you a team is looking for physical dominance.

## 2. Assess the weather forecast

Some of the best winning bets you strike may not require any rugby knowledge at all, just a scan of the forecast. Rugby is played in all seasons and all weathers, not always conducive to throwing, catching or running with a ball. Rain is always the first thing on a punter's radar but look out for high winds too. Poor conditions are a great leveller, hampering play and generally keeping scores down, making it harder for favourites to cover a big handicap.

*The team line-up not only tells you who is playing, it gives an idea of the style of play. A heavy powerful pack and a kicking fly-half? Sounds like a territorial game from a team looking to get the ball in their opponents' half as much as possible and put the squeeze on. A creative fly-half with lighting quick wingers and full-back? That looks more like an expansive, attacking game. There are so many clues there and the early announcement gives you time to work with them.*

239

**TOP TIP**

Information is key
so access as much
as you can and
keep notes – these
will help no end
when it comes to
pinpointing bets

## 3. Start at the beginning

Who's the favourite? Okay, I reckon they'll win. What's the handicap? Yep, they can cover that. Done.

How often do we do that – jump straight to the end and what the outcome will be? Far better to start at the kick-off and play the game out in your head. You know the teams and what the weather will be like, you've got the evidence of past results, so what do they tell you? What kind of game do these teams like to play and what sort of game will they be able to play? A kicking game, running game, forward dominated, expansive, territorial, possession-based? The clues should be there. And if you've read them right, you can start looking for a bet.

## 4. Keep records

Here we're stepping it up a bit and getting a bit more serious.

It's true of betting on any sport that you must have data to work with. And when it comes to racing or football, all the information is freely available in an easy-to-read format somewhere on the internet. But when it comes to rugby, the information a punter wants is harder to find all in one place. And the solution is to keep your own records.

The basic information I like to record on a spreadsheet are result, tries scored by each team, the best handicap for each team, and then a simple formula can tell me how far each team surpassed or fell short of the handicap.

Why is that useful after the event? Well, it acts as a kind of performance rating and over the course of a season, or several seasons, it allows you to look for patterns of when and in what circumstances a team put in its better and worse performances.

Other useful information that could be stored include weather conditions, a brief line or two about how the match played out, and any insightful quotes after the game from coaches or players. It comes down to what you find useful and have time to record, but it's important to be realistic about how much time you can devote. If you bite off more than you can chew at the start of the season you'll soon lose interest.

## 5. Don't be afraid to go with your gut

Keeping records will throw up all kinds of numbers, and there are plenty of other places to look for the minutiae of match data. A lot of it could be useful, some could be invaluable, but equally sometimes you have to look beyond it.

In sport people talk about putting their bodies on the line but in rugby that is sometimes literally the case. Professional players go to extraordinary physical lengths firstly to prepare themselves and then when they're out on the pitch. The game puts great demands on them, and sometimes it's about more than just who is the better team.

We've often said after the event that a certain team or player "wanted it more" and in rugby that's often a decisive factor. Perhaps a team are smarting after a heavy defeat, out for revenge, or motivated by personal factors. To quote Tony D'Amato from Oliver Stone's film Any Given Sunday, the team "who are prepared to die for that inch" is what you're looking for.

Conversely sometimes you'll suspect a team won't be able to fight for that inch. Perhaps they've just come off a big success, maybe in another tournament, or they're eyeing a significant fixture on the horizon. A short turnaround between fixtures, especially if travel and time zones are involved, can significantly affect performances, especially at the Rugby World Cup where rest time between matches varies enormously.

Look for the signs and don't be afraid to act on them.

*Angus Blyth secures the lineout ball as the Chiefs and Reds do battle in New Zealand*

So now you've taken on the golden rule, it's time to find a bet. But knowing where to put your money is not as easy as it sounds. When it comes to betting on rugby, it's often not enough just to know who's going to win. If it's England against Italy at Twickenham in the Six Nations, well most people know who's going to win. And while you're not going to get rich backing England at 1-100, you'll probably lose interest in a wager on Italy at 50-1 pretty early on in the match.

Granted, not all favourites are priced as short as that but it is quite striking how much the market can favour the jollies. All match odds naturally correlate to a handicap and it might surprise some that a favourite giving up just seven points can go off at 2-5 or 1-3 in the 80-minute markets. That's 1-3 about a team rated one converted try better than their opponents.

*Sam Skinner rises to claim the lineout during a Premiership clash between Exeter Chiefs and Northampton Saints*

Conversely, of course, that means the underdogs are on offer at something like 11-4 when they're rated only one converted try inferior, and often the value in the match prices is more likely to be found if you fancy an upset.

## MARKETS

### 1. Handicaps

Okay, so Italy are 50-1 to beat England at Twickenham. But give them a 30-point start and that puts a whole new complexion on the scoreline. You can back England to win by more than 30 points at 10-11 or maybe evens, or get the same price about Italy staying within the line. Whatever line bookmakers come up with the key point to bear in mind is that it is a figure of significance to us as punters but means nothing to the players on the pitch. One of the many frustrations with a handicap bet is that teams are not looking to win by a certain number of points. If there's one tale of woe that unites rugby punters it's the late consolation try scored by the underdog that has no effect on the outcome but blows your handicap bet on the favourite out of the water.

So often as punters we like to decide whether we think the handicap is right or wrong, but perhaps that isn't the way to look at it. The numbers bookmakers come up with are so often remarkably accurate and it doesn't really make sense to rule that when the scoreline is wildly different bookmakers have simply got it wrong.

What it does make sense to do is to try to discern what factors could have affected the result. Then go back to your records and see if those same factors can be picked up in other matches that have produced similar handicap outcomes. Perhaps this team struggles against a certain profile of opponent, against sides with a strong set-piece, top-ranked defence, exceptional pace. Or it could be that their performance is significantly poorer after a five-day break between fixtures compared to seven days. Whatever it is, there may well be clues in there that tell you when a team is likely to perform significantly better or worse than bookmakers would anticipate.

What you are also likely to find is that certain teams are treated less generously on the handicap than others and the reasons for that are understandable. In the case of England v Italy at Twickenham, bookmakers know that more bets will be placed on England winning well due to a combination of patriotic punters and people backing what they want to happen. So that England handicap will almost certainly be hiked up a point or two and a basic rule of thumb can be applied that the more unfashionable the underdog, the more likely their handicap start will be bigger than it should be.

Another key thing to bear in mind when looking at big handicaps is the weather. To cover a 30-point line a team must first score 30 points, and in wind and rain that's no given for any team.

The smaller the handicap clearly the tighter the difference in class and ability between the teams

## 2. Points

This is an increasingly popular market, although perhaps still not as popular as it should be, as it requires an easier set of judgements. You don't need to work out which is the better team or who will win, just predict the shape of the game.

Two big packs slugging it out on a cold, rainy December Friday night sounds like a low-scoring grind. But pit two open, attacking teams against each other in dry conditions, perhaps towards the end of the season with little at stake, and you've got the recipe for a high-scoring roller-coaster game.

It sounds simplistic, but ask yourself why bookmakers are slow to come up with points markets for weekend matches. Match odds and handicaps are often up early in the week then adjusted as teams are named on a Friday, but you'll be lucky to find a firm offering a total points line before the morning of the game.

The lowest points total in England's Premiership in 2018-19 was Sale's 6-3 victory over Bath in April (on a Friday night incidentally) while the highest was also at Sale, who beat Gloucester 46-41 in a pretty meaningless game on the last day of the season.

*'Whatever line bookmakers come up with the key point to bear in mind is that it is a figure of significance to us as punters but means nothing to the players on the pitch'*

O Of the 129 Premiership matches that produced a winner in 2018-19, 63 per cent were won by no more than 12 points

*'First tryscorer is usually the market that punters focus on first but it's a bet that can be scuppered early on in a match, whereas at least if you take a player simply to score a try your bet runs until the end of the match or he is substituted'*

More people bet on high points totals than a low one, presumably because they're backing what they want to see. And it's true that backing the total to go under the line makes it hard to watch a match as you're constantly willing the attacking team to drop the ball and mess it up. But bookmakers know that so the line they come up with is more likely to be pitched a little too high than too low.

## 3. Winning margin

Here you're picking not only who will win, but how much they will win by. That sounds as if you're making it twice as hard for yourself to win money, and in a match where there's a strong favourite you are. If a team are deemed handicap favourites by 20 points or more, who's to say that they won't win by 30, 40 or more?

The margins to focus on are the tighter ones, especially the increasingly popular five-way market.

Margins used to be priced up in bands of five – to win by one to five points, six to ten, and so on. That leaves only a narrow window. Ten-point bands offer more leeway, but the five-way margin allows you to back either team to win by one to 12 points or by more than 12 points, plus the draw.

At the top level, and especially in the northern hemisphere, games are more often close-fought, and in particular England's Premiership and the Six Nations tend to see more narrow wins.

In the 2018-19 Premiership there were 132 matches played of which three were draws. Of the 129 games that produced a winner, 81 (63 per cent) were won by no more than 12 points. And in the 2016 Six Nations, of the ten matches not involving whipping boys Italy, nine were settled by 12 points or fewer. The other was a draw.

## 4. Tryscorers

You can back a player to score the first try of the match, or the last, or to score at any time, or markets are available to pick a player in a certain position to go over first.

First tryscorer is usually the market that punters focus on first but it's a bet that can be scuppered early on in a match, whereas at least if you take a player simply to score a try, your bet runs until the end of the match or he is substituted. Anytime tryscorer markets don't offer the greatest value though, and speedy wingers will often by odds-on to cross the line. Tryscoring forwards sometimes offer more value, or look for someone switching position.

Some teams share their tries around while others may have a key player who is the focus of their scoring output.

Another thing to consider is the shape of a team, their style of play and the weather conditions. Usually it's odds-on that a back scores the first try of a match, but if you see a dominant pack running out in the wet, perhaps any forward at around 2-1 fits the bill better. Another favourite if a team is blessed with pace and attacking flair is to go for a back-three player (winger or full-back) to take the honours.

## 5. Spread betting

Many are nervous about spread betting and the potential risks, but rugby lends itself to the medium as it is high-scoring enough to get some leverage for profit while it is possible to limit the downside. Trading on a team's supremacy or match point is a straightforward enough trade and sometimes, though not always, offers a better opportunity.

One common strategy is to use the spread markets when you want to get behind a strong favourite. You feel the favourites are going to win comfortably so if they fall short of the line it won't be by much as there is the potential for them to go way past it. Conversely, if a team are huge underdogs, there is a good chance a supremacy sell will go wrong, whereas if you back them on the fixed-odds handicap market, you get paid the same whether they one point inside the line or 20 points, and your downside is fixed.

"

## EXPERT VIEW

Watching sport is meant to be fun – betting should add to the enjoyment – and there are plenty of bets to enhance your enjoyment of a game. Although rugby can be frustrating to watch, it has that rare appeal that it can have you on the edge of your seat, straining every sinew as you urge a team to power over, and if you get a winner at the end of it, it feels like a Grand Slam.

Go with your gut

Keep records – use your own data

Get ready for a rollercoaster ride

*Jonny May flies through the air to score England's fourth try in their Six Nations encounter with Scotland in March 2019*

# DARTS
## by Steve Davies

The spectacular growth of darts over the last couple of decades means there is little bookmakers and punters don't know about the game. That doesn't mean, however, arrers bettors should despair – they just need to be a good deal shrewder these days to hunt out value.

## A GAME OF TWO HALVES

Darts tournaments have short-priced favourites like no other sport. First it was Phil Taylor who, for almost 20 years, went off at cripplingly short odds pretty much every time he turned up. The Power's baton has been handed to Michael van Gerwen, a player the layers also take few chances with.

Thankfully, a tournament is made up of two halves and even if Van Gerwen looks a certainty (as he often can) to cruise into a final, somebody has to emerge from the other half. With the Dutch titan taking so much out of a book there is often plenty of decent each-way possibilities at nice prices to be found in the 'other' side of a main draw.

## STAY ON MAXIMUM
## STATS ALERT

There are myriad betting opportunities during matches – 180s, high checkouts, averages and so on – so you must know your stats.

But this is a width-of-the-wire sport every time a player toes the oche so those statistics shouldn't assume irrefutable proportions.

It can, when prudent, pay to swim against the tide, such as with 180s matchbets over short distances.

We all know the men who clobber the treble-20 bed better than most – Van Gerwen, Michael Smith, Daryl Gurney and Dave Chisnall spring to mind – and we presume the renowned big hitters will win their 180 matchbets more often than not.

*'With the Dutch titan taking so much out of a book there is often plenty of decent each-way possibilities at nice prices to be found in the 'other' side of a main draw'*

Yet at the 2018 Grand Prix, for example, nine of the 16 first-round favourites in most 180s betting flopped. At the Grand Slam 25 (52 percent) went down; at this year's Premier League 43 (or 60 percent) lost in the group stage.

The margins in darts are fine and in short games those expected gulfs between players are evidently not always seen.

## DON'T BE FLOORED BY FORM

Be wary of floor form. Many pros who look a million dollars at the PDC's bread-and-butter weekend Tour events at near-empty leisure centres, can fry on the big stage when the heat is on. All these stars can play but there's a reason why it's the usual suspects who repeatedly thrive under the greatest pressure.

*Dutch maestro Michael Van Gerwen's presence in a tournament means some decent each-way value can often be found*

# SNOOKER
## by Dave Clark

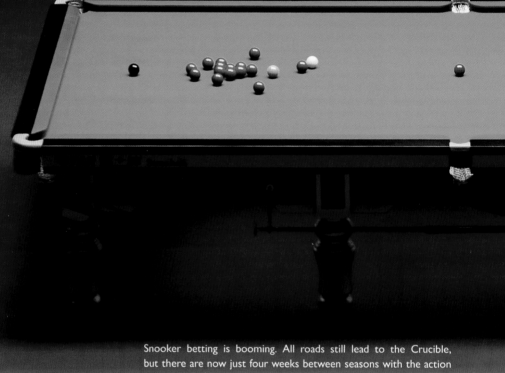

Snooker betting is booming. All roads still lead to the Crucible, but there are now just four weeks between seasons with the action coming thick and fast from all over the world and with that comes plenty of opportunities for punters.

## HECTIC SCHEDULE CAN BE DEMANDING

Gone are the days of only six tournaments per season, Barry Hearn has revolutionised snooker into a constantly moving and nomadic global sport – that can take its toll on the players.

It is worth noting that entry into every tournament is no longer compulsory, the elite players only take part in the tournaments they choose to.

With some tournaments scheduled only hours apart, monitoring draws and entries is a must with logistics and travel playing a part.

## KEEP AN EYE ON THE RANKINGS

Players' rankings are prize-money based and on a two-year rolling

system, there is also a one-year ranking system for the end-of-season lucrative FedEx Cup-style Tour Championship.

Whether it be a player fighting for tour survival, pushing for a place in the Masters or in line for a spot in the Tour Championship, there can sometimes be a lot more at stake than simply a spot in the next round of a tournament.

That added pressure can have an adverse effect on performance.

## KNOW WHERE TO GO FOR THE INFO

There are a number of useful websites to aid and educate snooker punters, none more so than cuetracker.net for head-to-head records and century stats.

Head-to-head record is hugely important, an overwhelming historical dominance can give one player the upper hand before a ball has even been potted.

The World Professional Billiards and Snooker Association website (wpbsa.com) is the place to go to monitor current and provisional rankings during the season.

# BOXING
## by Dan Williams

*Boxing is going through a boom in popularity in Britain with arenas and stadiums regularly filled and, after decades in the doldrums, the heavyweight division is now stacked with exciting talent and personalities, many of them British. Boxing is in many ways unique when it comes to sports betting and from time to time it can present golden opportunities for those with enough vision to see past the narrative*

## DON'T BELIEVE THE HYPE

The most successful boxers are not necessarily the best – neither are their opponents – but they are usually the most entertaining. Fighters are essentially self-employed and can fight whoever, whenever and for whatever they like.

Sometimes the biggest feuds can be bubbling along for years before the boxers actually get in the ring together – if they ever do – and promoters and TV networks pour huge amounts of money into promotion. Both fighters will try to convince you that they will beat up the other, and one of them may appear more convincing.  None of it really matters – it's an illusion. A loud-mouth and cocky bravado is easily shut down by a well-timed crisp jab.

With emotions running high, camps dug in and lines drawn many of those opinions will be based on warped logic and the information overload lead to bad judgement and confirmation bias. This may end up with you thinking that your chosen fighter is a sure thing and worth a bet regardless of the price, and that's a position that must be avoided at all costs.

Remember, any fighter can win or lose to any opponent in any round, it's just a question of probability. Having a rational, unbiased, emotionless understanding of a fighter's ability and ignoring the background noise is key to working out if the odds on offer are a true reflection of the probability, or if they are driven by hype.

## FORMING AN UNBIASED OPINION

If you were looking to hire a new employee you would start by looking at their CV, so why bet on boxing without knowing who you're backing. Sites such as boxrec.com are great for gathering stats and information. Fighter records are a mine of information and are an invaluable tool for punters if you know what to look for – and what to ignore.

The most obvious, and often most misleading, statistic on any boxer's record is the wins-losses-draws. A fighter may be undefeated with 28 wins, but does that mean they are any good? Not necessarily. The promoters will sometimes make a huge deal of undefeated records and amazing knockout ratios, but pay close attention to the level of opponents they have previously fought.

Sometimes promoters bring in foreign fighters to challenge their local favourites and talk them up as if they are world level, when in reality they are well out of their depth and most die-hard boxing fans have never even heard of them.

Always check both fighters' records – even if you think you know them inside out. Once you have studied all the information available, you should then check the odds to see if the match the model in you head. If they don't, then you may have found a bet. Remember, if you are betting on a fight you are trying to find the value, you are not trying to find the winner at all costs.

## BEWARE OF THE JUDGES

Many fights, especially at championship level, are decided by the three judges sat a ringside. Their verdicts are highly subjective, can be completely different and often blatantly wrong.

This can be a nightmare if you have money invested in the outcome. You have called it right and all the pundits, commentators and unofficial scorecards agree.

You are counting your money, but then the MC delivers the judges verdicts and it hits you like a sucker punch to the belly. If you are betting on boxing this will happen to you sooner or later – there is no way around it. Decisions can be influenced by a partisan crowds, reputations, high profiles, sheer incompetence and an unknown number of other factors.

Sometimes the odds often reflect an assumption that the judges will lean towards a certain fighter. There is little you can do to safeguard against a bad decision, apart from being aware that it happens on a regular basis. If you think it may be factor keep stakes low, or consider backing the fight to go the distance as your bet will win regardless of what is written on the scorecards.

## MIXED MARTIAL ARTS

*Mixed martial arts is relatively new concept and is often lumped in with boxing on sports betting sites. But beware, it is a very different and far more complex beast. Boxing is fairly simple to understand – one person punches the other in the head or body until someone falls over or the time runs out – but MMA merges every unarmed combat. There is an infinite amount of ways for a fighter to win or lose and with that comes punting opportunities.*

*It is impossible for anyone to master all the techniques, no matter how good they are.*

*Most modern MMA fighters are well rounded in a variety of skills, but they all have their strengths and weaknesses. Don't be afraid to back the underdog.*

# FORMULA ONE
## by Adam Scriven

The beauty of Formula One as a betting medium is that with only 20 drivers from ten teams contesting 21 races in a season it's relatively easy to have an in-depth knowledge of the form. Of course, that means the layers are also pretty clued up, but there are ways to get an edge.

## LOOK BEYOND THE MAIN MARKETS

F1 has a tendency for one driver or team to dominate and that can lead to prohibitively short-priced favourites, but the middle of the grid is usually fiercely competitive and there are regularly attractive odds-against bets to be found.

After qualifying has taken place a plethora of race markets appear and the advent of request-a-bet type specials has further swelled the options.

Top-six finish, points finish and both cars from the team to finish in the points (or not) are markets which often throw up findable odds-against winners.

# KNOW THE CIRCUITS

Most races will be won by the car with the best cornering speed but there are still circuits where engine power is more important.

On the 2019 F1 calendar Bahrain, Azerbaijan, Canada, Belgium and Italy are the raw power circuits, and cars that shine at one of those tracks will tend to do well at all of them.

The distance from the startline to the first corner is also something to bear in mind. The longer the run to the first turn the more likely the grid order is to change on the opening lap and the 'first-lap leader' market often fails to take that into account.

Some tracks also have a tendency for the cars starting on one side of the road to make better getaways than the other. Watch the starts of the support races for clues on how the F1 start may shape out. Formula Two and GP3 races are televised live.

## BE AWARE OF PENALTIES AND THEIR IMPACT

Strict technical regulations mean few drivers go through a season without incurring at least one grid penalty. But taking a three-place grid penalty at a circuit where overtaking is tough – like Monaco for example – can be more damaging than a five-place penalty somewhere else. Impending penalties are often known days in advance and are generally widely reported.

*'On the 2019 F1 calendar Bahrain, Azerbaijan, Canada, Belgium and Italy are the raw power circuits, and cars that shine at one of those tracks will tend to do well at all of them'*

# CYCLING
## by Nick Pulford

Cycling, which has gone from a minority sport to a hotbed of British success at the Tour de France and Olympics, has key fundamentals in common with other sports: class and form.

## SPOT A CLASS ACT

Fields of up to 200 riders may seem to have a random element but in most cases the list of likely winners can be narrowed down to 20, or even fewer, simply because not every rider has the class to win. Many riders are good enough to finish in the top ten of a big sprint finish, a smaller number can make the top four or five, but only a select few are capable of winning. The same is true of a summit finish or the overall classification in one of the big three Tours (France, Italy and Spain).

Richard Carapaz was a surprise winner of the 2019 Giro d'Italia in terms of his pre-race odds but he had been fourth the previous year and became the 15th consecutive Giro winner whose record included at least a top-six placing in one of the big three Tours. Filters like that can go a long way to finding big-race winners.

## FOLLOW THE FORM

As in horse racing, form in the right build-up races is important too. The Tour of Flanders is well known as Belgium's biggest bike race and one of the 'monuments' of one-day racing but more niche is the E3 BinckBanck Classic - yet that is a stepping stone used by every Flanders winner in the decade to 2019, with eight of the ten showing their form with a top-four finish at E3. Similarly, Geraint Thomas was in top form prior to his 2018 Tour de France triumph, having won the Criterium du Dauphine one-week stage race. Familiarity with the cycling calendar and the form lines is a vital tool.

Form is also important on individual stages of the major Tours - in the sprints or the mountains, riders who have been prominent on previous days often pop up as stage winners.

## TOP RIDERS CAN BE BIG PRICES

Carapaz was 80-1 for the 2019 Giro and Thomas was 25-1 for the 2018 Tour, making clear that cycling - similar to golf - is one of the rare sports where big odds are on offer for participants with the form and class to win. That does not mean the puzzles are easy to solve but big-priced winners are findable with good judgement and some luck. Try adding a longshot to your main bet in a race; you might enjoy the ride.

# REALITY TV
## by David Dew

Remember when Susan Boyle was long odds-on to win Britain's Got Talent? She stunned the nation with her voice and looked sure to win the third series of the hugely popular franchise in 2009. But it wasn't to be and over 13 million viewers watched dance troupe Diversity lift the crown instead. It was a similar story when The X Factor launched in 2004 and pop-opera vocalists G4 were a short price to win the final. The British public didn't agree with bookmakers, however, and Steve Brookstein was called the winner in a tense live show watched by more than seven million reality TV fans.

These reverses demonstrate there are decent betting opportunities to be had in this niche area of entertainment betting and, although the public ultimately decide who wins these shows, there are ways to gain an edge.

## IT'S ALL IN THE EDIT

*The way contestants are portrayed has a huge effect on what the viewer thinks of them. It therefore massively impacts the likely result. Take Love Island, for example. Sometimes it's easy to forget certain people are still in the competition such is their lack of exposure – while at the same time others get coverage night after night. Take the hint – if you don't see somebody regularly they won't win.*

## PRODUCER FAVOUR

There is plenty of armoury that can be wheeled out in a bid to sway public opinion. If you've ever watched judges discussing acts on the live shows of The X Factor and wondered if they're commenting on the same performance you've just heard, such ludicrous hyperbole can give away vital clues. If what you listened to sounded ropey but they're praising it to the hilt, it is a clear sign the contestant is wanted to remain in the competition and expected to do well. In the same way, you might notice one act is bathed in golden light during their act while another is surrounded by fire. Subtle clues, but ones that can prove very useful when it comes to second-guessing what is happening and who is favoured by producers.

## SOCIAL MEDIA

YouTube, Facebook, Instagram, Twitter and TV show apps can be very handy when it comes to a quick assessment of how an act or contestant is going down with the viewers. And to save valuable time searching these platforms for information, the excellent tellystats.com provides all the key data in a nutshell for every reality show you can think of. Using the stats is not a clear route to riches as those people who comment on social media are not always from the same group that vote, but you can certainly get a handy steer on who is liked and disliked.